RECONNECTING WITH AMERICA

A Stranger at Home

Robert J. Barra

CONTENTS

DEDICATION

Kyle Noll (1986 – 2023)

This book is dedicated to Kyle, a free spirit who wasn't bound by convention or the expectations of others. Even as he struggled in the bucket, he expressed kindness, joy, love of family, art, travel and a thirst for new experiences. We who knew him will always miss him.

ACKNOWLEDGEMENTS

I'd like to thank the people who helped me chisel a story out of the quarry that was my travel journal. First is Sarah O'Donnell, my friend, editor and coach. I couldn't have finished without her wise advice and tireless hands-on support. Several advisors offered suggestions and feedback on the early drafts that helped shape the final version; Georgie Dom and Peter van Eten, Henny Uilenreef-Jansen, Dieneke Hegenveld and Craig Carr who wanted to join me on the trip but wisdom prevailed. Many thanks also to Anne England for her thoughtful and meticulous review.

I want to thank all the people I met along the way who helped me reconnect with America through their open and honest conversations. I hope you don't mind that I changed some names to protect your privacy. I tried not to change your words. And finally, I want to thank Hanneke who overcame her bears, supported and encouraged me throughout this journey.

ILLUSTRATIONS
AND PHOTOS

The pen and ink illustrations that appear in this book are the original works of Martin Steyn. Martin is an artist from South Africa. He migrated to The Netherlands where he lives, works and teaches art. The illustrations represent a collaboration between the artist and the author. The author told the stories and wrote the text, the artist added his creativity and vision to it. Together we hope the illustrations inspire reflection. Find out more about Martin and his other works at http://www.martfineart.com or Instagram: martin.steyn.studio

The photographs in this book were taken by me during my journey, except the family and friends photo. It was taken before this trip.

FOREWORD

As the title suggests, I set out on the journey described in the following pages to reconnect. I wanted to reconnect both with my homeland and with my sons. The subtitle describes the feeling I was left with after the trip. I traveled across the country and met with both my sons. Along the way I spoke with a cross-section of Americans. I met a homeless wanderer who collected animal skulls in the desert and a recovering drug addict who was planning to open a head shop. I spoke with an insurance executive who lived behind a wall in St. Louis to keep out the riff raff and a retiree who was traveling across the country in a Prius to map his family genealogy. I spoke with students, immigrants and union workers. Each shared a story.

I set down this story to recount some of my traveling experiences, reflections and descriptions about riding across America. The heart of the story is in the conversations I had with the people I encountered. They spoke of what was important in their lives, what they cared about and what they worried about. I began to see patterns; recurring themes, shared concerns, common motivations and cultural blind spots. When I organized my notes, I discovered that their fears, challenges and rewards paralleled mine as I planned and carried out the journey. I hope that together our stories offer some perspective on American life.

When I started out, I was curious about the appeal of the populist movement and specifically the Trump mystique. What is it about Trump's message that resonates so strongly? Many Americans live stress-filled daily lives. They are surrounded by messages of fear. Some messages are subtle, like an insurance advertisement. Some are not so subtle, like the billboard beside the highway in Ohio, "WHEN YOU DIE YOU WILL SEE GOD". Americans are never far from some message about their fragile security. As one person described it, America is a bucket of crabs where people claw and fight for a place on the top. I concluded that Trump is selling fear to a fundamentally insecure population.

The following pages recount a motorcycle journey, but they also illustrate the toxic influence of fear and insecurity. I conclude with a suggestion about how we can make some progress toward reducing the baseline anxiety level of a stressed-out population.

I rode across America in the summer of 2019. I think the message is just as relevant now as it was when my journey started.

Robert Barra, 23 February 2023

CHAPTER 1: CROSSROADS

In 2003, I relocated from southern Massachusetts to The Netherlands. It was more a decision of the heart than the head. The heart thing didn't work out, but I decided to stay for a while and give this strange country a try. I held a temporary Dutch residence permit and enough money to support me for a few months. I found a job, rented an apartment and settled in to learn about life outside the U.S.

I spent my first few years in Europe becoming acclimated to an alien culture where doorknobs don't turn, there are twenty-seven political parties, customer service is a toll call and New Year's Eve is a national fireworks orgy. As time wore on, I became more acclimated though never entirely at home in my new environment. Now I bank online, pedal a bicycle to the center of town and slather mayonnaise on my *frietjes* instead of catsup.

I discovered to my embarrassment that most people were better informed about my country than I was about theirs. For starters, they could find mine on a map. I also learned that although my new friends and colleagues were pretty well informed about American life, a lot of their information was superficial, like mine was about their countries. It was a collection of stereotypes and generalities, gleaned from television, movies and news.

Though many non-Americans have cultural preconceptions about American life, they are thirsty for details. I found myself in the position of an unofficial cultural ambassador. Wherever I went, people asked me questions about American life.

- *America has two political parties, but what if you don't like either candidate?*
- *Why is there no national healthcare system in America?*
- *Is everybody in America a Christian?*
- *Do you have to tip in a restaurant?*
- *Why do Americans call it a bathroom?*
- *Does everyone own a gun?*
- *Why do Americans sue each other all the time?*
- *Why did they elect Trump?*

During the first few years, I was comfortable and confident fielding questions about American life. But the longer I lived in Europe, the more my American perspective faded. I tried to keep up with American current events: I watched and read American news, corresponded regularly with family and friends and I visited home once or twice a year. But over time a feeling of alienation from my country began to grow.

I was nearing retirement. My last business trip took me to Shanghai, where I planned to say farewell to colleagues and explore the city like a tourist. I indulged in an evening river cruise through the city center. In the sultry air, we gaped at a surreal view of bright lights flashing across building facades fifty stories high. Sparkling, animated messages in rainbow colors reflected off the flat, dark water. Later at dinner, a colleague asked about my plans.

"What are you going to do when you retire?"

A lot of our former colleagues started their own businesses, most became consultants. I think she expected something like that.

After a slight pause, I answered. "I want to travel across America and get to know my country again."

My response was so spontaneous that it must have been germinating in my subconscious waiting for an opportunity to blossom. I explained that after so many years away, I felt out of touch. She asked for details, but of course I had none. There was really no plan, it was just an idea. But it felt right.

When I returned from China, winter was softening into spring in Holland. Magnolia, crocuses and daffodils erupted pink, violet and yellow out of the deep green grass and the sky smiled. My life was evolving toward retirement. I spent my spare time planning finances and estimating pension income. I pored over expense records and calculated budgets. All the while, the idea for a journey to the U.S. simmered on the back burner of my mind. The summer saw me negotiate my job exit and by September 2018 I was free. Fiscal and career planning segued to excitement for a new adventure. The idea for a road trip began to take shape.

It occurred to me that I have always sorted out my life's crossroads on the road. A coast-to-coast ride in an old Chevy with a college friend punctuated graduation. When my teaching career ended, I paddled a canoe five hundred miles down the Yukon River. I rode west on a long, cold, March motorcycle trip past Pittsburg, then south to Florida seeking warmth and peace after my divorce. The Trans-Siberian railway carried me across Asia as part of my decision to stay in Europe and buy a house.

I've been a rambler all my life. I'll use any excuse to ride a motorcycle, a car, plane, boat or train to explore someplace new or revisit an old favorite. I started traveling on a budget because I had time but little money. It became my preferred method because it felt more real. I used to challenge myself to travel with as little money as possible. I once wandered about Anchorage with two dollars in my pocket. I started young and have remained a hobo at heart. Traveling helps me find my way.

Retirement felt like the right time for another trip. A cross-country road trip marked the beginning of my working career; another road trip would mark its end.

Even a hobo needs an excuse to set out. A journey needs a beginning point and at least the semblance of a destination. My excuse was to reconnect with my country. The inspiration that struck me in Shanghai still felt right six months later. The starting point was New England, where I grew up, now home to my son, Matt and his wife. The time frame for the trip would be the summer of 2019. My younger son Mike's home provided the destination, Lake Tahoe. What better way to rediscover my country than to visit both of my sons? I began to plan a June and July cross-country trip to relearn what it feels like to be an American. I'd ride from Boston to California – from son to son.

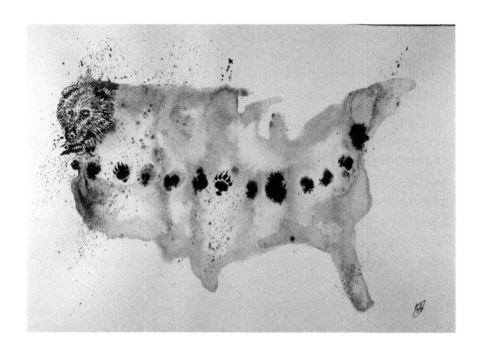

CHAPTER 2: BEARS

Why don't you just buy
a convertible?

I downshifted and began my turn. Suddenly, the front wheel slipped sideways. I was thrown to the ground like a rag doll. It happened in zero seconds. My helmet bounced on the gritty road surface. The engine coughed, died and began to smoke. Flashing black spots and little white stars filled my vision. Time stopped while I remained still and took inventory.

"I'm conscious and I can move my neck. That's good."

"My arms and hands move. Also good."

"My right leg is wedged under the bike and I'm pinned to the ground. Not so good."

"I can move my leg and wiggle my foot. Probably not broken."

"I smell gas."

Traffic was stalled at a red light on the other side of the road. The drivers and passengers had a clear view of the accident. As I lay trapped under the motorcycle, I imagined a parent turning to the teenager in the back seat.

"See, that's why I don't want you riding a motorcycle."

I reflected on the events that carried me to this little town in Pennsylvania where at sixty-seven years old, I found myself flat on my back under a 750-pound Harley Davidson.

* * *

The first time I rode a motorcycle, I was sixteen years old. It was one of those warm, clear, blue-sky days that hint at the turn of the season. Summer and freedom were just around the corner. The seniors had left school to meet their futures. We underclassmen were counting down the last weeks to the end of the school year and the teachers were just as anxious for parole. The school atmosphere was relaxed, anticipating the long holiday. My friend and I took advantage of the indifferent security and skipped out for an hour of borrowed liberty.

We hurried through the empty halls and out the back door to the student parking lot. His Honda S90 was leaning on its kickstand in a corner by the fence. He handed me a helmet and strapped on his. I was impressed by his expert tinkering on the side of the engine. Later I learned how to adjust the choke and turn on the fuel valve. He climbed on and kicked it to a coughing, smoky start. I climbed on behind him.

As we lurched out of the lot, I grabbed the bottom of the seat to keep from falling off the back. We rode behind Quincy Square to Bob & Ray's Sub Shop. We ordered large Italian submarine sandwiches with everything and ate them on a bench in the sun. By the time we returned to school, I was hooked. I needed a motorcycle of my own. I've been riding ever since.

As the concept for the trip started to take form, I considered the vehicle I wanted to use. In two months I could travel from coast to coast by bus, train, plane, car, van or camper. The logical choice was to rent a car. They are easy to drive and park and affordable to rent. A car has a trunk and a back seat that can carry lots of gear and clothes and keep it all dry. A cooler with drinks and food will sit nicely on the back seat, or on the passenger seat with maps on top. In a pinch, I could sleep at a rest stop or by the side of the road in a car. A car is a home on wheels. But I didn't want a home; I wanted a ride. Here again was a 'heart over head' decision.

Early on, I decided this would be a motorcycle trip. It wasn't a rational decision, it was emotional. I had no interest in cars, vans or campers. If I was going to spend a couple of months on the road, I wanted to do it on a motorcycle.

* * *

My second motorcycle was a gold Honda CB350 that resembled a tangerine more than a Krugerrand. It was sturdy enough to travel unpaved fire roads. It could negotiate the soft, leafy earth and dense tree growth in the forests. I bought a can of forest green Krylon paint to camouflage the fenders and gas tank. It wasn't pretty, but it was almost invisible leaning against a tree at a campsite.

In my early years of motorcycle camping, I'd strap my gear on the bike and ride for a week or weekend with no plan or direction. At the end of the day, I camped where I could find a likely spot. I'd ride along a secondary road at dusk till I found a path leading into the forest. I was looking for a fire road, or an old quarry or lumber road. My favorites were overgrown, with weeds sprouting in the middle. There are still lots of them in

New England.

I'd roll my forest-green bike into the woods in low gear with the lights off. I decided I had gone far enough when I could no longer see the lights from the road behind me, or from any houses. Usually the forest floor was thick with leaves or pine needles, too soft for the kickstand. I'd lean the bike against a tree, unpack and set up my stealth camp. For this was private property and I was trespassing. In the morning I'd rise early, break camp, leave no trace and be on my way.

As I got older, my motorcycles got bigger, heavier and less nimble in the woods. A cruiser big enough for a cross-country trip isn't built for off-road exploring or weaving among the pines. In a pinch, I'll camp as the need dictates these days, but for the most part, my stealth camping days are part of my past.

This time, I decided that I would explore America along a route that hopped between national and state parks and forests.

I bought an 'America the Beautiful' discount national park pass and a large, fifty-state wall map of the U.S. I mounted the map on the whiteboard in my den. I circled Boston and Tahoe City with a red marker and New York City and Denver in blue. A motorcycle can travel about two hundred miles between fill-ups. I expected to ride for four to seven hours per day. Including fuel, food and comfort stops; that translates to between two hundred and three hundred and fifty miles per day. I scanned my wall map for the green national and state parks within a day's ride of each other, then drafted an itinerary with the help of online maps and mileage estimates – all on secondary roads.

I traced an east-to-west route with little, yellow sticky notes. They inched their way across my map from right to left, roughly following U.S. Route 50. There is something about a visual aid that helps a concept move toward reality. As those little pieces of paper crawled across the miniature USA on my wall, I began to imagine myself on the road. I fixed a motorcycle photo on the top of the map for inspiration.

It wasn't long before my wall map was cluttered with little yellow flags, blue and red marks and colorful magnets. It looked like a plan. In New England, the sticky notes were scattered but close together. This part of the trip was made up of short visits to the homes of friends and family.

When I left New York City, I'd start camping. From there the flags stretched out, forming a connect-the-dots zigzag east to west. I'd cross New Jersey into Pennsylvania, riding south-west then west, in daily jumps between forests and parks. I'd cross through the middle of Kansas into Colorado and stop in Denver. After Denver, I'd cross the Rocky Mountains, then drop into the Utah and Nevada deserts.

* * *

In 2007, I'd been living in The Netherlands for four years. Things weren't going well. I had recently ended the relationship that brought me to Holland. I was living in the spare bedroom of a Dutch friend while I re-evaluated my choices and considered my options. As is common with me, I went on the road to clear my head. This time I drove to Sauerland.

Sauerland is a beautiful rural area of western Germany. The hilly farmland is blanketed with pine forests interspersed with verdant fields of corn, wheat and hay, populated by healthy, content cattle and the few people who are lucky enough to live there.

I stayed in a small hotel in the mountains; a hospitable, family-run inn, a little more than a bed and breakfast. The locals call them pensions. I've since stayed at a few of these in Germany. They offer a delicious continental breakfast of local vegetables, fruits, cold cuts, cheeses, breads, hard-boiled eggs, coffee and juices. For dinner, there's a simple menu. For example, on Tuesday, it's schnitzel. There's usually a simple bar with bottles of wine, local beer on tap and a few bottles of stronger stuff for those who want it. Guests mingle in the common rooms and on the terraces when they are not off exploring the forest trails or visiting local sights.

My hosts offered a barbecue on the terrace on Thursday evening. It was a clear, balmy summer evening with the scent of pine wafting on the mild breeze flowing up the mountain. We guests mixed and mingled, some offering helpful advice to the good-humored chef grilling steaks and corn-on-the-cob. Beer and wine flowed freely. Most of the guests were Dutch, some German and one American. I met Hanneke at this barbecue. She was also in Germany clearing her head in the mountain air. We talked late into the night and became friends.

After that long weekend holiday, she returned to the Utrecht area where she lived and worked. I drove back to Den Haag to look for a job. We stayed in touch, became closer and saw each other on weekends. It wasn't until seven years later in 2014 that Hanneke moved to join me in Delft, and we became partners. The Netherlands recognizes a partner relationship much like a marriage. I will not go into detail about Hanneke. She is a private person and would not want me to fit her into a character description. I'll simply say she's my partner, my conscience, my balance, my social director and the diplomatic liaison of our little democracy. She keeps me as honest as I can be. And she gives great hugs.

* * *

Hanneke always surveyed the map when she popped into my den with a snack or a cup of coffee. From New England to eastern Kansas, the map is tinted green. From Denver west, it fades to sandy colors and dark brown for the mountains. She has visited New England, but not the western part of the country. She asked me about the desert.

"What will you do if you run out of gas?"

"There are plenty of gas stations."

Hanneke put her index finger on the map, just west of Denver. She traced her finger over my yellow sticky notes from Vail to Lake Tahoe.

"What are those states?"

"That's Colorado, then comes Utah, Nevada and California."

"How many miles of desert are there?"

"It's not just desert, there are cities, with people."

"How many miles?"

"About a thousand. But with cities and towns in between, see?" I pointed to Grand Junction, Delta and Fallon.

"How many kilometers is that?"

"About fifteen hundred."

"What if you break down? What will you do?"

"I'll have tools with me."

"What if you get in an accident?"

"I'll be careful. I won't get in an accident."

"You can't promise that."

"I know. But I'll be careful."

She drew a link between lonely roads, old movies and threats to my safety.

"You'll be all alone. How will I know you're safe?"

"Safe from what?"

"You know, you saw that movie."

"Are you afraid I'll run into a gang of homicidal, kidnapping truckers?"

"Yes."

I admit to being somewhat dense when communication shifts to emotional fears. However, I have learned a few things over the years about Hanneke's way of looking at things.

Hanneke sees bears in new situations. Bears are usually a metaphor but sometimes they can be real. Like when Hanneke warned me about bears before a recent canoe trip to the Allagash Wilderness Waterway. The conversation went something like this.

"Are there bears in the Allagash?"

"There are all kinds of animals in the Allagash. It's a wilderness."

"Are there bears?"

"I've seen lots of moose, deer, eagles, otters, racoons, fish, frogs; yes, and a bear or two."

"So there are bears."

"Yes."

"What do you do about the bears?"

"I leave them alone. They leave me alone. It works out well for everybody."

"What if they attack?"

"They don't attack. They don't want anything to do with people."

"But what if they do?"

"Hanneke," (this is me trying to be patient). "A bear can smell you, I mean me, a quarter mile away. When they smell a human, they go the other way. For every bear you see in the woods, there are ten that you don't see because they don't want anything to do with you."

"How many bears have you seen?"

"You mean on my last trip?"

"No, in total."

"I don't know, a few."

"So there are ten times a few bears in the woods with you. And you have nothing but a nylon tent to protect you."

"I don't need protection; I've never needed protection. I've been camping and canoeing there forever and never had a problem with a bear."

"Do you hang your food from a tree?" Hanneke saw this on the Discovery Channel.

"Bears can climb trees. If there's food in a tree and the bear wants it, he'll get it. I store the food in little, blue plastic barrels – outside the tent."

"That's not making me feel better."

"What will make you feel better?"

"Tell me you'll watch out for bears."

"Really? That's what you want?"

"Yes, I want to know you'll be careful of bears."

"OK, I'll watch out for bears, and I'll be careful."

"Promise?"

"Yes, I promise."

The Allagash conversation taught me how to reason with Hanneke about the homicidal, kidnapping truckers waiting for me in the desert. I didn't argue that it was only a movie.

I said, "OK, I'll watch out for homicidal, kidnapping truckers." And Hanneke felt better about that bear.

"What about running out of gas?"

As the bears poked their heads up, one by one, Hanneke and

I talked them over and tucked them away. Sometimes they would reappear suddenly and unexpectedly, like the plastic moles at the carnival game that you hit with a rubber hammer.

The bears offered many plausible reasons to postpone or cancel the trip. I think when an adventure looms, a part of us wants to avoid it and stay safe at home. In all fairness, all the bears did not come from Hanneke. Some were introduced by friends and acquaintances. And of course I had my own, secret bears: insecurities, anxieties and doubts.

Age was a big ugly bear and a friend favorite.

"You're not a kid anymore. You could have a heart attack."

"You better be careful at your age. Reflexes slow by one percent a year from the age of twenty-four. Figure it out, you're functioning at about half speed."

"Admit it, you're going through a midlife crisis. Why don't you just buy a convertible?"

Midlife? I *wish*.

Others were more direct: "You're going to kill yourself."

This warning came up more than once: "You're being irresponsible. What's Hanneke going to do if you get killed or worse, maimed?"

Many of my bears were conceptual, little fears that grow like mushrooms in the dark soul. There were insidious doubts and fears specific to my journey.

- *If I get in an accident would the motorcycle insurance be valid? Would my Dutch medical insurance cover me in the U.S.?*

- *Would my high-tech navigation system guide me across the country? Would my phone and Bluetooth connection work?*

- *What if the bike breaks down in the middle of nowhere? What if I crash the motorcycle and get hurt?*

• *I'm planning to visit my sons. Would they welcome me?*

I was especially nervous about meeting my older son, Matt. He and I had fallen out of touch. I worried about my reception, or if he'd even see me.

I had lots of domestic reasons to delay or cancel the trip.

Hanneke put on a brave face, but two months is a long time. She would shoulder all the domestic responsibilities while I was away. There was the house and garden to maintain, bills to pay, repairs to manage. She became increasingly nervous as the end of May grew closer.

"Wouldn't a couple of weeks be enough?"

I promised to keep in contact from the road and support however I could. I left her a list of emergency phone numbers and contact information.

"What if you're robbed?"

I gave her photocopies of all my credit cards, driver's license and passport, with phone numbers in case they were lost or stolen.

She gave me a money belt.

CHAPTER 3: FOREPLAY

I was a trusting young fool

A trip is a lifetime experience made up of three parts; the plan, the execution and the memories. Planning an adventure – and every trip is an adventure – stimulates my imagination, prolongs the fantasy and increases my anticipation. Planning allows me to experience the trip in my mind before I leave home. It gets my heart pumping, adrenaline flowing and my mind spinning with exciting ideas and possibilities. I've always savored the planning process. Planning is foreplay.

I studied maps for hours at a time before I launched my canoe into the Yukon River. I read about the explorers, gold seekers, trappers and hunters who went before me. I read about the bears in the forests, the fish in the rivers and the voracious mosquitos everywhere. I read stories about the river. The Yukon is icy cold. It is almost two thousand miles long, two miles wide, and thirty feet deep. It is so muddy you cannot see your hand in the water from the wrist down.

Thousands of tributaries, large and small, flow into and feed the Yukon River with fresh water draining from the neighboring highlands. At the inlets, just before the tributaries meet the big river, are the best spots for good fishing. The waters at the merge are turbulent, clear, cold and clean. I found such a spot on one of my maps and marked it. During the cold winter nights of excited planning, I imagined standing on that gravel bank in the sub-artic sun. I cast into the rushing waters and hooked a grayling.

Six months later, I paddled to that tributary. I caught five graylings and built a campfire. While I cooked and ate the fish for lunch, I watched the forest for hungry bears. I spent many hours planning and dreaming about that two-hour fishing lunch. I savored that meal for thirty years.

A plan is not a commitment, it's a daydream. A detailed plan doesn't guarantee success, just as a vague plan doesn't mean failure. If my plan changes, it doesn't derail the trip. And the trip doesn't need to follow the plan. Often things go sideways, and I have to improvise. Planning for the joy of planning is its own entertainment. You have to like it to do it. I do a lot of planning because I like it, not because it's necessary.

I spent more than six months preparing for my two-month motorcycle ride across America. Every part of the plan bumped my anticipation up a notch. As the departure date approached, my excitement grew. Planning filled the gray Dutch winter with bright possibilities.

I'm more of a tent than a motel guy. I'll stay in motels in a crunch, but given the choice, I'd rather sleep under the stars.

Additionally, the tent freed me from organizing a complicated travel itinerary with scheduled motel stops along a fixed route. The U.S. has a wide network of state and national parks, forests and conservation areas that are popular and inexpensive.

I have always found it easier to meet and talk with people at a campsite than in a motel. People at campsites start off with a common bond, an affinity for nature. Plus, I've always found that a campfire facilitates conversation more than a television.

* * *

My first wilderness camping experience dates back to when Nixon was President. A college friend and I studied a map of the northeast United States. We searched for the largest green patch within a day's drive of Boston. That's about as far as I trusted my old Chevy. We discovered the Allagash Wilderness Waterway, north of Millinocket, Maine. We scraped together some primitive camping gear, bought some food and drove north. We rented a canoe at Prays General Store and paddled for two weeks, camping along the way.

The days were rainy and windy and the nights were wet and cold. We burned our food, boots and hands over smoky campfires. We lined our packs with plastic trash bags that did little to protect our clothes and sleeping bags from the rain and breaking waves. Without map-reading skills, we navigated a serpentine route across deep, glacial lakes, quiet, shallow sloughs, and portaged muddy trails. We broke a paddle and lost a life jacket in the wind-driven three-foot swells on Chamberlain Lake. We dragged, scraped and carried the aluminum canoe through low water, and over rocks and gravel banks. We were two happy idiots with only a benevolent universe to protect us from the elements and ourselves. Somehow, we survived.

I sometimes marvel that we ever went camping again. We returned damp, filthy, tired, scratched, burned, bug-bit and happy. It was a defining trip. There were more reasons to quit camping than to repeat the disaster. You have to love camping to do it again after a trip like this. Since then, I've done a lot of canoe/camping trips. But the Allagash is where I grew up.

It was an easy transition from canoe to motorcycle camping. A motorcycle is a canoe on an asphalt river, except with less storage capacity. You've got a couple of saddlebags and maybe a duffel or two strapped behind you. You have to pack efficiently.

When I mentioned the trip in conversations with friends, in addition to their helpful observations about the dangers and my sanity, some expressed interest in following my progress. They suggested I blog along the way. But social media is not a big part of my life. I use email but I'm not really a Twitter, Instagram, or Facebook person. But maybe a blog?

I know me. I've always kept a paper journal. I use a fountain pen because I like the smooth way the ink flows onto the paper. Writing is as much about the process as the result. When I read an old trip journal, I remember where I was. I remember if it was rainy or sunny. I remember the feel of the picnic table, if it was wooden or metal. I can almost smell my pipe and feel the warmth of the campfire. Sometimes my writing was tight and cramped because I tried to squeeze in the last line before turning the page. When the pen went dry, I remember if I ran out of ink or I was reclined in my tent with gravity working against the flow. When blue ink shifts to black, I remember why. When I shift to pencil it means I lost or wore out my pen. The coffee-stained pages and raindrop-smudged ink bring back memories of their own.

I visualized myself at the end of the day surrounded by wilderness and beauty, with a laptop on a picnic table squinting at a computer screen and I decided: no blog. I trimmed my technology list to a mobile phone, a camera and an e-reader. I would charge the phone from the bike battery while I was riding and my e-reader and helmet receiver when I stopped for the night. It all took up very little space and worked pretty well.

If you imagine a breakdown on the road far from home, there is no limit to the tools and replacement parts that come to mind. I'm not a mechanic, but I've muddled my way through a few repairs. And I've done a lot of maintenance work on my motorcycles and cars over the years. Youth and poverty helped me identify the limits of my mechanical skills. A bargain vehicle isn't a pile of junk, it's an opportunity to learn. I bought my first motorcycle before I owned a car, even before I had a license to drive.

* * *

After my first motorcycle ride, I returned home filled with excitement. I announced to my parents that I was going to buy a motorcycle. My mother was horrified. I'm sure her head was filled with images of Hell's Angels and her broken and bloody son spread all over the road. My father was thoughtful. They promised to discuss it. The next day I was thrilled when my father told me they had decided to let me buy a motorcycle. In fact, he knew someone who might have one for sale.

"How much money have you got?"

"I have $300 in the bank. Is that enough?"

"I think he might sell it for $300. How about if I ask him?"

The next weekend, we drove his Chevy Bel Air to look at the bike. The black 1963 Honda Dream 305 cc leaned against a wall in the back of the garage. His friend cleared the boxes, trash barrels and lawn mower from around the bike so we could see it.

"I haven't used it in a couple of years. It doesn't start. But all it needs is a tune-up."

I asked my father what he thought. I was so excited my suspicions were not aroused when he said: "I don't know anything about motorcycles. It's up to you."

We rolled the bike out of the garage onto the driveway to look at it. The chrome handlebars and muffler pipes were pitted and flaky with rust. The mirrors were bent sideways, the black gas tank and fenders sheathed in gray dust. The engine was grimy. The front tire was low and the back was flat. It looked beautiful.

I was a trusting young fool with stars in my eyes and rocks in my head. I happily handed over his asking price. It was all I had, four years of allowances, part-time work, odd jobs and babysitting money. We loaded the bike so the front tire hung out the back of my dad's trunk. He tied the lid down with clothes-line rope and drove it home.

I soon discovered that it needed a lot more than a tune-up. A part-time summer job helped me earn money for tools, parts and fluids. I bought a shop manual and began my education as an amateur mechanic.

My father was somehow never available to help me work on the bike. Once in a while, he'd look in the garage as I sat on the floor surrounded by a growing pile of greasy parts and ask how it was going. After the first week, I felt cheated and blamed him. I became even more determined to repair and ride my motorcycle.

It wasn't until years later that I understood my father's plan. I can imagine my parents' discussion. They conspired to let me spend all my savings on a wreck of a motorcycle in hopes I'd give up and forget it as a fleeting whim. I grudgingly admit that it was a much wiser strategy than arguing with a stubborn, starry-eyed teenager.

That summer I learned the basics of motorcycle maintenance. I installed new tire tubes, battery and muffler. I drained and changed the oil and replaced the fuel, oil and air filters. I installed new points, spark plugs, headlight and some wiring. I removed, flushed and cleaned the gas tank. I replaced the fuel lines and rebuilt the carburetor. I removed, lubricated, reinstalled and adjusted the clutch, gas and brake cables. I flushed and bled the brake lines. At my father's insistence, I also scrubbed the concrete garage floor with a hard bristle brush and solvent to remove the rusty gas-tank vomit. It took all summer, but I remember the thrill when the engine coughed and sputtered to its first smoky start.

By October, I was the proud holder of a Massachusetts learner's permit and the owner of a motorcycle that passed the state safety inspection. Looking back on my entry into the world of motorcycling, it sort of compares to my introduction to camping. There were more reasons to quit than continue. I think my father was pretty smart, but he underestimated my passion.

Since that time, I've always owned a motorcycle and always carried a tool kit. But in planning for this trip I realized that I seldom used tools on the road. I used my tools almost exclusively at home in the garage. Before I travel, I make sure my motorcycle is in good shape. I have used tools; I have worked on motorcycles; I just haven't used tools much on trips. So why should I bring them on this one? A tool kit is heavy, bulky and takes up a lot of space. Did I really need a tool kit? I thought it over. Maybe I was already carrying the only two tools I'd need: a phone and a credit card. What could I really fix on the road anyway?

In the end, I decided that I'd be more comfortable if I carried some tools. I always carry a Swiss army knife in my pocket. Two months and eight thousand miles is a long way to go without a wrench or screwdriver. I put together my own kit from the tools in my garage. It just made me feel better knowing they were there. The tool kit all fit in a small canvas bag that rested in the bottom of a saddlebag. And over the course of that summer, I was glad I had it. (If you're curious, you can find the list in the Appendix.)

I already owned most of the camping equipment I'd need, but I borrowed a tent from Hanneke's son and his wife.

I assembled a simple kitchen kit that fit into one saddlebag. The other saddlebag held my tools, stove fuel, water bottles, motor oil, and rain gear with some space left over. Behind me on the seat, I strapped a Harley Davidson waterproof luggage box for my clean clothes, towel and toilet kit. As part of my promise to Hanneke to ride responsibly, I always wore my multilayered, Kevlar-reinforced motorcycle jacket.

By the time spring arrived, I had assembled and field-tested all my gear. I even cooked a meal on my stove in the back garden. I used my camping pans, plates, cups and utensils. I loaded everything on my Dutch motorcycle and took a ride in the Netherlands. My equipment was ready.

CHAPTER 4: THE HARLEY

The beast started with a roar
like a prehistoric monster.

My plans were progressing well, but without a vehicle, they were still just a plan. To make my fantasy a reality, I needed wheels. Shipping my Dutch motorcycle to the U.S. for the summer would be problematic, bureaucratic and just too much trouble. I resolved to search for a good, used cruiser in the U.S. I needed more than a motorcycle large enough to cross the country, I needed all the U.S. paperwork that makes it legal; a title, registration and insurance. This was a daunting roadblock, especially for a non-resident.

Paul's my oldest friend. We met at the Quincy YMCA when he was fourteen years old and I was sixteen. Paul grew up in Hull, Massachusetts; a tough guy, from a tough town. Pound for pound, Paul was one of the toughest judo players I ever knew. He wasn't afraid of anyone, no matter their size, weight or rank. He loved to fight. And he never gave up. There was no meanness in Paul. He fought for the challenge, for the competition, for the joy of the battle. He fought to win. He never fought to hurt. He was a clean competitor, no dirty tricks. He was a fighter who combined energy, strength and technique in equal measures. And he was fast. He was fun to watch and scary to fight. But that was fun too. Because you could fight Paul without fear. You might lose, but his technique and sportsmanship guaranteed you would not get hurt. You might fly through the air and land flat on your back, but his skill was so thorough that it would be a fast, painless ride. And you'd probably both be smiling at the end of it. I know he would. And I did plenty of times.

Paul joined the U.S. Navy when he was eighteen years old. He was always vague about the details. I may be wrong, but I suspect it was part of a deal to keep him out of jail. After he joined the Navy, he visited when his travels brought him back to New England. Our friendship continued to grow. He is one of those rare friends that whenever we get together, no matter how long we've been apart, our conversation continues as though we started it yesterday. We know each other so well, there is no need for new introductions. Paul has been my friend for over fifty years. He traveled the world and retired after putting in his twenty. Paul supplemented his Navy pension after retirement with a job as a security supervisor in New Hampshire.

When Paul and I get together, we sit on his back deck overlooking the New Hampshire forest that surrounded his home. We discuss the meaning of life like two old friends with seriousness and humor, lubricated by domestic beer. In his job, he meets the public under sometimes stressful circumstances. If there is anyone I'd want to protect me, it's Paul. He keeps a cool head and a firm resolve. He will not abuse his authority. He is a strong, tough realist but not a hot head.

In the autumn before my trip, Hanneke and I sat with Paul and his wife Caroline on the deck in back of his house enjoying the warm sunshine of an Indian Summer, under the rainbow-colored trees.

"Paul, you were a logistics guy in the Navy. I need some advice on a "logistics" problem."

"I was in procurement. That's not logistics."

"Same thing."

"It's not the same thing, Barra; you don't know what you're talking about."

"That's why I need you. How about a hug?"

"Maybe later."

"OK. Here's my procurement/logistics problem, I need a motorcycle to ride across the country next summer."

"Why don't you rent one?"

"Do you know how much that costs?"

"Too expensive?"

"It's too expensive for me. I want to buy a used one here."

"Shit, Barra, you can buy mine. I'll give you a good deal."

I took a sip of beer. Paul watched me and sipped his. "Are you serious?"

"Sure."

"Do you want that hug now?"

"I'm getting my gun."

"Really, you want to sell your bike?"

"Not really, but I haven't been riding it much and I want a pick-up truck with a plow for the winter."

"Paul, let's think about this for a minute. I need the bike next summer. Not now."

Paul lit a cigarette. "You can keep it in my garage till you need it."

"Wow, Paul. This might work."

"Sure it'll work. Want to take a look at it?"

We walked out to his garage. The gleaming, black Harley stood poised on its kickstand, ready for an adventure. I was thrilled. It was just what I wanted for a long tour. It looked solid and powerful with a windshield, leather saddlebags and a chrome sissy bar.

"How big is that engine?"

"1450 cc and it's only got 17,000 miles on it. It's in great condition, nothing wrong with it."

"How old is it?"

"2001"

"Sold!"

"Don't you want to take it for a test ride?"

"Good idea."

Paul wheeled the Harley out of the garage into the driveway and pushed the starter. In The Netherlands, I ride a BMW R1200C. The engine ticks quietly and smoothly. This beast started with a roar like a prehistoric monster.

"It's loud," Paul said.

"I noticed."

"I like it loud. I mounted those pipes to get that sound."

I climbed on and rode it down the road and around the corner, probably the shortest test ride ever. I rode directly back to Paul's house where Paul, Caroline and Hanneke were waiting on the lawn. All three of them were smiling; so was I. Just as Paul promised, it ran perfectly.

"I love it."

"I knew you would. I hate to sell it. Hell, I'd like to go with you. But I can't. So the bike is yours if you want it."

"It's perfect for a long ride."

"You bet it is."

I wrote Paul a check before he changed his mind. I was excited. Though I have owned a motorcycle of one type or another for more than fifty years, I had never owned a Harley. I was unprepared for the learning curve ahead of me.

I flew back to The Netherlands at the end of October in high spirits. I carried the shop manual for my 2001 Harley Davidson Heritage Softail Classic in my suitcase. My trip had changed from a dream to maybe a reality. I was a Harley owner.

I didn't realize how different my new motorcycle was from all the other bikes I had owned and ridden before. Riding the Harley would require me to develop an expanded set of skills. But that was a surprise that was waiting for me to discover on the road ahead.

CHAPTER 5: SETTING OUT

*Nothing of value originated
from America.*

Friday, May 31

Flat, channeled polders verged the highway, cloaked in fog from Delft to Schiphol. Paris was shrouded in clouds and it was a slate gray afternoon and raining when I landed at Logan Airport in Boston. I cleared Customs and merged with the crowd hurrying to the exits. I waited at the sidewalk for the bus that would carry me to Portsmouth, New Hampshire.

After twenty years navigating airports in Europe and Asia, I was already viewing Boston with new eyes. Logan Airport has been a rat's nest of reconstruction for as long as I can remember. Its landscape is cluttered with Jersey barriers, orange cones and traffic control signs in seemingly random and ever-changing configurations. I spent most of my life within fifty miles of this city. Yet every time I travel to and from Logan Airport, I get lost. I get so confused by the traffic congestion, detours and unintelligible road signs that I panic and often end up driving in the wrong direction. So, I was delighted to rest in my seat and leave the navigation responsibility to our patient bus driver. I rested and let my mind drift.

Rain-streaked diagonal soot lines down the wide windows as we bounced north out of Boston. Rush hour traffic oozed along slick, asphalt channels. The bus approached one of the dark funnels that characterize the inner-city freeway system. Traffic crawled and merged. Six lanes squeezed down to two. I may have recognized a few fuzzy traffic signs through the window, but I wasn't trying very hard. My eyes were filled with a Milky Way of reflected vehicle brake lights and flashing yellow caution lights. I relaxed with the gentle rocking motion of the bus, content that the bewildering maze was not my problem

At six o'clock on Friday morning, Hanneke drove me to the airport. The flight crews carried me to Paris then Boston. The bus driver would deliver me to Portsmouth, where Paul would pick me up and drive me to his house. By the time I met Paul, I'd have traveled four thousand miles in other people's care. That's the distance across America. When I arrived at Paul's, I'd need to prepare and pack the motorcycle. That was for later. For now, it felt good to float and reflect.

Ten years earlier, I rode the Trans-Siberian Railway across Europe and Asia. Four friends traveled together for six weeks. We were an odd group; a Dutchman, a Filipino, an Indonesian and an American. In a restaurant in Mongolia, one of our group revealed her view of America. She said it casually, sharing an

American truism everyone knew.

"Nothing of value originated from America. There is no American cuisine, no art, philosophy or religion. America is a country without a soul. The only contribution America has made to the world is the hamburger. Even that is a lie because it's not ham."

I was surprised and hurt. My response was defensive.

"If America is so bad, why does everyone want to move there?"

"Because it's rich. Poor people want to move there for a better life. They think everybody in America is rich."

"So America is the land of money and hamburgers?"

"And guns. Americans love guns."

Over the years I've listened as non-American acquaintances casually season conversations with their impressions about America and Americans, stereotypes they accept as reality.

They accept opinions and rumors as fact and incorporate them into their belief systems. Many non-Americans judge us very much as my Filipino friend did: as rich, loud, greedy, fat, aggressive, Christians, prudish, lovers of baseball, barbecues, guns and gas-guzzling, eight-cylinder engines, who don't care about the environment and are ignorant of geography and languages. They see Americans as wealthy but ignorant.

It's not all negative. Not everyone hates us. There is a grudging admiration of U.S. economic success. People buy and imitate U.S. products, fashions and music. They follow U.S. news.

They are not much into U.S. sports but very into U.S. movies, TV and travel. They love the U.S. National Parks and Forests, wilderness areas, the multi-lane highways, free parking, Disney World, New York City, New Orleans, Smithsonian museum, California coast, redwoods, the Grand Canyon, barbecues and lobster.

They respect America's financial strength and imitate the systems that support it. In fact, those systems are changing European life. Fast food restaurants, mega-supermarkets, warehouse stores, health maintenance organizations (HMOs) and liability lawsuits are just some examples of U.S. business models that have migrated. They have even adopted our holidays as commercial opportunities. The Netherlands doesn't celebrate Thanksgiving, but Black Friday marketing campaigns are prolific. Halloween and Christmas celebrations are growing business opportunities.

Another side of the world view of America is not so positive. Many people view our world postures as aggressive and political positions as macho bravado. Loud American tourists reinforce that image on a personal scale. Many Dutch people, with characteristic candor, express the view that Americans are shallow and superficial. They cite the greeting, "How are you?" They see this as an empty expression, meaningless and hollow, a waste of words. They can't imagine anyone would or could care how a stranger feels. So why ask? The Dutch aren't alone in this opinion.

Non-Americans criticize and at the same time depend on U.S. military strength. They question the motives of U.S. political and military interventions in Cuba, Vietnam, Afghanistan, Iraq and others. They also criticize the U.S. when it does not interfere in conflict areas, like Syria, and Eastern Europe and Ukraine. They resent and criticize the U.S. intelligence community; the CIA, NSA, TSA, FBI, while at the same time they imitate them.

They recognize their dependence on the U.S. military. They acknowledge the need for a strong world peacekeeper to enforce international agreements. They can't and don't want to do it. They don't have the resources, so they contribute to U.S. military actions as required by international agreements. They recognize the benefits of aligning behind the U.S.

They acknowledge, sometimes reluctantly, that this system provides a more secure balance of world power. Their citizens pay lower taxes for military spending in their own countries because the U.S. military is so large. European politicians and other U.S. allies gain political leverage by speaking to local popular opinion. They publicly criticize U.S. actions while quietly supporting them with diplomatic agreements. Just as American politicians do.

I've lived in this schizophrenic society for almost twenty years, trying to make sense of what I observe and experience. I've engaged in many discussions with knowledgeable and ignorant, curious and critical friends, colleagues and strangers. People often ask me to explain why America did this, why the President said that. They want to know about the real America and Americans. I've tried to explain, defend, apologize and express pride in my country.

I learned that when you're away you become an ambassador for your homeland. People see you as the example of life where you are from. When you meet people from other countries and cultures, you are a representative of your country. Many of the people you interact with have little or no direct contact with your country or the people in it. They watch how you act and listen to what you say. You are American. Just as visitors to America represent their countries, Americans abroad leave a lasting impression. If you are loud, Americans are loud. If you are happy, Americans are happy. If you are patient, Americans are patient. It's a big responsibility, but it's real.

I discovered that people in other countries know more about America than we do about them. They speak our language. The most common language in the world is bad English. Two billion people speak it. They know the names of our President and Vice President. They probably know at least some of the Cabinet Secretaries and Supreme Court Justices. During an election, they know the candidates and their positions. They broadcast American movies, watch American television, listen to American music, read American news and play American video games. They know there are somewhere between forty-eight and fifty-two states, and they can probably name more than the average American high school student. If they haven't been there, they have friends and colleagues who have. So, though you are their real, live representation of America, they have already formed opinions and are eager to learn more. So they ask questions.

Over the last few years, I began to recognize that I was becoming disconnected from my country. This feeling intensified with the 2016 Presidential campaign and even more with the election of Donald Trump. Like most of my friends and colleagues from all over the world, I was surprised. I guess even Trump was shocked, because he had already prepared to challenge the election results as a Clinton fraud before he discovered he'd won the electoral vote.

I was disillusioned by the vitriolic American campaign that sensationalized character over issues and hyperbole over facts. Is it possible to be disappointed by your country, embarrassed? I was confused. People asked for my opinion. They were also confused and concerned. They asked what was going on in America. I realized I didn't know. I wasn't able to answer their questions.

Instead of offering answers, I quipped a quote attributed to P.T. Barnum, "You never go broke appealing to the lowest common denominator."

However, that wasn't really an answer. My ignorance confirmed for me that I had lost touch with my country. After spending so many years in Europe, I was not really connected to American culture or Americans. What was happening in America was as foreign to me as it was to my Dutch friends. I was seeing America as an outsider. I listened to European perspectives, watched Dutch television, read and heard international news and opinions. But I wasn't listening to Americans. I wasn't speaking with people who lived and worked in America. I was far from their reality. I no longer shared American experiences, challenges, ambitions and fears. I did not have a feel for the American way of life. I've lived in Europe so long that I've absorbed a new cultural perspective. My thinking was muddled. My purpose for this trip was to try to repair that.

Outside, the rain had stopped. The late afternoon sun was breaking through. The bus pulled into the Portsmouth terminal. I hauled my heavy duffel bags from the luggage compartment and lifted them onto a wheeled trolley. I called Paul, then sat on a bench to wait. The rain had cleared and cooled the air and scrubbed it clean.

While I was wool gathering, Paul and Caroline pulled into the parking lot. I stood, waved and smiled. Paul had cultivated a ZZ Top-style beard in the time since we last saw each other. His stocky frame had widened since we were teenagers together at the Quincy YMCA and he filled the driver's seat. He smiled as he pulled up and stroked his hand over his bald head.

I jammed my luggage into the back of his compact hatchback and folded myself into the back seat. Paul drove. Caroline sat in the passenger seat. It was cool and breezy in the late afternoon. The sun shone through clouds that were breaking up and hurrying off to the horizon. We stopped for pizza and beer.

Paul and Caroline live about five miles from the ocean. For Paul, that's far enough from the craziness that descends on the southern New Hampshire beaches with the summer tourist migration.

Caroline walked into the house. Paul and I went directly to the garage. The roll-up door stood open. I dropped my bags on the concrete apron. For a minute, I just stood and looked at the motorcycle. It leaned on its kickstand, polished black and chrome. It looked beautiful, eager to leap out onto the road. I felt the thrill of anticipation up my spine and in the pit of my stomach.

Paul extracted a beer for each of us from his garage fridge. We got right to work. Bike parts and tools littered the concrete floor. Paul removed the tarnished round mirrors from the handlebars and installed new rectangular glass. I removed the seat and installed the new battery.

I fired up the bike and took it for a quick test ride before it got dark. The Harley felt hulking, heavy and powerful. Back in the garage, I emptied my duffel bags onto the floor. I repacked my gear for the ride. I filled the saddlebags and mounted the gear and clothes bags on the back of the bike with straps and bungee cords. Everything fit as planned. The bike was packed and ready to go.

In the house as darkness fell, we sorted out the registration, insurance and ownership papers. It was a bit of a treasure hunt, but Paul managed to find everything. We talked about liability concerns.

"Barra, this bike is insured in my name. What if you get in an accident?"

"Does the insurance cover someone using the motorcycle?"

"I don't know. Anyway, you're not using it. You bought it."

"The title is still in your name, so technically it's still your bike. I'm just test-driving it."

"I don't think they'll buy that in Nevada."

"What do you think we should do?"

"Be very fucking careful. You get in an accident and I'm fucked."

"Paul, I know it's my responsibility. I'll cover the damages if something happens."

While we talked at the kitchen table, Caroline listened from her seat in the living room. She was not entirely comfortable with this arrangement. I guess none of us were. I was taking a risk. So was Paul. Only the very young, very stupid, or best of friends put faith in this kind of agreement. Paul and I have been friends for over fifty years and there was the answer. We ended the discussion about liability. I hoped I didn't have to make good on my promise, but I would if necessary.

It was nine-thirty in New Hampshire, three-thirty in the morning in Amsterdam. I was exhausted. Paul showed me to his guest bedroom. It served as an office and storage room when there were no guests. I washed up, popped an allergy pill and crawled into the bottom bunk. I was asleep as soon as my head settled on the pillow.

CHAPTER 6: MATT

I want my son back.

Saturday, June 1

I woke at five o'clock Saturday morning. Paul's house was quiet. As I dressed, I collected my thoughts about the next stage of my trip. Today I'd head south to my son's house in Leominster. I was anxious about this visit.

When Matt was eight years old, we packed my rusty, diesel pick-up truck with food and camping gear. We roped the canoe on a two-by-four frame over the cab and cargo bed. It was an eight-hour drive from our home south of Boston to the hotel in Millinocket. The next day we navigated three more hours through the North Maine Woods on muddy, washed-out lumber roads. Water flowed and pooled in vast swampy puddle-lakes at the low points in the road. This was Matt's first overnight camping trip. I was thrilled to share my love of the wilderness with my son.

I wanted this trip to be special and it was. It rained, drizzled and misted all week. When it wasn't raining, it was cloudy and threatening rain. One golden afternoon, the sun broke through for a couple of hours. We rejoiced. We grabbed the opportunity and hung our wet clothes and gear to dry in the warm sunshine. Before dark the rain returned, but our clothes were dry and our spirits high.

Mornings, we heated hot chocolate and oatmeal on my tarnished, brass stove. We ate at the picnic table protected from the dripping sky by a blue, nylon tarp. We cooked our dinner over a smoky fire while the rain and wind rattled the fragile cover over our heads. Life was simple.

During the day we explored the winding paths through the woods, searching for the deer and moose who made them. We collected fallen trees and cut firewood. We discovered a natural spring in the forest. It formed a pool, leaking through moss-covered bedrock. Rising from deep within the granite, it delivered fresh, cold drinking water. We shared high hopes of pan-fried trout for breakfast. Every day we cast our lines into the deep, gray water. We joked that Maine must be home to intelligent fish who loved worms but avoided the hooks.

Matt never complained about the weather, about his wet sleeping bag. or the bugs and pine needles in his SpaghettiOs. He was always cheerful, always happy to go for a walk in the dripping forest. He volunteered to fetch water by himself. He didn't notice me following him at a safe distance all the way to the spring and back.

For that week Matt and I spent all our time together and mostly alone. A retired couple camping in an RV shared our campsite by the lake. Except to say hello, they went about their holiday on their own. At the end of their stay, as they were preparing their departure, the lady from the RV came over to say good-bye. She said she never saw a father and son get along so well.

It was true, but I didn't think about it until she mentioned it. Matt and I never argued. We discussed each decision and came to agreements. We didn't gripe about the terrible weather. We talked, we walked, we explored and we enjoyed our time together. There was no stress, no strain, no conflict. Just a father and son in tune with each other and the world around them.

After that trip, we explored a new section of the Allagash every year. Sometimes we enjoyed clear skies and warm days. First, it was just Matt and me. When Mike was old enough, he was happy to join. Each trip was a new success. Matt was a great example for Mike. And Mike embraced the wilderness with as much energy and joy as his older brother. Both my sons are grown now. I don't visit the Allagash as much as I used to. But I was excited to hear from Mike that he and Matt kayaked the northern wilderness together along the route we took when they were young.

The closeness faded when Matt turned sixteen. He connected with friends who offered more exciting diversions. We argued and I did my best to balance his need for freedom with my concern over the direction he seemed to be choosing. He went his own way in high school. Matt and I have had a rocky relationship since he began to test boundaries. It's an old story: the concerned father struggling with the rebellious teenager. Things didn't improve in the subsequent years that included his time at university and his parents' divorce. I miss the intimacy we shared.

* * *

Paul prepared coffee, eggs and thick bacon for breakfast. He talked about buying a house and moving nearer their children who lived in Keane. He worried that his pension wouldn't be enough for a new mortgage. Caroline sat with the puppy in her lap in front of the TV. Virginia Beach news: twelve people fatally shot at work by an angry co-worker. I was distracted, anxious to get on the road and find my way to Leominster.

After breakfast, Paul offered to lead me to the highway. I gratefully accepted. In many ways, Paul helped make this trip a reality, first by offering me his motorcycle, then arranging the pre-trip maintenance, and dealing with the paperwork, and now he was relieving me of another worry by getting me started in the right direction. Paul is a good friend.

It was an awkward good-bye. I followed Paul to the highway and parked the bike on the side of the busy road. Paul hopped out of his pick-up truck, gave me quick directions and a hug then jogged back to his vehicle. I heaved the bike off the kickstand, started the engine, clicked it into gear and merged into traffic. Paul turned right and headed home. I turned left toward the interstate. There wasn't even time to wave. Starting mileage on the odometer: 17,215.

* * *

Unsummoned memories of Matt filled my thoughts as I rode south. There were many events during Matt's teenage years that I wish I had handled better. One in particular haunts me because, thirty years later, I still don't have the right answer.

Matt wrestled for his high school team. It was the end of a successful season. Matt had qualified and won the regional championship. He was competing for the state championship at a weekend tournament. Between matches, he paced back and forth across the gym with nervous energy, head down, with a stern, tight face, totally focused on his sport. During matches he wrapped himself like an anaconda around his opponents, overcoming them with skill, strength, and patience. His muscles pulsed with energy like tightly strung piano wire. As he moved through the division, winning one match after another, he met stronger and tougher opponents.

I watched his struggles and progress with a father's pride and anxiety. I cheered his successes from the sideline, and I worried for his safety. These were big, strong guys trying to tear his head off. I wished him the joy and pride of victory and the feeling of satisfaction from hard work and training. I wanted him to win the trophy and save it with pride all his life. Mostly, I wanted him to win because he wanted it.

I watched his most difficult match, against a young man with more strength than skill. I was concerned; Matt seemed to struggle and lacked energy. It was a different match than any of his others. It played out in slow motion. Matt appeared tired; he looked to be weakening. He was more skillful than the other young man, but the other's strength was wearing Matt down. It all came down to strength of will, determination and perseverance. In the end, Matt wrapped his long body around his muscular opponent and won the match. I was relieved but concerned. He would face more challenging opponents ahead. He needed to gather his strength, find his inspiration and his heart.

Matt walked toward his mother and me at the end of the match. He was smiling. He was proud to have won. This victory qualified him to compete in the finals. As Matt approached, I faced an important decision. I asked myself, what does Matt need now? Praise for the win, or a challenge to motivate him? Should I be a coach or a father?

It didn't matter to me if Matt won or lost; I loved him anyway. It only mattered that he was satisfied with himself. I did not live vicariously through the successes of my son. His victories were his, not mine. But I wanted him to be satisfied and have no regrets. I wanted him to finish knowing that he gave it his best, win or lose.

Looking back on it now, I don't know if I made the right or

wrong decision. It still haunts me. I'd do it differently now. I think Matt needed his father's praise. Instead, I offered a coach's advice. I think I disappointed him.

* * *

The weather was sunny, cool, breezy with no threat of rain. A perfect start to the trip. I used the seventy-mile ride to Matt's house to settle myself into the bike seat, feel the shift of the luggage; which made me a bit nervous and experiment with the throttle and think about Matt.

Leominster was an hour and ten years away. I suppose it's good that the bike was unfamiliar and unwieldy. The immediate anxiety distracted me from my nervousness about meeting with Matt. The traffic, as always, was heavy near the Massachusetts / New Hampshire border. I could feel my gear bags shifting behind me. I reached back to check how much they had moved and pulled them back into place. I was satisfied they would hold till I got to Matt's. I would make some adjustments there.

In the twenty years since my divorce from his mother, my relationship with Matt has eroded. It did not suffer from the fire of an argument or the fatal explosion of a fight. We had no disagreement or confrontation. Over the years, his responses to my cards and emails slowed and shortened. Our communication broke down to only the briefest responses to my queries and his reluctant but polite agreement to accept an occasional visit. A corrosive acid slowly ate away the structure of the bond between us. I learned that Matt was married in 2017 when, on a hunch, I asked his brother. Matt and I seldom communicate and when we do, it's a different Matt than the camping partner I remembered.

I have always been curious, as the children grew up, what parts of our shared experiences they would remember. Often, when we did things together, I wondered if we were creating memories. One summer day long ago, little boy Matt let go of the string holding his helium balloon. He was standing in the front yard. He cried as he watched it drift up into the air. It became trapped in the branches of a tall pine tree beside the driveway. I climbed into the tree to retrieve it while he held his mom's hand and watched. As I climbed higher and higher, I wondered if this was something he would take with him or was it something only I'd remember. Would he remember playing catch beside the house? Skiing and sledding in the backyard? Building a snow cave on the front lawn? Riding through the woods in the old jeep? I don't know what Matt remembers because he doesn't speak to me about those things.

Growing up, Matt was a loving, friendly, happy child. He liked to hug more than Mike, who liked to wrestle. Matt was a caregiver who protected his little brother and his friends. Matt was a sociable young man, who would follow a charismatic leader. He was also independent, stubborn and strong-willed. He was competitive in sports and academics. He excelled at math and science. He chose his own study program. He submitted only one university application and was accepted. He worked for several years to finance it. He stuck with it. While many of his friends dropped out, he graduated as a mechanical engineer. Then he continued his studies for a Master's degree.

My wish for this visit was to reconnect with Matt, to open the door to closer ties. Now that he was married, I hoped he would start to develop a new perspective. I was cautious, managing my expectations. Matt is conservative and slow to change. In the past, he'd refused to discuss the issues that divide us. I tried to be realistic and not expect too much. I brought a gift – a not-so-subtle reminder of the history that I remember, a photo album. It could be titled, "This is your life (as I remember it)". It's my collection of photos of Matt as he grew up. I was hoping it would trigger some memories of the good things from his childhood.

I rolled up in front of Matt and Jessica's house just after noon. I greeted Matt, Jessica and their two dogs. Matt showed me the renovations he made inside and outside his house and garage. He accepted the photo album and handed it to his wife. Jessica flipped through it while Matt and I toured the house. I had also brought a gift for Jessica, a silver bracelet I had found during my travels in Malaysia. She put it on and showed it to Matt. I invited them to lunch. They held hands under the table. Their mutual affection was heartwarming.

They were polite. Matt has always been respectful. The conversation revolved around things; jobs, plans for a new house, selling their old house, home improvements and their pets. At one point in the conversation, Matt confided he wanted a job where he can make a contribution (to humanity). Jessica nodded in agreement as he said it. It was an uncharacteristic expression of personal feelings. I'm not used to that kind of openness from Matt.

Matt gave me a copy of their wedding photobook. The date on the cover told me they'd been married eighteen months. The photos show a small wedding with a few friends and no relatives, nobody I recognized. What happened to the closeness we shared when he was young?

I asked Matt for some advice about securing the bags to the motorcycle. I wasn't confident they were balanced and stable. He quickly saw the problem. He switched the packs. He moved the nylon duffel to the back and mounted the Harley luggage box on the seat behind me. It served as a back rest while I rode. It took him less than five minutes to figure it out, move things and tie them down, tight and neat. Of course, he's an engineer, and it shows. I used his method for the rest of the trip. It worked perfectly.

Matt and Jessica were excited about their new house. It was situated on five acres of wooded land in a rural town west of Boston. They planned to move in while I was away. He invited me to visit on my return trip. I promised to call when I got back to New England. The visit with Matt was cordial but too brief and superficial. I tried to convince myself I was OK with baby steps. But in my heart, I knew that the three-hour visit did little to rebuild the bond we once shared.

I rode away from Matt and Jessica at three o'clock and headed north toward Lebanon, New Hampshire, to visit my college friend Dan. It's about one hundred miles from Matt's to Dan's. I avoided toll roads and followed secondary roads north. The weather remained cool and breezy. The sky was filled with fluffy cumulus clouds drifting like ships at sea. I had no map and no working mobile phone, so no GPS. I navigated using route signs with compass directions. I generally headed north looking for city names I recognized and connectors to route I-89. It was Saturday afternoon. The roads weren't busy and I was in no hurry. It was only about two hours to Dan's so I cruised, feeling the bike and the road and thinking about Matt and Jessica.

I had been worried they would avoid our meeting, claiming to be busy or just not have the spirit for a visit. I'd hoped to get our differences into the open, air them out and talk them over. But Matt doesn't want to do that. Rather than push the issue, I try to be satisfied with occasional contact. It's better than none. But I wanted more. I wanted my son back. I wanted the camping Matt. I was encouraged by how well he and Jessica were getting along. It was good to see the affection they shared. Meanwhile, I felt like a stranger.

I'm a bit off balance by their lifestyle. The house and garage were cluttered with more technology than I've ever seen. Video games, computer disks, digital game boxes, laptop computers, charging cables, adaptors, hard drives, computer monitors and thumb drives littered every horizontal surface, including the sofa. A large, flat screen TV hung on the wall connected to a complex stereo system stacked in an open cabinet. A dozen speakers decorated the walls up to the ceiling. The garage was the same with an automotive flavor. Tools, parts and equipment were stacked and racked everywhere. The same was true for the cellar. It was clear that Matt is an enterprising young man with a diverse skill set. He has a bigger collection of tools and technology at forty years old than I ever had.

As I rode north, I moved thoughts of Matt and Jessica into a file cabinet in the back of my mind and focused on finding my way to Dan's. I cruised the secondary highways north in the sunshine, listening to the confident thrum and growl of the engine. I weaved from side to side to feel the balance of the bike. It was louder and lower than my BMW. It felt strong and comfortable. I liked it.

CHAPTER 7: OLD FRIENDS

It'll be good to shake
up Washington.

June 1-2

I stretched the hundred miles from Matt's into a three-hour ride. It was a pleasure to savor the quiet, New England country roads. I didn't know it then, but that would be my riding style for the next two months. I added two hundred miles to my odometer on my first day. The bike felt smooth and comfortable. I was almost sorry the ride had to end when I made the turn into Dan's driveway that evening. He strode out of his garage to greet me as I pulled up to his house. His gray hair and mustache were a welcome sight. I hadn't seen Dan in three years.

"You're late. The pizza is cold." He led me to the kitchen.

Dan's house is nestled on the top of a hill, overlooking route I-89 in northern New Hampshire. It's hard to spot from the highway. The earth tones, green shingled roof and clever architecture, all blend into the grassy hilltop and pine tree background. Until you make the last turn on his long, winding driveway, you might think you were climbing into a forest meadow. From his triple-paned, sliding glass windows, you can see snow-capped mountains rising to the horizon a hundred miles away. Vehicles traveling north and south on the highway below are toys on a black ribbon track. Occasionally, a growling truck, downshifting to climb the hill, wrinkles the silence of the surrounding pine forest.

Dan and I met as clueless freshmen in college. We stumbled upon each other during our first semester of ignorance and confusion and had stuck together ever since. Dan was a Psychology major. I studied History and Business Administration. Dave was the third member of our trio. We were an unlikely threesome. Dan's family owned a lumber mill in upstate New York, Dave's family were western Pennsylvania farmers, and I was the local guy from Quincy. We became fast friends. Dave dropped out in his sophomore year to marry his high school sweetheart. Dan and I graduated together and he named his second son Dave, after our old friend.

After graduation, Dan didn't return to New York to join the family business. He chose to find his own way. I'm not sure I'd have had that strength of character. He worked at part-time jobs to support himself, an anonymous, single young man in a city far from home, family and security. Dan finally found the right opportunity to suit his skills and gregarious personality. He moved to New Hampshire and has lived and worked there ever since. Dan spent the last forty years building a family, a home and a successful business. I admire Dan and respect what he's accomplished. He could have gone to work for his father. Instead, he risked everything and forged his own success.

I've visited Dan many times since he relocated to Lebanon. Our children have grown and moved out on their own. At the time of my visit, Dan and Carolyn lived alone in their house on the hill.

Life for all of us has evolved. But our friendship remains. A trip to the U.S. would not be complete if I did not spend a day or two with Dan. My visit to Lebanon gave me a chance to visit with my friend and at the same time make the final preparations for my journey across the country.

Saturday night, we ate cold pizza and drank non-alcoholic beer. We philosophized under a canopy of stars by a campfire, smoked cigars and revisited old memories.

"I have to decide whether to sign a new five-year lease or find a new building," Dan told me. "The landlord raised the rent. I might as well be in Boston."

"Why don't you retire?" Dan is six months older than me.

"What would I do if I retired?"

"You could learn to ride your new motorcycle?"

"I was thinking I could ride it to work."

"Two-fifty cc's is a nice size for around town."

"I took a safe riding course and they told me to sell it."

"Are you going to renew the lease? Five years, you'll be seventy-two."

"I just don't know what I'd do if I gave up the business. I like my work."

"Is it still making money?"

"If Clinton got in, I probably wouldn't renew the lease. But with Trump, I think I have a chance."

"What do you mean?"

"Clinton would have taxed the shit out of me. It just wouldn't have been worth the trouble. Trump's a businessman. He's an asshole, but he knows what it's like to run a business."

"But a country isn't a business. You can't fire citizens."

"No, but you don't have to give away everything to them either. I don't trust Hillary, or the Democrats. They've had it too easy for too long. They don't know what it's like to work for a living."

"And you think Trump will make things better?"

"He's an outsider, not a politician. Washington is filthy with politicians who never had to work for a living. Trump will do things differently and we need somebody different. It'll be good to shake up Washington."

Sunday, June 2

I woke at five-thirty and started my "to-do" list. When I heard them moving around, I joined Dan and Carolyn for coffee in the kitchen. Dan and I drove to the phone store where I arranged a U.S. mobile phone account. I bought some supplies for the road: coffee, oatmeal, raisins, honey, tuna, stove fuel and pipe tobacco.

We unloaded the bags at Dan's house, then I pulled out my tool kit and got to work on the motorcycle. The Harley rode lower to the ground with a lower center of gravity than my BMW back in The Netherlands. That made it agile in the turns but caused concern when I stopped in traffic. When I pushed the bike forward, like at a stop light or in a parking lot, my heels caught under the rear footrests. I suppose with experience I would get used to it, but I was concerned that I'd forget and trap my foot, tip over or twist an ankle.

I removed the passenger footrests and stored them in Dan's garage. I'd collect them when I returned. I had no room for passengers on this trip anyway. I also worked through my checklist of tasks to arrange navigation and recharging:

- Mount phone holder on handlebar
- Install USB charger and quick connect to bike battery
- Install helmet Bluetooth receiver and test it.

Later that afternoon, I repacked my bags for the long trip.

Sunday night, Dan barbecued thick, juicy steaks and vegetables over a log fire spiced with apple tree branches. We spent the evening philosophizing like so many nights before over the years, in comfortable friendship.

Monday, June 3

It was an easy two-hour ride in the sunshine to my cousin's house in Haydenville. Jim and Cindy were not home. They were celebrating Jim's birthday in Aruba. They had left me the garage door code, so I could use their house while they were away. They had left plenty of drinks and food in the fridge and three pages of Bed and Breakfast information on the kitchen table. In spite of their absentee hospitality; I was asleep by eight thirty – jet lag, I guess. In the morning, I wrote a thank you email.

Dear Jim and Cindy:

Thanks for letting me use your house on my outward-bound trip. You have such a nice place and the firemen are so kind and friendly.

Bob

CHAPTER 8: NEW YORK CITY

They found another body.

Tuesday, June 4

Tuesday morning, my fourth day on the road, I was winding my way along the secondary roads in western Massachusetts searching for I-91 south toward New York City. I felt jet-lagged, slow-witted and sluggish, not at all comfortable on the bike. We were not riding together. I rationalized; we were still getting to know each other. It felt like the Harley was trying to train me. I was ready to learn but felt tense, mechanical in my motions. I was only steering and driving. That's OK in a car, but you have to *feel* a bike. I was unfocused and distracted.

There seemed to be so much to remember. I stopped to fill the tank and laid my sunglasses on the top of the saddlebag. Half a mile down the road I realized I wasn't wearing them and pulled over. They were still resting on top of the leather bag. There was too much on my mind and I was not enjoying the ride, I was struggling, fighting it. My thoughts should have been on the ride, instead they darted around a circular list of tasks and responsibilities.

A thousand details spiraled in my head, a barber pole of worries.

"The bike insurance is in Paul's name. He took a big risk. I have to be careful."

"The Pensacola house hasn't sold yet."

I pre-paid six months insurance.

"I hope it sells before I have to pay a second installment".

"I'll probably have to lower the price."

"I should be riding, enjoying the road."

"What's the matter with my navigation system? I can't hear the speakers in my helmet."

"They worked in The Netherlands."

"You were riding a BMW. The Harley pipes are loud."

"You're talking to yourself."

"I know but I'm not answering."

I tried to adjust the volume but couldn't feel the tiny controls through my leather gloves. I fumbled at the buttons on the side of my helmet. Suddenly loud static filled my ears. I had pressed the wrong button and switched to FM radio.

Before GPS, I used maps and hand-written directions viewed

through the scratched, plastic pouch in the gas tank pack. It was not perfect, but it was simpler and reliable. Maybe I should have used paper instead of technology. I thought maybe the battery was weak and I should charge the receiver.

I pulled over to the side of the road and removed my helmet. I disconnected the receiver from the helmet and plugged it into the USB charger on my handlebar. I slid the receiver into the pocket of my gas tank pack so I could see the red charging light. My phone was mounted on the handlebar. I'd use it to navigate without audio while the receiver charged. I watched for road signs to route I-91 south.

The big American bike felt strange, unfamiliar and unwieldy, frustrated by the heavy traffic. I tried to relax and learn its language. "Do I go left or straight to I-91?"

"I think straight through the intersection."

"There's the sign."

"Lucky guess."

I looked down and a chill gripped my stomach. The Bluetooth receiver was no longer in the pocket of my gas tank pack. It was gone. The white USB cable was dangling off the handlebars, hanging out of sight in front of the bike.

"Oh no!"

I looked for a parking lot, certain that my navigation receiver had dropped off in traffic. Years ago, the wind pulled my sunglasses away from my face when I turned my head. A following car crushed them to splinters. I feared the same had happened to my Bluetooth receiver. I pulled over and stopped the motorcycle and hurriedly fumbled the kickstand, almost tipping the bike over. I felt clumsy, awkward and anxious. Even the kickstand was different from the BMW.

Sitting on the motorcycle seat in a parking lot, I gently reeled in the USB cable, afraid to reach the empty end. When the last of the cable came into view, there, at the end of the line like a fish on a hook was my Bluetooth receiver, still attached. It had not dropped off. It had pulled out of the pocket of my pack when I turned the handlebar.

"Stupid, Why didn't I think of that?"

The charging indicator light glowed green. It was fully charged.

I felt like a drowning man who suddenly held the rescue rope in his hands. I said a brief thank you to the universe and blessed the gods that protect idiots. I snapped the Bluetooth receiver onto the helmet, reconnected it to my phone and listened for the reassuring voice.

"Bluetooth connected."

My tour director was still with me. My hands were shaking. I was sweating, nervous, and unbelievably relieved that I didn't have to start my trip without GPS navigation. At the same time, I felt embarrassed and stupid. Why was I so dependent on this technology? Why was I afraid of losing it? Not for the first time I considered bypassing New York City. Maybe it was better to head west and avoid the chaos, confusion and dangers of the city.

"Maybe this was a sign that we should skip New York City."

"That's stupid."

"Are you sure? How do you know it's not a sign?"

"You're just scared."

"Yes, I'm scared."

"We're going anyway."

I found I-91 south and merged with the traffic crawling out of the suburbs toward the city. The Harley and I may not yet have been in sync, but we both agreed that we hated traffic. Even during off-peak hours, it was bumper to bumper. Occasionally we reached speeds up to fifteen miles per hour. For the next two hours I rethought my decision. New York City is a scary place, with millions of people, congested streets, confusing signs, construction barriers and who knows what other hazards.

"Where can I park the motorcycle?"

"I can't leave it on the street all night to be towed or stolen."

"Maybe it was a bad idea to start my trip with this stop."

As I inched my way south with a million other commuters, I recalled my reasons for this visit to New York City.

* * *

At eight-thirty on Tuesday morning, September 11, 2001, I arrived at Tufts University in Medford, Massachusetts for a nine o'clock appointment. The meeting never got started because the news on the television captured our attention. Two days later, I was wearing a full-face respirator and climbing through smoking rubble, testing for airborne and surface contaminants. I spent most of the next six months in New York City. In 2019, I was riding back to revisit Ground Zero.

When the two towers crashed to the ground, more than fifteen nearby buildings were damaged. Five were completely destroyed. I was called in to assess the environmental hazards in the area. My job was to lead the recovery of business assets and personal belongings of the office workers who evacuated the area. I was an environmental, health and safety consultant with a client at Ground Zero.

I spent most of the first morning working through security procedures to acquire my Ground Zero ID badge. All of us who worked on site were documented, photographed, photocopied, videotaped, fingerprinted, scanned and interrogated under the gaze of unsmiling soldiers armed with automatic weapons. At the last checkpoint, an armed soldier handed us a respirator.

We exited the security checkpoint to a scene of burning destruction. An army of firemen sprayed rivers of water on a fiery, twelve-story iron skeleton. It was twisted and teetering atop a mountain of rubble enveloped in flames and black smoke. Water arched over acres of steaming debris.

Hoses snaked across gray mud from a fleet of pump trucks. The cityscape was replaced by scarred, smoking ruins of crumbled brick and twisted steel. Weary, grimy, hard-hatted rescue workers wearing yellow and orange vests dug in the debris, climbed through mountains of rubble and sweated in the sun.

Burning concrete, plaster, PVC, copper, plastic, steel, and asphalt combined to create a soup of air pollution that burned eyes, nose, throat and lungs. We all worked with the knowledge that thousands of bodies lay crushed and buried within the smoldering wreckage. During the first few days, soldiers stopped us often to check the ID badges hanging around our necks. We stumbled to the worksite through the debris, and the mud created by the pools and streams of fire hose water.

With two other scientists, I entered the client's building through a shipping door, blocked open by a cardboard box filled with laptop computers. Inside, the air was cleaner and it was quieter but just as disconcerting. The pristine financial office space I had visited just a few months earlier was now a scene of destruction, disorder and chaos.

We donned Tyvek suits and respirators and crunched around the office space in awe. All the windows on the north and east sides, the sides facing the towers, were shattered. Glass and debris, blown in from the towers, littered the floors and desks and stuck to the walls. Gray dust coated the walls, floor, computers, printers and copy machines. It rose in clouds when we walked and stuck in our hair and on our clothes. Flat-screen monitors, gray with dust hung high on the walls. No longer busy and bright with news and stock quotes, they were silent and dark; some were cracked and broken. The electric power blew out with the windows.

The office walls were water-stained by the fire suppression system, smeared with grime and already mottled with spots of mold. The underground main had shattered, shutting down water service. When the towers collapsed, a hurricane of debris blasted through the building. All the double-paned glass windows below the tenth floor were shattered. Glass shards littered the floor like confetti in the dust at our feet. Above the tenth floor, 75 percent of the windows were broken or cracked. Above the twentieth floor, some of the windows survived. Above the thirty-fifth floor, most of the windows remained intact and the offices were deserted, silent and clean.

The view from the upper-floor windows was more dramatic than from street level. Through an empty window frame I looked down on a panoramic scene of catastrophe. A twelve-story section of the north tower remained upright. It was a canted concrete arch, simultaneously a chimney and fuel for the flames that still burned. Bent, twisted metal girders stuck like broken twigs from the ragged sides of the frame. Melted, deformed beams merged with concrete rubble to form smoking foothills, each with a team of firefighters spraying water in all directions. Clouds of steam, black smoke and flames rose, obscuring the blue sky.

The scene around the perimeter was little better. All the surrounding buildings were wounded and scarred. Many bore gaping holes in exterior walls, exposing the interior offices. It was like looking through the smoking wreck of a car accident at the wounds of a crash victim before the ambulance arrived. Hundreds of workers scurried in every direction throughout the site.

Hundreds more were beginning the clean-up work inside the buildings that remained. My heart and mind rejected the concept that human beings could cause this destruction and think it was good.

Fire hoses pumped millions of gallons of water to cool the piles of super-heated concrete and steel. Billows of white and black smoke rose from the yellow flames, sending tons of soot into the air over the city. Fifteen hundred police, fire and New York Port Authority officials patrolled the site twenty-four hours a day. Emergency vehicles, construction equipment, rescue workers, demolition teams, fire trucks and ambulances roamed and dug in the debris. At night, the work continued under the glare of generator-powered searchlights. Three and four-story steel skeletons with charred concrete skin staggered and fell or were later knocked down.

Within the first two days, all the access points were blocked and within a week it was impossible to get a view from the street. Soon after, the buildings were covered with facade screens so no one could see the damage from the outside.

The Jersey barriers, police tape, roadblocks, military guards and New York City police stopped unauthorized access into the site, but they didn't stop contaminants from escaping. The super-heated concrete smoldered and burned for months. Firemen sprayed water on the hotspots continuously. Steam, smoke and dust rose from the hot debris piles, floated on the wind and blanketed the city.

There is a common misconception that scientists know how chemicals affect people. In some cases, it's true. We know for example that small dust particles entering the lungs can increase the chance of asthma. We know that dust is dangerous and asbestos can cause cancer. And we know that often, a dose-exposure relationship exists. In other words, the more of a contaminant you are exposed to, the greater your chance of disease. But the volume of information we don't have is huge.

When the WTC was bombed, thousands of chemicals melted, burned, merged, flowed, vaporized and drifted into the air, water and land in and around New York City. A chemical cloud floated over eight million people on the island and millions more in the surrounding metropolitan areas. And the sad truth is no one knows what damage it did.

The filter respirators distributed to all Ground Zero workers could protect against dust, but not against soluble contaminants like acid. Many workers found their respirators inconvenient and used them inconsistently, incorrectly or not at all. Many New York City residents acquired their own respirators. Some people used paper masks, some used filter cartridges; others just covered their faces with handkerchiefs. But pretty much everyone worried about the effects of exposure.

The Environmental Protection Agency (EPA), the NY Department of Environmental Protection and many private organizations, including mine, performed regular air sampling in and around Ground Zero and at many points in the city. Scientists who knew the facts were skeptical when government spokespeople declared the air around the financial center "safe to breathe." Many of us on site suffered from what came to be known as the 'World Trade Center cough.'

The offices where I worked served as a financial document repository and customer service center. The site housed a secure vault and a multi-floor operations center. Thousands of people evacuated the offices when the World Trade Center was destroyed. Some fled to the nearby pier and jumped on ferries that carried them across the Hudson River to New Jersey. Many wandered through the dust and ash, heading north into the city, walking for miles because no other transportation was moving. The fleeing workers left their business and personal possessions behind. My job was to evaluate the health and safety risks and salvage the business assets and personal property.

My team's project was only one small part of the general clean-up. Ours was limited to disaster recovery for one client. Over the next few months, my team grew from three to fifty scientists, engineers, technicians and laborers. One of them was my son, Matt, a recent engineering school graduate. I recruited him to perform air quality sampling. This was an historic event. I wanted him to be part of it. He worked with me for a week.

We set up our recovery operation on the fifth floor of the building. We installed a clean room with HEPA ventilators, generators, plastic sheeting and duct tape. We wore Tyvek suits, rubber gloves and respirators. We tested, inspected, cleaned and transported all the personal property of the employees and as much of the business assets as we could salvage. We cycled everything from microfilm files, teddy bears, photographs, computers, printers, copy machines, and coffee cups to a file cabinet from the fourth-floor safe containing $865 million in bearer bonds, through our process.

In addition to asbestos, the laboratory found human bone fragments in some of our dust samples. Smoke from the burning buildings drifted in the open windows until they were closed with plywood. After the flames were extinguished, the smoldering debris piles belched smoke and steam for two months.

I worked at Ground Zero for six months. I stayed in hotels near Times Square and lived out of a suitcase. The subway under the WTC was destroyed. Every morning our team trudged the last half mile to our worksite, through narrow alleys, along rough, plank boardwalks, past the guarded perimeter and across Ground Zero.

The days became routine. I almost forgot I was working in a disaster area surrounded by smoke, destruction and death. One morning I was walking through Ground Zero on my way to work, sort of daydreaming, on autopilot, blind to the rubble and wreckage. A uniformed NY police officer stepped in front of me, held up his hand, and put it on my chest to stop me. I came out of my daze and looked up. It was a familiar face.

He said, "Hold up, Bob. Wait a minute."

I looked around and asked, "What's going on?"

"They found another body."

We removed our hats; everyone did.

Somber firemen wore yellow slickers, boots and hard hats. They carried a blanket-covered stretcher to the waiting ambulance. I had not noticed the change in the activity around me until the police officer stopped me. No one on the site was working. No one was moving. Everyone had stopped to watch the small group, accompanied by a German Shepherd dog, slowly making their way out of the debris.

They loaded the stretcher into the back of the ambulance. We stood silently as the ambulance drove, slowly over the muddy ground and out the gate. I was never able to forget where I was or why. None of us were. Almost three thousand office workers, including three hundred and forty firefighters, seventy policemen, a chaplain and two paramedics lost their lives when the towers were destroyed.

I didn't expect to like New York City. In fact, I was a bit intimidated by its reputation. We've all been exposed to the hype about the unique personality of the City, about the cynicism and worldly wisdom of the people who live there and about the crime and dangers that lurk in every alley and dark street corner.

To my surprise, I found New York City vibrant, energetic, busy, noisy but with a purpose. Everyone seemed to know where they were going and why. I became comfortable with the city, the subways, the shops and I found the layout of the streets easy to navigate.

In all fairness, the fall and winter of 2001-2002 was not a "normal" time for New York City. It was not business as usual. There was a community atmosphere in the city. It was a time of unity after a catastrophe. People came together, were willing to stop, answer questions, and help each other. Of course, at the beginning in September, everyone was stunned, suspicious and afraid. They were quiet, shell-shocked. But as the initial shock faded, they got up, got moving, got back to work, opened up, held out their hands and helped each other.

I lost my mobile phone twice during my six months in New York City. It was one of those with a clip that slipped over my belt. It fell off when I was working at Ground Zero. Even before I noticed it was gone, a stranger sought me out to return it. The second time was at nine o'clock in the evening. It fell off my belt. The taxicab drove away with my phone in the back seat. The next passenger found it, contacted my company outside of Boston and returned it. It was a special time in New York City after the bombing of the World Trade Center.

Over the months, I watched Ground Zero evolve from a flaming, burning chaos of twisted steel and mountains of smoking concrete populated by the dirty and dazed zombies, to become an orderly construction site occupied by an army of skilled workers.

Soon after the mountains of debris stopped smoking, the politicians arrived. I heard sirens. I thought they signaled the discovery of another body. I looked out from a fifth-floor window. A limousine with a convoy of SUV's, police and a media escort rolled down Liberty Street and parked in front of our building. Funny how I thought of it as "our building".

The driver ran around to open the rear door. A suit emerged

and was escorted around the building to a clearing on the WTC side. The suit donned a new hard hat, shook some hands, smiled at the ad hoc semi-circle of workers, frowned when he spoke at the cameras and was escorted back to the car. The whole entourage was gone in fifteen minutes.

The play was re-enacted daily, sometimes two or three times. A construction crew built a raised deck behind our building so the politicians and their courtiers didn't scuff their Guccis. Day after day, Ground Zero photo ops disrupted the workflow, blocked traffic and highlighted the local evening news. Based on the frequency, I think pretty much every U.S. politician and candidate made an appearance.

Sometimes, I watched the evening news. The speeches were all more or less the same. They expressed outrage, sadness and promised retribution. They condemned the monsters that perpetrated this horrible mass murder on innocent Americans. They would make sure the evil masterminds behind this would be captured and punished. "Vote for me."

But what I missed was any discussion of why. Why did people from halfway across the world attack America? We were well aware of what they did. We heard who they were, but we never heard any discussion of why they crashed two planes into the World Trade Center and one into the Pentagon. Why were they so angry with us? No one answered that question. In 2001, no one even *asked* it.

I watched from the fifth-floor window when a crowd of firemen and their families marched onto the site from the north. They were met by their brothers in blue who were ordered to turn them back. The firemen protested New York Mayor Rudolph Giuliani's order that reduced the number of NYC firemen on the site from five hundred to fifty. The mayor argued overtime was threatening to bankrupt the city.

My part in the WTC clean-up ended a year later. I attended the Liberty Street building reopening ceremony to sign off on the completion of the clean-up. The building was renovated like new, polished, glass, chrome, marble and brass. Ground Zero was bulldozed flat, graded and prepared for rebuild. The facades of the surrounding buildings were shielded from view and still under repair but the site was swept clean. Ground Zero had transformed from war zone to construction site.

My work in New York was a crossroad. It was my largest environmental, health and safety project. It made a huge impact on the way I look at the world. I struggle to understand how anyone can think of death and destruction as a positive contribution. But I continued to wonder about the other side of the story. My experiences in New York City set me on a path that would move me from my home outside of Boston to start a new life in Europe.

* * *

Sixteen years later, I was returning to New York City for the first time since September 2002. I wanted to see what had changed. I wanted to see the City. I wanted to visit the World Trade Center Memorial. I wanted to visit the building where I worked to put my memories in perspective. These were the thoughts on my mind as I creeped south to New York City praying my Harley wouldn't overheat and stall.

My Harley was not happy in large, slow-moving crowds, but maybe I was projecting. We inched our way through construction projects that funneled the flow, squeezing five lanes down to two, sometimes one. The air-cooled engine was suffocating. I could feel its heat radiating through the fabric of my jeans. A familiar burning rubber odor warned me that the clutch plate was overheating and the brakes squealed in protest. I fought with the heavy bike, and it wobbled every time I lurched to a sudden stop. I struggled to keep balance.

Finally, the speaker in my helmet whispered an instruction to turn. I was in Manhattan. I strained to hear the directions over the street noise. I circled my way around the busy one-way streets to Amsterdam Avenue and found my hostel. I parked the bike on the sidewalk around the corner and locked it. I unstrapped and carried my bags half a block to the entrance, sweating under my heavy black motorcycle jacket.

A hostel is an inexpensive alternative for a night in NY City. The staff was friendly. It was a dynamic environment of young people and many internationals. My room was an eight-man dormitory. The accommodations included a bunk bed and a locker. I jammed all my gear into the big metal box and secured it with a padlock.

My first order of business was to find a safe place to store the motorcycle. I had no intention of leaving it on the sidewalk all night. In the first place, it's illegal. In The Netherlands you can park a motorcycle pretty much anywhere it will fit and nobody will bother it. But in the U.S. a bike is the same as a car. You have to use a legal parking place. The sidewalk won't do. I didn't want it stolen or towed.

I found a private parking garage beneath an apartment building nearby. I rode down the ramp and introduced myself to an enterprising parking attendant willing to make a deal. Cash still worked in NY. For twenty dollars, he let me tuck the bike into an unused corner of the garage. My biggest worry about staying in NYC had been how to keep the motorcycle safe overnight. I walked away from the parking garage with a sense of relief and boarded the subway to Times Square.

Danielle returned my call while I was wandering around like a tourist, gaping open-mouthed at the crowds, the traffic and the tall buildings. Yes, she said, she was in NYC and could meet me that afternoon. She suggested a coffee shop near the Ground Zero site. I returned to the subway and made my way to the south end of the island.

I've known Danielle since she was in diapers, a fact I didn't mention during this visit. She's Dan and Carolyn's middle child, bookended on both sides by brothers. She grew up to be a beautiful young woman. When I was working in New York City, Danielle was 13 years old.

We walked around the reconstructed World Trade Center site, now the Memorial. I felt the generation gap open between us as she described her job. She worked for an information technology company in New York City. They design programs that track internet shoppers and target them for "use-based" advertising. Cookies recognize your computer, tablet and phone. They send you advertisements based on what you searched for and even what you looked at on web pages.

"If you go into a mall, they send advertisements for the store you're in."

"It sounds like, 'Big Brother is watching'," I said. She didn't register my   Orwellian reference.

Before I fell into the chasm dividing us, I changed the subject. I described the site we were walking through from my memory. It was a warm, sunny early June afternoon. There were thousands of tourists in Liberty Park, but it didn't feel crowded. And in spite of the many people, it seemed unusually quiet for a city location. The area had a peaceful, respectful and open feel. It was large yet comfortable. I found it contemplative, inviting and subdued.

As we toured the site, I talked with Danielle about the memories of my experiences after the bombing. I was impressed how the area seemed to invite reflection. Trees offered shade and if not solitude, a bit of personal space. There was plenty of room around the two infinity pools to rest, read names and watch the black water disappear down the bottomless wells. We walked at street level, then found our way to the building where I worked so many years ago. It too had changed. It was again under reconstruction.

A walkway that formerly connected to the Twin Towers now

leads to Liberty Park. I remember the Twin Towers before the attack as a huge, busy office complex. After the bombing, it was a burning disaster zone. In 2019 it was a park, a monument and a museum. I became disoriented and distracted trying to align my memories of the site to the current floor plan. Finally, I gave up. That was not the point. I wanted to feel the site, not recognize how it was compared to how it is. You can't ever go back. Danielle was patient with my descriptions and my long silences.

From Liberty Park we walked to a near-by mall for a quick dinner. She suggested a trendy burger joint. She ordered a shake; I got a burger and shake. She described her week on the Colorado River rafting trip with a friend.

"Danielle, you don't seem like a 'wilderness girl' to me."

"No, not really. But my friend had an extra ticket because her boyfriend couldn't go. So I thought I'd give it a try."

"Was it tough, I mean physically challenging?"

"It might be something for you and my dad. Most of the people on the trip were your age."

"Ouch."

The mention of her father opened up a new topic.

"What do you think about your father's big change, giving up alcohol? That's a pretty big decision."

"But now he's smoking."

"I guess we all challenge our mortality in one way or another."

"What do you mean?"

"Well, look at you. You just got back from a rafting trip down the Colorado river. Isn't that risky?"

"Not as risky as a motorcycle trip across the country."

"Yah, sort of like that. Maybe we are all self-destructive."

We talked about her work, her boyfriend and her recent Mother's Day visit to Boston. We hugged goodbye on the street corner. She headed back to her apartment in Soho, me to the subway and my hostel.

I went to sleep that night in an upper bunk of a dormitory room to the sounds of snoring young men and NYC traffic. I felt older after talking with Danielle. Maybe too old for this trip.

CHAPTER 9: JUST RIDE

*Getting killed having a bad
time is just wrong.*

Wednesday, June 5

A light rain was beginning to fall as I packed the motorcycle for the long trip south and west. I passed a fuel station on my way out of the city. It was situated at a busy corner, on the other side of a congested intersection. I was anxious to put NYC behind me and sure there would be more fuel stations along the route. The gas gauge mounted on the tank indicated it was half full. I didn't know it at the time, but this was a learning opportunity. I'd like to say I took advantage of it and gained valuable experience. I should have. But it wasn't until Utah that the message finally penetrated my thick skull.

By ten o'clock the light rain had stopped. I was swept along with the fast-moving traffic in the left lane on I-78 west. I was distracted, struggling to hear the route directions through muffled speakers. The highway system around NYC was complicated by the dizzying collage of route and information signs. The mobile phone screen was too small to serve as a guide. I focused my attention on the low volume audio directions and struggled to find my way through the frantic freeway maze of the late morning commute.

Suddenly the motorcycle engine hesitated, coughed, choked and shut down. I squeezed the clutch lever and speed-shifted to neutral. I scanned the road ahead for an escape route and checked the rear-view mirror for approaching vehicles. I glided across to the middle lane, coasting without power and losing speed fast.

"What the hell is going on?"

"You're out of gas."

"I should have stopped at that station."

"Too late now."

"Switch to reserve."

Traffic was flowing by on both sides as the bike continued to slow. I spotted an opening in the stream of traffic and merged into the right lane. I reached down with my left hand and fumbled to locate the reserve tank valve.

"You should have practiced this before. You'll probably kill yourself trying to find it."

I steered with my right hand while the fingers of my left hand explored the side of the unfamiliar engine.

"Where is that damn fuel valve?"

Leaning forward to feel along the engine I checked the mirrors for a gap in the traffic. I guided the bike into the breakdown lane. Finally I found the valve. I turned the valve up and restarted the engine. I shifted into gear and regained speed. My heart was pounding in my chest. I crossed a solid line and made a quick exit off the highway. A police car parked in the breakdown lane ignored me. I was grateful for his apathy.

The Harley had a range of about one hundred and eighty miles in the main tank. It varied with road conditions, speed and type of fuel. As I searched for a gas station, somewhere south and west of New York City, I made a mental note to keep better track of my odometer.

I exited the highway and wound along secondary roads searching for a fuel station. I fueled up and thirty minutes later found my way back to route I-78 and continued west.

This was an anxious day on the road struggling with my doubts.

"What am I doing here?"

"What am I going to do for two months?"

My goals were to reconnect with my sons and my country. I didn't feel up to either task. I hadn't made much progress with Matt. I worried about my riding competence and my physical fitness. My bears began to rear up and growl.

"Can I do this? I don't feel comfortable on this bike."

"You shouldn't have run out of gas."

"I was distracted."

"You've been distracted a lot on this trip."

I worried about every noise, bump and rattle. I worried because I couldn't hear my speakers and I worried that the navigation system would fail.

I worried about the phone-charging system. The cable was

connected to the battery but the phone wasn't fully charged at the end of the ride. I didn't know why.

I worried the police would stop me and ask for my license and the registration that was not in my name.

I worried that I wouldn't find any answers. I worried about Matt and Mike.

My worries spiraled, circled and filled my mind and heart.

I tried to think my way out of it. "You can't find answers if you spend all your energy on worries."

Then I worried because I worried. I told myself to think of something else.

I had lost my toilet kit in the hostel. I left it in the men's' washroom by the sink. When I went back, it was gone. "Who'd want someone else's toilet kit?"

I tried to remember exactly what was in it.

> "You don't have to remember because you have the list in your bag."

> "I'll have to put another toilet kit together. I'll start with a toothbrush."

> "Who'd want my toothbrush?"

> "Forget the toilet kit. Focus on the ride."

> "Right."

At about one o'clock in the afternoon I was in Pennsylvania. My empty stomach cried protest to inform me it was time for food. I pulled off the highway in Fredericksburg where I saw a sign for Esther's Restaurant. It looked more inviting than a fast-food burger place.

Esther's was on the right. I downshifted and began my turn. Suddenly the front wheel slipped sideways. I was thrown to the ground like a rag doll. My helmet bounced on the gritty road surface. It happened in zero seconds. The engine coughed, died and began to smoke. Flashing black spots and little white stars filled my vision. Time stopped while I remained still and took inventory.

"I'm conscious and I can move my neck. That's good."

"My arms and hands move. Also good."

"My right leg is wedged under the bike and I'm pinned to the ground. Not so good."

"I can move my leg and wiggle my foot. Probably not broken."

"I smell gas."

Traffic was stalled at a red light on the other side of the road. The drivers and passengers had a clear view of the accident. As I lay trapped under the motorcycle, I imagined a parent turning to the teenager in the back seat, "See, that's why I don't want you riding a motorcycle."

The bike was lying in the middle of the parking lot entrance, leaning on the right-side crash bar with me under it.

I replayed the fall in my mind. The parking lot surface was gray, stone dust, like sand. Some of the stone dust, dragged by car tires, had accumulated on the asphalt apron at the entrance. I didn't notice it on the pavement. When I turned into the parking lot, the front tire slipped on the fine stone dust, like on ice, and the bike went down.

Two men and a woman arrived on foot.

"Are you alright?"

"Yes, I think so."

Without asking, one of the men turned off the gas valve. I was surprised, "How do you know how to do that?"

"I have a bike."

The two men lifted the bike enough for me to drag myself out from under. It's possible for one person to raise seven hundred and fifty pounds of cruiser onto its wheels alone, but I was grateful for the help. Together we lifted it to vertical. We four stood in the driveway and I thanked them all. They asked again if I was alright, and I assured them I was OK. I pushed the motorcycle off the street into the parking lot. It felt heavy. I felt clumsy. The bike was awkward to muscle around in the sand. I parked the bike in the back of the lot, set it on its kickstand and took a deep breath.

The three Samaritans were gone. They just walked off. If they went to their cars or into the restaurant, I never saw them again. Alone in the parking lot, I inspected the bike. The first thing I noticed was that the luggage, even the phone, had remained secured in place during the fall. I would have to remember to tell Matt.

The engine crash bar had hit the ground first, trapping but protecting my right leg. The bar was scratched but looked solid and intact. The windshield was scratched on the right side where it had hit the sand but was not cracked. The handlebars were not bent or twisted. The accelerator grip was not damaged. The back of the right mirror was scratched but the glass was not broken. All in all, the bike came out of the fall in good shape.

My appetite was gone but I needed some time to regroup. I could feel my heart pumping in my chest. My hands were shaking when I picked up my gas tank pack. I walked into the restaurant and made my way to a quiet booth by a window where I could keep an eye on the bike. I peeled off my coat, gloves and rain pants. I should have, but didn't think of going into the men's' room to wash up and look over my wounds. Instead, I sat at the table. When the waitress brought over a glass of water and a menu, I ordered a tuna salad sandwich.

I took a second inventory at the table. My rain pants and jeans were torn and stained with blood where I had scraped my knee. The leather on the side of my right boot was torn. I had twisted my ankle and could feel it beginning to swell. My lost toilet kit contained an elastic ankle wrap and ACE bandage, no good to me now. My shoulder, neck and head ached. My hand trembled when I picked up my water glass.

Bike riding is all about confidence. I promised myself long ago, if I was worried about it, I wouldn't ride any more. I had to admit; after the fall, I was worried. The trip had only just begun and I was already on my ass. I thought about quitting, selling the bike; hell, just leave the bike. I could rent a car and drive to Tahoe. I even considered taking a bus to California or a taxi to an airport. I considered giving up the whole stupid idea and going home. I spent about an hour in the restaurant considering my options. I forced down half my tuna sandwich only because I knew I should eat something. Finally, I paid the bill, put my jacket back on, got back on the motorcycle and continued south and west.

I filled up a few hours later at a station in Fayetteville, near Caledonia State Park. Again, I had run it well into the reserve tank. I bought a toothbrush, toothpaste and a comb in the general store and a can of Chef Boyardee ravioli for dinner.

It was four o'clock when I pulled into the ranger station parking lot. I climbed off my bike just in time to watch the ranger exit the building, lock the door, get in his car and drive away. The after-hours phone number posted on the board in front didn't work. Too exhausted to look for another place to stay, I rode into the campground and selected a vacant campsite.

I parked the bike, unloaded my gear and set up my tent. I smoked my pipe, sipped water from my bottle and spent some reflection time with my journal. I reconsidered my decision to ride across the country.

"Maybe this wasn't such a good idea after all."

I faced some facts of life about motorcycle riding. A rider is vulnerable; a motorcycle has no airbag, no seat belt, no safety glass and only two wheels. A flat tire can be fatal. And it can flip over in the blink of an eye. I asked myself, "Are you sure you want to do this? Hanneke will kill you if you get hurt or die."

I made a 'What have you learned?' list.

- I am not a young man anymore.
- The motorcycle is heavy. Even getting it off the kickstand takes muscle.
- I can't push it up any kind of grade. I've got to park it facing out if I can.
- I need to respect, and be cautious of, gravel, stone dust and sand.
- The fuel gauge is not reliable. I need to use the odometer.
- I must fill up between 150–175 miles. I've got about twenty miles in reserve.
- Google Maps is pretty accurate about the mileage, but not about the time. It takes longer than you think. Not a problem but I need to keep it in mind.
- I must co-ordinate food, fuel and comfort stops to save time.
- I should gas up at premium stations. They accept credit cards and don't require a zip code. (This turned out not to be consistent. Zip code requirements continued to plague me.)
- Interstate highways are soulless, high-speed asphalt canals. There is no scenery, no peace and no fun.
- Air wash from high-speed truckers can blow me off the road.
- I like to travel on two-lane secondary roads. There's much more to see and the riding is more relaxed.
- Finally, I have to find my rhythm. I'm trying too hard to do everything right. I forget things like my toilet bag in NY City, strapping my helmet, sunglasses on the saddle bag and connecting the phone to the charger. I'm too tense. I'm thinking too much.

My spill could have been a lot worse. I was lucky. I needed to relax and just ride, not worry about getting everything right. I decided to change my riding style. It sounds clichéd, but it's real. I needed to become one with the bike. I needed to know it, to make it mine.

Until now, I thought of it as Paul's bike. I was just using it. I had to change that perspective; I had to own it. I began to recognize that this ride is a marathon, not a sprint. It wasn't about speed and performance or getting from point A to point B and it wasn't about doing everything right. It is about enjoying the ride. And up to now, I wasn't really enjoying the ride, the road or the bike. I was fighting the bike. I wasn't connected to the ride. And I wasn't having any fun.

> "Getting killed having fun is one thing. Getting killed having a bad time is just wrong."

The fall in Pennsylvania was a turning point. I decided to ride for fun. Riding for fun is a sensory experience. I enjoy the feel of the road, the smell of the air, the sun on my face, the sound of the engine, the vibrations, the bank of the turns, the scenery, the hills, the trees, the farms, the heat and the cold. I enjoy the connection between me and the motorcycle. When we are traveling along the road as one, linked, my hands and feet are part of the motorcycle; the shift, clutch, brake and gas. It's a union of man and machine. I wanted that feeling back.

> "I want to forget all the individual details, all the things that separate me from the bike and let us merge and just ride."

> "Sounds like a good plan."

> "Right. Now you just have to do it."

> "Remember, there are only two types of Harley riders; those that have dropped their bike and those who are about to."

Caledonia State Park was my first campsite. Until then I had slept in other people's beds. I was on my own. It felt good. As I sat at my picnic table, making notes in my journal, I kept an eye out for my neighbors. Across the road from my little tent, two RVs, one a large tow-behind, the other a camper van, were backed into the campsite. Their picnic table was covered by a plastic tablecloth with a colorful floral design. Four citronella candles in green glass jars held the corners from blowing away in the wind. A yellow, canvas awning decorated with red and white Christmas tree lights, stretched from the side of the larger RV to shelter the table. A purple bug light hung from a pole, connected to the back of the RV by a heavy-duty, orange electrical cord. A smoky campfire burned, unattended in the pit beside the table.

In the interest of full disclosure, let me take a minute to describe the way I collected and recorded the opinions of the people I met along the way. To achieve my goal, to get the feel of my country again, I wanted to meet and talk with people. I was nervous about how to accomplish it. I'm not an extrovert, or a naturally gregarious, outgoing person. I don't usually seek out people to talk to. I'm not the kind of person who approaches strangers in public places to pass the time in casual conversation. To carry out my plan I had to step out of my comfort zone, take initiative and reach out. I had committed to do whatever it took to meet people during this trip and initiate conversations.

It turned out to be pretty easy. Typically, I'd approach a neighboring campsite, in the late afternoon, always before dark. Usually it was occupied by an RV. Often the people were sitting in plastic lawn chairs around their fire pit.

I used a variety of methods. Sometimes I'd ask if I could burn some paper in their fire. One time I asked if they wanted a package of firewood I had found. My most common icebreaker was to start off with an apology for my noisy motorcycle. This was easy because it was true. The bike sounded like a fireworks explosion in the quiet morning.

This is how it usually started:

Me: "Hello, I'm your next-door neighbor. I'm camping over there. My name is Bob."

Neighbor: "Hi, how are you?"

Me: "Good, thanks. I just wanted to say hello. I'm riding that bike; it's pretty noisy. I want to apologize in advance if it wakes you up in the morning when I leave."

I'd pause and we'd look over at the low, black Harley leaning near my little tent.

Neighbor: "Oh, that's OK. I have a motorcycle too. I don't mind."

Me: "Well, thanks. I just wanted to warn you."

Neighbor: "It's no problem, we're up early anyway. You probably won't wake us."

People along the way, were for the most part cordial, positive and encouraging. If they didn't own a bike they used to, or had a husband, boyfriend, neighbor, brother or sister who did. But nobody complained and it was a good conversation starter.

From there I moved on to, "Where are you from?"

I used this method throughout my trip; it was simple, easy and it worked well.

A word about the quotes I've included. I kept a daily journal. I wrote when I had time, usually at the end of the day. Sometimes I stopped for lunch and took out my notebook. I did not use a recorder to capture conversations and I did not take notes while people spoke. Neither did I fact-check what they said. And generally, I did not challenge their arguments. I listened to what they had to say, then wrote it in my journal when I was alone at the picnic table, in my tent or motel room.

In my notes, I recorded the message and tone of the people I talked with as accurately as possible. Sometimes people used phrases I wanted to remember. I took care to jot them down in their exact words. The dialogue is as close to what people really said as my short-term memory could retain.

I did not use a list of prepared questions to tick off at each meeting. Sometimes I asked questions to better understand. Generally, I let the speaker lead the conversation. I tried to be open, to listen, hear, understand and absorb their messages.

One other point, and it's important. The conversations were not interviews and certainly not debates. Political opinions in America are like religion. People are very willing to talk about theirs and they feel strongly about them. But they are not very interested in hearing about yours, unless you agree with them. A discussion between opposing points of view quickly degenerates into an emotionally charged argument. Both parties end up angry with nothing accomplished. I found that the best way to hear what was on people's minds was to admit ignorance. I explained that I'd been living outside the country for more than fifteen years. I didn't know what was going on. I was trying to find out. And this was true.

My first evening on the road I met and talked with Bob and his wife, Sun. Bob covered his gray hair with a John Deere cap. His blue eyes, framed by bushy eyebrows, were active and lively. Sun was a head shorter than Bob; short, dark hair framed her oval face and dark almond eyes. When she smiled, her eyes sparkled. I used my noisy motorcycle apology and he was fine with it. I spent three hours speaking with them at their picnic table by the campfire. They shared their dinner with me. When I returned to my tent after dark, I wrote in my journal by flashlight.

He's seventy-two years old, from Ohio. She's sixty-six from South Korea. They're retired and live in Pennsylvania. They met when Bob was in the Army. Bob installed broadcasting equipment and satellite uplinks for radio stations all over the world. The radio stations broadcast American news and music programs to third-world countries.

Bob is proud of their three children, all with successful jobs, good spouses, new cars and second homes. One daughter is an emergency room nurse, the other is a medical technician. Both live in Pennsylvania. His son manages a bikini warehouse in Los Angeles. If he said whether this was retail or wholesale, I don't remember. I got distracted by images of a bikini warehouse in LA.

Bob bought a new mobile home this year. He gave his old one to his daughter and her husband. Bob and Sun live in a three-bedroom home with a gazebo, a greenhouse, a woodworking shop, internet, cable TV including Netflix and HBO, and a family plan for multiple mobile phones. They each have electric bikes,

Bob receives a comfortable pension; he's got a 401K retirement plan and social security income. His wife is a naturalized American citizen, legally immigrated to the U.S. She will be eligible for social security this year. Bob collects knives and pellet guns. His collection of fifteen pellet rifles and pistols includes weapons up to fifty caliber. He explained that you don't need a permit to own a pellet gun. He owns over two hundred knives that he describes as tools, not weapons.

The conversation shifted to my camp. Compared to his home away from home, mine looked small and meager, with only a small tent, and a motorcycle parked beside it.

Bob: "What are you using to cook?"

Me: "I have a little one-burner liquid gas stove."

"I have a Solo Stove. It's better."

"What's a Solo Stove?"

"An environmental stove made out of stainless steel. It uses scrap wood, sticks, charcoal, even pinecones for fuel. You don't need to buy gas or butane. I have three of them."

"Three of them! Why do you need three stoves?"

"Different sizes. Come on, let me show you."

I followed him to the back of his van. It was packed with camping gear. He pulled out a plastic box.

"Look at this."

He opened the molded, blue box to show me a pellet pistol. It was nestled in custom-cut, black foam with three compressed-air cartridges and a round metal box holding fifty pellets.

"It's .22-caliber for target shooting. I haven't even used it yet. I'll take my granddaughter into the woods tomorrow to practice. She's a good shot."

Next, he pulled out a silver two-section pan. It looked like a bucket with a flat bail. It was about eighteen inches tall and a foot in diameter. He carried it to the picnic table where he opened the pan to show me the two sections.

"See, you put the fuel in here at the bottom, turn the top over and you can cook in it."

I picked it up and looked it over. It was shiny and new, never used.

"It looks like a good idea. But it's a little big for a motorcycle."

"They have a small size for backpacking. That would fit on the bike. I have one of those too. This is the middle size. I have the big one on order"

"What is the bigger size for?"

"Barbecues. When I bought the other two, the big one was out of stock."

He carried the stove back to the van and locked it, then asked me where I was from.

I told Bob a version of my story that I repeated many times over the next seven weeks.

"I live in The Netherlands. I've been there for more than fifteen years. That's sort of what this trip is about. I retired last September. I thought this would be a good time to get to know America again. Find out what's going on."

Bob nodded. "Yah, it's a good time. A lot is going on."

"OK, tell me, what's going on?"

"OK, first, you should know, I don't listen to the news. The news is all bullshit. The media hates Trump. OK, Trump is an obnoxious asshole. I know it, everyone knows it. I don't like him. But he's trying to do what America needs. He's the only candidate who's not a politician. He's a businessman.

"The Clintons, they're crooks. They have that fake foundation. It's just a money-laundering machine to hide foreign campaign contributions.

"The last straw was when Bill got caught cheating on his wife. The guy's a scumbag. You can't trust a man that cheats on his wife."

Although I avoided debates, occasionally I asked a question for clarification.

"But didn't Trump cheat? What was her name?"

"Stormy Daniels. But that was never proved and he wasn't impeached."

Then he moved to other subjects in quick succession.

"The worst thing that happened was the Democrats winning a majority in the House.

"The biggest mistake the Republicans made was not funding the wall when they had control of the House."

"Don't get me wrong, I'm not against immigrants. Hell, my

wife's an immigrant. Legal immigrants are OK; my wife is a legal immigrant. We had to hire an attorney and go through military interrogation. She has relatives in North Korea. They wanted to make sure she wasn't a spy. It cost us a lot of money. But she's legal.

"There's 1,000 illegals coming across the Mexican border every day, 100,000 last month. These people couldn't make it in their own country. They got no skills, no education, tons of kids. They come here; drug addicts, thieves, rapists. All they want is a free ride. I worked all my life. Now I got a pension. Why should I give it up to pay for them?

"I work hard for what I have. Nobody has the right to take it from me. I will fight to protect what is mine."

I asked, "Who's going to take what you have?"

"Are you kidding? Everyone, anyone. There are lots of people out there who don't work, who never worked, but think they have a right to what I worked for. And there's people who want to give it to them."

"Do you mean welfare?"

"You bet; welfare, immigrants, druggies. They all want what's mine and the Democrats want to give it to them. I'll tell you what, Trump is doing the right thing with that wall. Keep them out, that's what I say. Why should they come here and get for free what I have to work my ass off for?"

He continued, "That's why people voted for Trump. He's a businessman, not a bleeding-heart socialist who wants to give away the country. I won't co-operate with anyone who wants to give away what's mine. That's why I collect pellet guns. They're not registered, I don't need a permit, nobody knows I've got them, so the Democrats can't take them away. And I can protect what's mine."

The sun went down while Bob talked. His wife cooked

vegetables and sausages in aluminum foil on the grill over the campfire. Their ten-year-old granddaughter took a break from her video game in the RV to join us for dinner. The meal was hearty and delicious. When the meal was done, we piled the paper plates into the campfire and the plastic cups, forks and knives into trash bags. I thanked my hosts, bid them farewell and returned to my camp to think about our meeting.

Later that night, I reclined on my sleeping bag, with my flashlight hanging from the roof of my tent. I was writing in my journal when I heard the sound of approaching footsteps in the dark. Bob presented me with a gift for my travels; a strong, LED flashlight. He said it was better than the one I was using. I thanked him and repeated my apology about the noisy motorcycle engine.

"Don't worry about it. I'll be awake before you. Have a safe trip."

After Bob returned to his RV, I considered the ambiguities he presented. Bob was neither unkind nor selfish. He was proud of his family, proud of his own accomplishments, and continued to accumulate toys. He supported a wall to protect against immigrants stealing into America. Yet his wife was an immigrant. He vowed to protect what he owns from anyone who tried to take it. He resents welfare recipients. But he invited a stranger to his dinner table and gave me a flashlight because he believed I needed it.

CHAPTER 10:
TROUBLESHOOTING

They attacked her in her
home for drug money.

I guess I'm getting old and responsible. I'm just not a stealth camper anymore. I could have avoided the ranger station on my way out of the park. Instead, I stopped to check out and pay the camping fee. My next stop was Shenandoah National Forest in Virginia, one hundred and twenty miles away. My helmet speakers and phone-charging system were still an irritating nuisance. The audio volume was too low and the phone was not charging during my daily ride. My high-tech navigation system was turning into a pain in the ass.

It was mid-afternoon when I rode into Matthew's Arm Campground and selected a site. The day was warm with bright sunshine. I parked the motorcycle on the asphalt driveway in the shade beside my campsite. I unpacked the motorcycle and set up the tent, zipping it closed to keep out the insects. I inflated the sleeping pad and used it for a cushion on the picnic table bench.

I wanted to clean up. This campsite offered a well pump but no shower facilities, so I filled my pans at the water pump. While they warmed in the sun, I set out to troubleshoot my navigation system. My task for the afternoon was to repair the charging system and increase the helmet speaker volume. I was worried. I needed this system to work, and it was not dependable.

If you think about it, the word 'troubleshooting' starts from a negative perspective. You've already accepted that you're in trouble and you decide to shoot it. You have no guarantee that you will hit your target. Intrinsic in the word 'troubleshooting' is the concept of failure; failure of the system being shot and failure if you miss. If you shoot and miss, the system fails and must be cast away or replaced. Troubleshooting, or problem solving therefore is often accompanied by stress maybe even fear. Sometimes it's easier to live with a problem than to try to fix it.

Troubleshooting exposes all the bears. When I troubleshoot, think of the system as a whole and I ask what is the simplest thing that could have gone wrong? I don't start with the most difficult problem. I look for the least expensive and the easiest way to fix something. Of course, that doesn't always work. Sometimes I must take the whole thing apart or even throw it out and start over. But that is the last resort.

In this case the solutions were simple. After a little

investigation I discovered a faulty USB cable and replaced it. That fixed the phone charging problem. I repositioned the helmet speakers and solved my volume problem. In a little over an hour my tools were packed up and my phone and speakers were mended. It was time for a bath.

The afternoon was still warm and sunny when I gathered my pans. The water from the tap wasn't warm but a couple of hours in the sun had taken the chill out. I laid out a change of clothes on the picnic table and looked forward to a pan-bath.

I stripped down and sat on the picnic table bench. I washed with the bar of soap I had recently purchased from the gas station and rinsed with clear water. I dried with a towel in the sunshine, put on clean underwear, t-shirt and socks and felt much better. I examined the scrape on my right knee for the first time since the accident. I picked out little grains of stone dust from the swollen and raw skin with the tweezers from my Swiss Army knife. The wound was open and ugly but didn't seem infected. I washed it and applied antiseptic and bandages from my first aid kit.

I stuffed the seven-day-old t-shirt, sox and underwear into a plastic bag in the corner of my duffel. My jeans were slightly torn at the knee, but still serviceable, so I put them back on. When I was dressed, I ate the other half of my tuna fish sandwich with a bottle of water, sitting at the picnic table.

I was pleased with myself for solving my little electrical problems. As I smoked my pipe after dinner, I thought about how we approach problems; worst-case scenarios or best case? It is easy to get caught in the trap of thinking about everything that can possibly go wrong. That kind of thinking can turn a little problem into a catastrophe. It most often turns out the simplest solution is all that is needed. Simple doesn't always work. But I'm not sure that looking at the worst possible outcome is best either. And worrying about the worst outcome doesn't do any good.

I was pulled from my thoughts by unwelcome visitors after my pipe went out. My brother says black flies exist in two universes simultaneously. They are neither wholly in our time and space, nor out of it. They phase into and out of our universe, oblivious of spatial orientation. That is why they move so randomly, why they fly such erratic patterns and why they fly suicidally, up our noses and into our eyes and ears. These thoughts inserted themselves into my conscious thought and occupied my mind as I slapped, waved and clapped at air-borne time/space vampires in the early evening. I lit my pipe again, grateful that in whatever time/space reality they exist, they don't like smoke.

In the early evening, two women drove in and set up two tents at a campsite across the road. I waited till they had finished setting up their camp and lit a campfire, then made my approach. Cleaned, fed and rewired, I walked over with a handful of scrap paper and a full bottle of water.

After a brief greeting, I asked, "Do you mind if I throw some paper in your fire?"

Pat was a small-framed, dark-haired physical education teacher, studying physical therapy. Her friend, Rose was a tall, blond retired university laboratory manager. They lived eighty miles north. This was an impromptu weekend camping trip.

Not long after I arrived, John, Pat's brother, and his wife rode up on his new, R1200 BMW motorcycle. It was a rough terrain vehicle with high suspension and heavy-duty aluminum side boxes. He and his wife wore matching riding outfits, pants, jackets, gloves and full-face helmets with Bluetooth communication. John explained they could hear the GPS directions, talk to each other, receive phone calls and listen to music while they rode. John stood on tiptoes to reach the ground from the high ride seat of the big bike. His wife sat back with her feet on the passenger pegs.

Our discussion focused on how expensive it was to live

in America. John worked for an elevator repair company, a union job with high pay and good benefits. Rose worried her retirement pension would not be enough to live on. Pat worked two jobs and still couldn't afford to buy a house. At fifty-five years old, she didn't think she could ever afford to retire. Her career as a teacher was insecure. Budget cuts were a continued threat. She was laid off a few years ago and expected it again. She loved teaching and wanted to keep her job. But she wanted to be prepared. She was studying physical therapy at night school. She hoped it would increase her marketability.

We talked by the fire as the sun set and the black flies time-warped in and out of our reality. I described my situation; living in Europe, traveling to visit my sons. I admitted I was trying to find out what was happening in America. They were open to share their perspectives.

John: "You can't listen to the news. It's all biased for or against Trump. OK, sure Trump is an asshole. Everybody knows that. But what else have we got? Nothing but socialists on the other side. They want to give away the country."

Pat: "Nobody calls Trump the education President. But at least he's trying to protect working people. He's going to reopen the steel mills, bring jobs back to this country."

Rose: "My neighbor was almost killed. She hired contractors to work on her house. She paid cash. After the job was done, some men came back and broke in. She came home while they were inside and was almost beaten to death."

Pat: "They attacked her in her home for drug money. They beat her so badly she was hospitalized. The medical bills cost her thousands. It's been months and still she can't work. She might lose her house."

Rose: "Oxycontin is going to bankrupt this country. When they can't afford Oxy, they use meth. It's cheaper but it's deadly. Hospitals, EMTs and police are overwhelmed. My town is firing teachers to hire police to deal with drug crime."

Pat: "That's why I'm taking physical therapy courses. I'll probably get laid off. When I do, I need another profession."

Rose: "I don't know if I can afford retirement. Nothing gets any less expensive. Medicare doesn't pay for my prescriptions. How can we let illegal immigrants come to this country and give it all away for free? OK, I don't like the idea of the wall, but what other choice do we have?"

After dark, I bid good night to the group and walked back to my camp. I made a small campfire, smoked my pipe and reflected on our discussion. I was impressed with how much of their discussion was filled with anxiety and insecurity. They all felt that their lives were fragile, vulnerable and out of their control.

Friday, June 7: Wayne National Forest, 325 miles, 9 hours

At six o'clock in the morning, I woke from a confusing dream. I had come home from college. We lived in a small house with a grassy front yard. There were two men sitting on lawn chairs drinking beer in front of the house. My family was there; my father, mother, two brothers and my sister. I got the feeling that something was going on that I did not know about.

I walked into my room to change clothes. Suddenly the house started to shake. It lurched up and down and from side to side. Then one end started to rise like a capsizing ship. Then the whole house upended with me in it. I braced my arms and legs against the walls inside a closet until it stopped. Then I climbed out of the rubble.

No one outside seemed to notice or care when I told them. They continued to drink and socialize.

I yelled at my father, "Will you get off your ass? We've got some shit to do." Everyone was shocked. But my father got up. Then I woke up.

I packed the motorcycle and was ready to move on by seven o'clock. Pat and Rose approached from across the road as I was climbing on the bike.

Rose: "A bear woke Pat up this morning. Did you see it?"

Me: "No. What happened."

Pat: I was sleeping in my tent. I woke up when the bear's nose touched my head."

They told the story in turns.

Rose: "I was asleep in the other tent."

Pat: "My tent was open at the ends to let some air through."

Rose: "A black bear came sniffing up to Pat's tent. You didn't hear her scream?"

Me: "No."

Pat: "I woke up when his nose pushed through the net screen and he sniffed my head."

Rose: "She scared me when she screamed. You didn't hear it?"

Me: "No. I didn't hear anything."

Pat: "When I felt it, I jumped up and screamed. The bear backed off. I turned around and watched as he walked slowly back into the woods. He wasn't upset at all."

Rose: "You didn't see him?"

Me: "No, I would have liked to get a picture."

Pat: "He looked like he was moving slowly but he was out of sight in no time."

Me: "I guess he wasn't hungry."

Pat: "I don't think he liked my shampoo."

We shared a morning cup of coffee by their fire pit as we talked about bears, each of us with an eye on the woods around us. I bid them farewell, climbed on my motorcycle and rode away with a wave.

I rode Skyline Drive through the mist rolling down from the Blue Ridge Mountains. I cruised for nine hours through the Appalachian Range from Virginia, through West Virginia to Ohio. I rode through ancient, lush, pristine forests from Shenandoah National Park, through Monongahela National Forest to Wayne National Forest. I crossed under but never merged onto a major highway.

The scenery was breathtaking. I pulled over and parked off a secondary road beside a quiet lake to watch the wind ripple the water and riffle the leaves. I cruised along quiet, neighborhood roads, by small farms, general stores and clapboard houses with pick-up trucks parked in the driveways. When an occasional vehicle appeared in my mirror, I slowed to let it pass. I wanted to savor this ride, not rush through the mountains.

Nine hours sounds like a long time to ride a bike. But it didn't feel like a long ride. It felt like I added a day to my life. After riding the winding road from Virginia to Ohio I cannot imagine choosing an interstate highway route. William Least Heat-Moon called them "Blue Highways". This trip more than any other imprinted on me the value of the Blue Highways over the Interstates. I passed through unincorporated towns with names like Elk City, Wolf Summit, Deer Walk. Many were just small clusters of houses with a few families and sometimes a general store.

I passed graceful homes, picturesque mansions atop rolling, grassy hills, with fenced horse corrals and ponds with row boats and fishing docks. On closer examination I noticed that many of the farm fences needed mending. Tractors leaned on flat tires. Clapboard houses cried for paint and repair. And there were more than a few empty stores on Main Street with boarded windows. The roads were grooved, cracked, bumpy and patched. The cars were dented and pock-marked with rust.

Fast moving eight-cylinder pick-up trucks rattled up behind me with leaky mufflers and tailgated around turns. I slowed, pulled over and waved them by. I could feel the poverty in this part of the country. People were struggling. I spotted more than one burned-out house that shouted, "Meth Lab, out of business". I recalled the conversation with Pat, Rose and John about drugs.

Bible-Belt billboards lined the road and shouted warnings in bold font.

"WHEN YOU DIE YOU WILL SEE GOD."

"WHERE WILL YOU SPEND ETERNITY?"

"ABORTION IS THE END OF LIFE."

"THERE IS A HELL"

"INJURED IN AN ACCIDENT? ONE CALL IS ALL IT TAKES."

I arrived at Burr Oak campground in Ohio just before five o'clock, tired but content.

That evening I spoke with my neighbor at the next campsite. Jim rode a Triumph 1200. He retired from the Navy and now he works for a pharmaceutical supplier. As we spoke, I wondered if he sold Oxycontin. He warned me of bad weather ahead. Thunderstorms and heavy rains were predicted for the next three days to the south. I had planned to ride in that direction. My meticulously planned itinerary put me in Daniel Boone National Park in Kentucky tomorrow.

Jim's advice convinced me to consult my map and detour north.

CHAPTER 11: BAIT AND SWITCH

Are you ready to fly?

Saturday, June 8

I rode north to outrun the thunderstorms. I merged onto the interstate racetrack outside of Columbus. I had been happy on the peaceful, two-lane secondary roads, winding through the countryside at a relaxed pace. The highway ride was an intense change of pace.

President Eisenhower is credited with the development of the Interstate Highway. He recognized that America needed an efficient system of roads to move equipment, goods and people long distances. Highways allow millions of Americans to cross the country in a hurry. I seldom rode the interstates during my trip. My decision to avoid the thunderstorms caused me to reprioritize my riding pleasure. On this day, pleasure took second place to efficiency.

I followed the by-passes around Columbus and Cincinnati to avoid the city centers. Though I was riding at midday and avoided rush hour traffic, it was still an endurance ride, not at all the pleasant trip I had planned before my detour. Instead of the gently winding, rural roads I had become accustomed to, this speedway was straight, smooth, flat and noisy with cars and trucks flashing past. The only vehicles smaller than mine were those of local motorcycle riders, rocketing past everyone. They traveled in the high-speed lane or weaved in and out, passing other vehicles right and left, leaning low over their gas tanks to slide through traffic like the wind.

I stopped at a Denny's at Jeffersonville, between Columbus and Cincinnati. The sign on the wall advised:

Think adventure is dangerous? Try routine, it's lethal.

At four o'clock, I stopped at a motel in Bedford, Indiana, one hundred and twenty-five miles west of Cincinnati. Rain was spitting out of the gray sky. I was sore, tense and tired. My ears were ringing from the noise and wind and my right hand was tingling from holding the throttle in one position for hours.

Every country has characteristics that appear confusing, maybe illogical, to visitors. In The Netherlands, doorknobs don't turn. When you walk up to a front door, turn the key and grab hold of the round, brass knob, it doesn't move. The doorknob is fixed, locked in place. What's it for? To open the door you turn the key firmly in the lock and push. Sometimes there are two keys.

You must use the keys in the correct sequence or the door

doesn't open. It's not an electrical code; it's mechanical, top lock first, then bottom. Do it the other way around and the door stays closed. So what is the doorknob for?

I asked my Dutch friends about this: "Why install a doorknob if it doesn't do anything?"

Dutch friend: "That's just the way it works."

I experienced an American doorknob shortly after I climbed off my motorcycle in the motel parking lot in Bedford, Indiana. I took off my helmet and stuffed my gloves into the helmet. I lifted my pack off the gas tank and carried it with me into the front entrance. I spoke to a young woman behind the reception desk.

"Hi, do you have a room available?"

"We have a room with a king-size bed or one with two queens. Both cost the same, $108 for a night. It's the weekend rate."

"I forgot it's Saturday."

"Which one do you want?"

"It's just me. I only need one bed."

"OK, king size it is. That'll be $122.36

"I thought it was $108?"

"That doesn't include tax and cleaning fee."

"OK, I guess I'll take it."

I handed over my credit card. She did whatever they do back there to make sure there was money connected to the account. She pushed some buttons, and some paper came out of a machine. I signed something and she gave me a key.

"Is there a restaurant in the hotel?"

"No, but I can get you a 25 percent discount at PaPa John's. They deliver free."

"What do they sell? Like sandwiches?"

"Sure, pizza, sandwiches, wings."

"OK, how about a sandwich? How much is a cold-cuts sandwich?"

"That's $5.25. But they won't deliver an order for less than $8. They have a large pizza for $10."

"OK, let's do that." I figured $7.50 for dinner was OK.

"That'll be $13.64."

"Is that with the 25 percent discount?"

"Yah and that includes tax. There's no discount on the tax, or tip."

Instead of a $5.25 sandwich, my discount pizza ended up costing me $17.64 with a 25 percent discount, 15 percent tip and I-don't-know-what percent tax. It was cold and greasy when it arrived an hour later.

I asked my U.S. friends and relatives about this way of doing business. Isn't this bait and switch? They gave me the same answer.

"That's just the way it works."

Sunday, June 9

I rode out of Bedford on Indiana's Historic Pathway, a welcome relief after the interstate. I headed southwest. It was sprinkling when I passed through Bryantsville but dry by the time I reached Huron. The sun peeked through the clouds and the day warmed as the road wound down to Willow Valley in Martin State Forest. By the time I crossed the east fork of the White River, it was dry and warm.

The day became progressively more sunny and warm. The quiet roads flowed past sleepy farms and quiet woods in long, gentle curves and calm swells. I rolled along below the speed limit enjoying the feel of the road and the sway of the turns.

I drifted toward the center line and leaned into the turns. The ride was calm and scenic.

My memory book took me to the first time I flew a plane. It was more than thirty years ago in Johnstown, Pennsylvania. Tim owned a Cherokee 140, a single engine, four-seater. It was a warm afternoon under a cloudless sky. We took off from the airport and climbed to ten thousand feet and leveled off. I occupied the front passenger seat.

Tim: "Are you ready to fly?"

Me: "What do you mean, fly?"

"Take hold of the wheel."

He took his hands off the wheel and held them in the air in front of him.

"It's all yours."

"What if I crash?"

"Even if you wanted to, you can't hit anything for two miles."

He explained how to keep the wings level, how to turn, how to pull and how to push the wheel to fly up and down. He sat back, lit a joint and left me to fly the plane. After a few anxious minutes, I forgot my fear and relaxed.

Below us the rolling hills of western Pennsylvania and Ohio stretched out for a hundred miles. The land was green and yellow with mid-summer hay, corn and wheat. White farmhouses framed by board fences, red barns and silos with silver caps decorated the countryside like a Norman Rockwell painting. Tiny trucks, tractors and irrigation equipment dotted the farms and fields. Dark ribbon roads connected each island farm to tiny towns with white churches.

Riding a motorcycle feels like flying that plane. There is a sense of weightless freedom. Time does not exist. Balance replaces gravity. Wind is the only link with speed. Both vehicles offer 360 degrees of visibility and maneuverability with a twist of the controls. At twelve hundred pounds, Tim's Cherokee was about four hundred pounds heavier than my motorcycle. But both are weightless while they cruise. Tim's plane's top speed was about a hundred miles per hour, the same as my Harley.

Riding west through the farm roads of Indiana and Illinois I was flying again, in balance, weightless, timeless, at peace.

I stopped for fuel in Decker and crossed the Wabash River from Indiana to Illinois at Mount Carmel then turned south. I stopped in Harrisburg for a large cold-cuts sandwich and ate half of it sitting at a table in a booth with plastic upholstery. I wrapped the other half and packed it into my saddlebag to save for dinner.

Shawnee National Forest Headquarters is just outside of Harrisburg. The office was closed on Sunday and the parking lot was empty. Outside the building, a National Forest kiosk offered camping information. Printed brochures filled the slots in a wooden box beneath a detailed map of the national forest. I picked out a couple and leaned my butt on the seat of my motorcycle with my legs extended as I read them in the warm sunshine.

I picked a camp near Lake Glendale. Whenever possible, I chose a campground near water where I could swim or bathe if necessary. Oak Point looked like a good prospect. It was about twenty-five miles from the parking lot. I followed a winding, two-lane country road south through the Shawnee National Forest. A gas station with a general store was the only service on the way to the campground. My ride was undisturbed by other vehicles, traffic signals or road signs. A few unmarked, unpaved side roads disappeared in the shadowy forest.

An honor system, self-registration kiosk greeted visitors to the Oak Point campground. The posted instructions became familiar as I traveled across the country. Campers remove a pre-printed envelope and select an unoccupied campsite. We complete the form on the envelope with personal information and note the campsite number. The fee is inserted by cash or a check into the envelope. Campers deposit the envelope into the steel lockbox at the kiosk. A ranger or attendant collects the envelopes at regular intervals. My America the Beautiful pass qualified me for a 50 percent discount on the twelve-dollar camping fee.

Most of the state and national park and forest campsites I visited across the country offered the same self-registration system and generally the same camping facilities. There was a fairly level place to park the vehicle. Most parking areas were asphalt, some were gravel or stone dust.

They were all spacious enough to accommodate a couple of cars or an RV, sometimes all three. I had no trouble parking my motorcycle. Additionally, the campsites offered a grass or gravel area to set up a tent. They provided a picnic table and a fire pit. Some sites offered an electric connection for an RV, primitive sites did not.

Most sites offered drinking water from a local well. Some toilets flushed with water; some were dry holes hovering over hand-dug pits. Some campgrounds offered showers. Oak Point campground offered drinking water and flush toilets but no showers. A lake was nearby.

I selected a campsite near a family, hoping for conversation. There was no one else in the area. I pulled my bike into the gravel parking area and unloaded my gear. My neighbors at the next campsite scurried into a circle of lawn chairs around their campfire. They ignored me as I unpacked and set up my tent.

I peeked at their campsite while I went about my business. Their site was crowded with a large, tow-behind RV, a dented, heavy-duty pick-up truck, with faded paint, a trailer hitch and a double-rimmed rear axle. In the center of their site, they set up a family-sized, nylon tent. In addition to the truck, a small, red compact car was parked near the road. Several coolers of varying colors and sizes were scattered on the ground. A stand-up four-burner stove attached to a 5-gallon propane tank stood by the picnic table. Children's pants, shirts, underwear and towels hung limply from a line strung between two trees. A column of smoke drifted into the trees above the fire pit. A mongrel dog, chained to a tree, barked in my direction.

The man was about thirty-five years old, thin, wearing work boots, jeans and a sleeveless 'wife-beater' t-shirt. His stringy brown hair haloed his head under a John Deere cap. A can of beer was attached to his right hand. The woman was dressed in jeans and a loose-fitting flannel shirt. She wore no hat over her straight brown hair. She bustled between the fire, the RV and the three children. Country & Western music drifted over to my campsite from the battery-powered boombox on the picnic table. The children sat by the smoky fire silently eating sandwiches, stealing glances in my direction.

After lunch, the mother gathered the children and herded them into the car and they drove away; to swimming was my guess. Beer guy poked the fire with a stick, shut off and carried the stereo inside, locked the RV, closed and zipped the tent, collected the dog, climbed into the pick-up and roared off in a cloud of dust.

The warm, humid early afternoon became suddenly quiet. Alone at the campground with the afternoon to myself, I longed for a swim in the nearby lake. I changed into shorts and sandals and set out to explore the campground. A network of worn paths spider-webbed through the forest. The lake was north, so I headed in that direction. Within a few minutes, I saw sunlight sparkling on water through the trees. I followed the path to a wooden bridge. It connected the high ground to the edge of an expanse of shallow water dotted by little islands of lily pads, ferns and tufts of tall grass.

I stood on the footbridge in the peaceful wood. The body of the lake was visible in the distance but not accessible through the swamp. Insects hummed in the air. Long-legged water spiders skittered across the surface of the still pool below. Birds chirped, banked and sailed over and through the trees. A woodpecker hammered in the distance. Children called to each other while they splashed, out of sight on the distant shore.

I waved ineffectually at flying insects as they dived and swooped around my head. Mosquitos, several kinds of flies and a few butterflies orbited randomly in their gravity-free universe, blissfully unaware of my existence. Then they found me. They started to bite. It was time to move on. I hurried off the bridge to escape out of range. I stumbled in my sandals, stubbed my toe and scratched my arms on the underbrush in my haste.

I lost my way. It had seemed a short walk to the lake. Why was it a long one back? I circled, following the path but it led deeper into the woods. Silly, I thought; which way was my campsite? After a few misturns, I spied a clearing through the trees and made my way in that direction.

Though it was the wrong campsite, I could see mine off to the left. Somehow, I had stumbled onto the wrong path. It led to another campsite. I looked over the new site: I liked it. It offered more privacy and plenty of shade. A pile of firewood was stacked near the fire pit and the grassy, flat area for the tent looked softer than mine. I considered relocating. In the end, it was just too much trouble to break down my tent and move my gear. But, this was a good lesson. I vowed to be careful selecting my campsites in the future. I would take a good look around before I settled in.

When I returned to my site, I discovered several insect bites and scratches on my face, neck, arms and legs. I sat at the picnic table, sipped some warm water, smoked my pipe, jotted in my notebook, and then read some John Sanford in my e-reader.

My neighbors returned at about five o'clock. They chained the dog to a tree, revived the smoky fire, set the boombox on the table and prepared dinner on their stove. They sat around the smoky fire holding paper plates on their laps and wielding plastic forks. They continued to ignore me.

The situation was comical. We occupied the only campsites in view. A few short yards separated us. They could see me and I could see them. They behaved as though I was invisible. I looked for an opening to initiate contact. I waited till they were finished with their meal. I gathered some scraps of paper, took a deep breath and walked across the stretch of pine needles between our campsites. The woman saw me first and alerted beer man. He stood to intercept me, chest out, arms stiff at his sides with his elbows bent, as I approached. She gathered the children and retreated to the picnic table.

It's a campsite courtesy not to enter someone's camp until you're invited. I walked to the edge of his site and stopped. He walked to the boundary on his side and stopped. We spoke from a short distance over the demilitarized zone.

Me: "Hello, I'm camped just next door."

Beer guy: "Yah, we saw you."

"Pretty nice RV. How long are you staying for?"

"What do you want?"

"I saw your campfire. Do you mind if I toss in some paper to burn?"

"Why?"

"I'm not going to light a fire. It's too hot. I'd like to get rid of this."

I showed him a couple of brochures from the information kiosk and a gas receipt.

"Yah, OK."

He turned and walked back to the smoky fire pit. It was the closest thing to an invitation I was likely to get, so I followed.

The smoky pile was more a trash dump than a campfire. A few charred logs smoldered in the center of the circle. They were covered with half-melted Styrofoam cups and plates, a plastic shopping bag, a food box, some elbow noodles and a charred can of dog food. I tossed my handful of paper into the few weak, yellow flames flickering at the edges of the debris. Beer guy sipped from the can and watched silently. His family eyed me suspiciously from the table a few feet away. Even the dog was quiet.

"Well, that's it. Thanks very much. I'm traveling light. I don't want to carry anything extra."

"Yah."

"I'll be leaving tomorrow morning. I hope my motorcycle doesn't bother you. It's pretty loud."

"I heard ya ride in."

"I know, I'm sorry about that. The guy I bought it from liked loud pipes. It's pretty noisy."

"Yah, it is."

He stood by the fire pit, sipping his beer.

"Well, OK, thanks again. Have a nice evening."

"Sure."

Life at the other campsite returned to normal as I walked away, even the dog started barking again. Beer guy's wife and kids returned to the fire pit. Beer guy popped open another can. I returned to my campsite, reclined on the picnic table bench and reopened my e-reader. But my mind was on the family next door. Their vehicle license plates told me they were local. I had hoped to strike up a conversation, find out a little about their lives, maybe tell them a little about mine. But that was not to be. The experience stayed with me. I wonder why.

CHAPTER 12: BIG MUDDY

*The streets were rivers and the
farms white-capped lakes.*

Monday, June 10

The tent zipper rasped like a cross-cut saw in the silent forest at five-thirty the next morning. I slowly opened the screen and tossed out my bags, one at a time, then followed them and zipped the tent closed to keep the insects on the outside. No one was moving at the family campsite. I was quiet as a thief loading my gear on the bike.

My clothes fit into the waterproof Harley luggage box, strapped to the seat behind me, which also served as a back rest during the ride. The nylon duffle was not waterproof. It stored my sleeping bag, pad, tent, sandals and sneakers. It rested on the frame behind the sissy bar, secured with three bungee cords.

A small bag secured to the gas tank with magnets functioned as a day pack. It contained my valuables and the small things I might need during the ride: wallet, passport, insurance and registration papers, credit cards, some cash in an envelope, a little camera, my journal, a pen, a bottle of water and a small road atlas. I was confident that no one would touch the gear attached to the bike, but I couldn't risk losing the tank bag. I always carried it with me during stops for gas or lunch.

I'm an early riser. The Harley could wake a hibernating bear in a cave five miles away. I delayed my morning departures until about seven-thirty or until I saw people moving around. I used the time before my neighbors woke to make notes and check my maps. By seven-thirty there was still no activity at beer guy's camp. It was time to be on my way. I woke the beast and roared out of the campground; confident I wouldn't offend any friends.

I had been on the road for an hour, headed toward the Mississippi River, when I saw the first sign,

"Caution – water on pavement."

The heady, rich smell of muddy water triggered a long-forgotten boyhood memory. Riding toward the river, my mind recalled unsummoned images of a pond, ferns and frogs near my home sixty years ago.

* * *

We had hiked through the woods; three brothers out to explore our neighborhood wilderness south of Boston. We discovered a pond full of life, fed by a seasonal stream, high in the spring, swampy and fern-covered in the summer. In the winter we hiked in with snow shovels, sticks and skates to play ice hockey on its frozen surface. I was transported to an Indian Summer, when golden leaves sparkled in sunshine filtered through trees and reflected on the flat water.

Insects buzzed and feasted on young arms, legs, ears and necks. We slapped dirty hands, smearing ourselves with muck. We slopped in the shallow, muddy water, mucking through ferns, snapping dead twigs, stage-whispering, hunting big-eyed, green amphibians. Buffalo silent, we stalked frogs, salamanders and black and yellow garter snakes. We snatched at them, bare-handed and clumsy. Still we managed to catch a few, the old and deaf or young and stupid. But the real thrill was to spot a snapping turtle. They shared the pond and we sometimes spied them sleeping in the sun.

We were strictly 'catch and release' hunters. We loved the thrill of the hunt and the excitement of the catch, but we had no long-term plans for our quarry. We didn't keep trophies or wild pets.

We loved to hunt and catch them and feel their slimy skin and shells. Sometimes we teased a turtle with a stick for the thrill when he snapped it. The bigger the turtle, the bigger the snap. We'd set the turtle free and watch him waddle to the woods or disappear into the murky water. It was our pre-adolescent, pre-video game adventure.

Three neighbors followed us to the pond to join our expedition. They lived at the end of our street but we didn't know them very well. They didn't join in our neighborhood pick-up baseball and football games. We built tree houses and explored the forest behind our house, but not with them. However, when they followed us to our hideaway, we were happy to include them. We pointed out likely hideaways for frogs and turtles. Together we hunted and splashed in the mud.

Though we were about the same ages, they seemed older, more experienced, not sophisticated as much as tougher, cooler. They were unimpressed with the wonder of our wilderness pond. They joined us a few times and tried their hand at snagging wildlife.

One day, we walked by their house on our way to collect friends for a ball game. We intended to invite them to join us. We spotted them beside their house. In those days the forest surrounded all the houses. They were walking on the border where their lawn and the wood met. The three of them were laughing and yelling excitedly. They did not see us.

We stopped to watch. They had caught a large snapping turtle. Two brothers were holding the ends of a heavy tree branch, carrying the turtle between them. Its jaws were clamped onto the middle of the branch. The other boy was beating the turtle with a stick. The turtle hung on to the branch while the boys carried it into the woods. They banged the turtle against a tree, but it would not let go of the stick. The stick was too big and green to snap. The turtle was locked on and wouldn't or couldn't let go. They mounted the stick between forked branches of a tree, so the turtle hung in mid-air above the ground. They each picked up a stick and beat the turtle. Still the turtle held on. Tiring of swinging sticks, they collected rocks and began throwing them at the turtle. We silently walked away. They continued their game.

On our way home after the ball game, we passed their house. The brothers were nowhere in sight. In the dirt beside the road, we saw the mutilated remains of their victim. They had discarded the body in the gutter. The shell was shattered, the body smashed, the neck extended and the head crushed. After that day, we saw them play the same games with frogs, snakes and toads. Sometimes they employed matches, fireworks and knives. They became bored quickly and tired of hunting at our pond. They moved on to other adventures, without us.

For our part, we were shocked and confused by their violence. We didn't understand their sadistic pleasure from hurting the helpless. My brothers and I continued to frequent our wildlife refuge, sometimes catching and always releasing whatever we found. We crafted waxed albums of fall leaves and birch log candle holders as Christmas decorations. We avoided the family down the street. I am ashamed I did nothing to stop them from killing the turtle. I was a young coward; afraid they would turn their wrath on me and my brothers. I marvel that one sniff of damp mud can spark such vivid ancient memories.

* * *

I rode west toward Cape Girardeau to cross the Mississippi River into Missouri. Heavy rains had blurred the boundary between river and flood. The damp air chilled and gusty winds shook the bike from side to side. I tightened my grip on the handlebars for the illusion of control. A sign warned of possible washouts ahead. I rode close to the middle line to avoid the muddy berm beside the pavement.

A wide expanse of water extended far to my right and left. Wind-whipped waves washed brown foam onto both sides of the road. The throughway was a dike between two lakes. Fifty yards from shore a billboard stood in water so deep, waves broke against the bottom. "Farmland for Sale." The phone number beneath the headline was submerged. I realized that I was not riding between two lakes. The road bisected flooded farmland.

A half-sunken, plastic tank bobbed in the surf, anchored to submerged irrigation equipment. I passed an orange sign warning of water on the road. I geared down and steered clear of the waves lapping the right shore. I edged toward the high ground in the center of the road. I prepared for a quick stop or a

U-turn if the road was closed ahead. The road was narrow, but open, just higher than the farm/lake. Both sides were washed by waves, the road surface was wet but passable.

I approached Big Muddy surrounded by water as far as I could see. It was impossible to distinguish the course of the river. Only the tree tops were visible above the viscous, brown, swirling soup in the valley below. I reached the Bill Emerson Memorial Bridge. Thick brown water flowed dangerously close to the steel framework. Orange-and-white-striped traffic cones sprouted from the asphalt like spring narcissus. Concrete construction barriers and hundreds of cones formed a trail along the only passable route. I slowed and followed the pavement directly under my wheels, navigating through the obstacle course to the other side.

Spring storms had dumped huge amounts of water on the middle of the country for weeks. The earth was saturated. The Mississippi River offered the only outlet to the Gulf of Mexico, six hundred miles away. The river swelled and overflowed its banks flooding the adjacent lowlands. In Illinois the farms were lakes.

On the Missouri side, the river drowned the town. The side roads were under water, exit ramps impassable and the buildings awash. Shops, gas stations, restaurants, post offices, churches and homes were awash to the ground floor windows.

Fire trucks and emergency vehicles and motorboats churned in the muddy flood among the buildings. Construction crews clad in hard hats, yellow vests and rubber waders sloshed in the thick soup to operate backhoes, dump trucks and pumps. But there was nowhere to pump the water. The streets were rivers and the farms white-capped lakes. The water was still rising. The off ramps resembled boat launches more than roads. On the west side of the river the land rose out of the water. I climbed out of the flood into the Missouri hills.

In the afternoon, I stopped at the U.S. Forest Service

headquarters for the Potosi-Fredericktown Ranger District. Whenever possible, I stopped and spoke with the people that managed the campgrounds where I traveled. They were always friendly, helpful and informative. I asked about campgrounds in the Mark Twain National Forest. A friendly ranger suggested Berryman Campground, about twenty miles west. He printed a map and even helped me select a route from Berryman for my trip west.

I asked him another question.

"What is the difference between a National Forest and a National Park?"

He explained that National Forests are managed by the Bureau of Land Management of the U.S. Forest Service. National Forests are large tracts of land purchased by the federal government. The land may not be contiguous because it is purchased at different times from private owners. Some land is donated.

He pointed to the map of Mark Twain National Forest on the wall. The map was a patchwork of green and white.

"The green sections are public land. The white sections are private land.

"National Parks are managed by The National Parks Service. It's a bureau of the Department of the Interior."

"Do they offer the same kind of experience?"

"National Parks have a theme, like Arches, Glacier, Grand Canyon, Crater Lake, and Mammoth Cave. The tourist appeal and level of services in a National Park are generally higher than in a National Forest."

"Which system is bigger?"

"Well, we manage about one hundred and ninety million acres of National Forests. And there are about eighty-four million acres managed by the National Parks Service."

"So you're more than double their size."

"You can say that, but we don't do the same thing. We manage forests and grasslands. They do that and they manage tourist attractions too. I'll show you how to get in and out of Berryman but won't give you a tour."

I rode out of the ranger station toward Berryman Campground. I took the ranger's advice and stopped at the gas station and general store to pick up some food for the night. It was about four o'clock, sunny, breezy and warm when I rode in. Berryman offered eight primitive campsites, free to the public. No registration was required. There was one pit toilet for the campground. Each site provided a picnic table and fire pit. There was no cell tower within range, no electricity and no drinking water. I was alone.

I circled the campground and selected my campsite. I parked the bike on the gravel drive, facing out, unpacked and set up my tent. I collected dry, dead leaves, twigs and branches from around my campsite, broke up the sticks by hand and piled it all by the fire pit. One flick of my butane lighter was all it took to start. I opened a can and cooked my dinner and heated water for coffee over the fire. After dinner, I sat at the picnic table and smoked my pipe till the mosquitos drove me into the tent for the night.

I enjoyed a lazy, peaceful, quiet evening. Probably much different from the families who lived and worked in the fertile land that bordered the Mississippi River. What were they doing tonight; all those people, families, business owners, farmers displaced by the flood? What did they do today? What will they do tomorrow? Next week? Where are they living while their homes, cars, clothes and furniture rotted in the muck? What will they find when they return? The destruction will take a long time to clean up. I wonder how many billions of dollars the disaster cost in personal property, crops, and business loss this year, last year, every year.

Maybe instead of investing in a wall at the border with Mexico, we should invest in a dike.

CHAPTER 13: WINDMILLS

All change is bad.

Tuesday, June 11

Tuesday morning, I sat at the picnic table studying the map. I was headed toward Kansas City. I could find no likely state or national parks anywhere close to my intended route. I decided to ride west from KC and find a motel when I was tired. A soft bed and a warm shower wouldn't do me any harm.

I rode away from Berryman at seven-thirty. It was a cold, windy morning. I wore a long-sleeved shirt, plus all three layers of my motorcycle jacket. I wore my rain pants over my jeans for added insulation against the wind. I peeled down as the sun climbed into the sky and the day warmed. As I rode north then west, the road became rough and bumpy. A billboard beside the road displayed two children and an adult, with a cross in the background. Printed below the picture was the question:

"HAVE YOU PRAYED WITH YOUR CHILDREN TODAY?"

This idyllic region of the country was dotted with farms, grassy fields, forests, lakes and rivers. But it felt stressed, like a rubber band stretched too far. It seemed a bit frayed, tired, maybe not as resilient as it used to be. A motorcycle rider feels the roads in a way the automobile driver cannot. A car is built for comfort and safety. My bike was comfortable as bikes go, but I felt the imperfections in the road surface. Every bump in the road was transmitted from the tires to the frame to my feet, hands and up my spine. Smooth roads were a pleasure, but they were the exception, not the rule.

The roads through this part of Missouri were a creative quilt of endless repairs. Old crumbling roads were patched, filled and plugged. Holes and cracks were hidden under coats of viscous asphalt. Black ribbons filled cracks along the road surface. Long, narrow ropes of coal glue were painted across the concrete. The patches formed geometric shapes of stripes, circles, squares, rectangles, and rhombi. From inside the cabin of a car, road patches are innocuous. The driver might feel a slight double thump dampened by the shocks, springs and independent suspension.

It's not the same on a motorcycle. A motorcycle rider feels all those economical road patches and small repairs. They bump and thump and jar. I felt every stripe, square and circle patch along every mile. I tried navigating between the long, thin strips of black tar. Road fractures don't follow straight lines. The repairs follow the cracks. I could ride between lines of tar when they ran parallel, but not when the pair converged or drifted to the other side of the street. I could delay but not avoid thumping over them. The same was true with the bigger patches: bump, thump, rattle. I tried shifting my weight off my seat onto my feet to cushion the shocks. At sixty miles an hour, they jarred my spine to my shoulders, stiffened my neck and rattled my teeth.

My right hand gripped the throttle and felt little electric shocks, sometimes all the way through my elbow and up to my shoulder. My left hand and arm suffered less. I could release my grip and ease the pressure. My feet, even on the high crash-bar pegs, did not insulate me from the vibrations that rattled my body from knees to neck. Patched roads are hard on motorcycles and their riders.

The other travelers piloted their multi-wheeled vehicles, equipped with efficient springs and shock absorbers, at high speed. They accelerated quickly from stop lights, turned without signaling, tailgated and passed on the left and right. Traffic speed cameras have not been embraced by Americans. I saw none on my trip. Speed limits seemed more like suggestions than regulations.

American roads and bridges were wearing down, so were the buildings that lined them. The landscape was rife with abandoned structures along the secondary highways and in the town centers. I passed empty, deserted gas stations, general stores, factories and homes. I saw barns with collapsed roofs and broken windows. A burned-out two-bedroom RV was abandoned in a lot beside the road. The land around it and driveway were overgrown with weeds. An old pick-up truck, also burned, settled under a tree on rubberless rims. Even the occupied buildings showed signs of neglect, peeling paint and uncut lawns; weedy, unpaved car parks and driveways.

Though the roads were rough, many of the vehicles that traveled on them were not. They presented a sharp contrast to the condition of the infrastructure. A multitude of late model, high-end RVs, SUVs and pick-up trucks cruised the roads. Many were towing expensive toys like campers and trailers carrying boats, dirt bikes, snowmobiles and jet skis. I shared the road with multi-bedroom land yachts accessorized with expanding living rooms, electric sun awnings and satellite dishes on the roof. They towed cars, carried bikes or motorcycles and flew the American flag.

I stopped at McDonalds for coffee. There were two media options, Democrat or Republican. It was easy to identify the local politics with a quick look at the TV news station. The flat screen in the restaurant was set to Fox News – Republican. I sipped my coffee and watched a commercial for a litigation attorney who promised to, ". . .Get you what you deserve".

I had been spoiled by the tranquil, scenic secondary roads over the past few days. My anxiety level started to rise about fifty miles outside of Kansas City. The world seemed to suddenly increase in intensity. The highway became faster, wider, noisier and crowded, all at the same time. The number of travel lanes expanded from two to three, then became four. Traffic speed increased as though the city was at the bottom of a long hill and nobody had brakes. Where did all these cars come from and where were they going? They were entering, exiting, continually changing lanes, like black flies, flying from everywhere, all in a hurry to be somewhere else.

As I approached Kansas City, the energy of the highway intensified. Someone was turning the dial on a huge variable speed transformer, increasing the pace of the world. The sound from my navigation speakers was lost in the din of the road. The glare of the sun blotted out my mobile phone screen. It was impossible to absorb the multitude of traffic, route and safety information posted along the road. I focused on avoiding collisions with other vehicles, negotiating safely around the construction detours and finding a route west without getting run down.

There are two Kansas Cities. I guess I knew that but the reality was a shock. The two KCs are side by side. Somewhere along my high-speed flight through the confusing highway, Missouri turned into Kansas. Six travel lanes wound through the city, all vehicles streaking along at upwards of eighty miles per hour. Road construction barriers, orange and white cones, men and equipment, speed-control signs all failed to slow the midday traffic frenzy. Everybody was in a god-awful hurry in all directions.

After my peaceful ride through the back roads of Illinois and Missouri, the Kansas City twins were a rude awakening. At KC, tranquil U.S. Route 50 merged with I-35 and became a super-highway. My peaceful rides of the last few days were snatched from memory. I felt like an old lady, out for a Sunday ride, who had wandered into the middle of Le Mans.

I managed to negotiate the Harley through the complex megalopolis of the Kansas Cities speedway. About a hundred and twenty miles west of Kansas City, Route 50 splits away from I-35. With a sigh of relief, I pulled in at the first motel where I gladly paid $43.80 for the $37.92 hotel room and didn't ask why.

I took advantage of the hotel Wi-Fi and cell connections to make some phone calls. I called Kyle in Denver to let him know I was on my way. He helped me make an appointment with a Harley dealership to install a new rear tire. After two thousand miles, the front tire looked fine but the rear tire was worn. From Denver, I would climb into the mountains then cross the desert. I wanted good rubber under me.

Jim and Cindy were home from their birthday celebration in Aruba. I shared my location with Jim via Google Maps. He'd been following my progress and sent me occasional messages. He invited me to stop at his house on my return.

I phoned my brother Mike, who doesn't ride a motorcycle and hasn't followed me on Google Maps. He was stressed about his impending move. He had wanted to move to Florida for thirty-five years. There was always a reason they couldn't; jobs, kids' schools, health insurance. Their kids, now grown with their own families, are happy to have parents in Florida to visit.

Me: "So you're finally making the big move. You must be excited."

Mike: "It's a pain in the ass."

"I thought you wanted to move to Florida."

"Yah. I guess."

"So what's the problem?"

"It's a big change."

"It is, but it's what you always wanted. That's good, isn't it?"

"Change is bad."

"It's hard, but it will be better for you. That's not bad"

"All change is bad."

"So you got the health insurance figured out?"

"Sort of but it's not great."

"What do you mean?"

Mike explained. "Massachusetts has better insurance than Florida."

"Insurance companies offer different coverages in different states?"

"My insurance company doesn't do business in Florida."

"Why not?"

"I guess it's not profitable."

"Is it a big difference? I mean big enough to keep you tied to

Massachusetts?"

"Up till now it has been."

"So you were trapped in Massachusetts for health insurance?"

"That's about the size of it."

"Why?

"I can't afford to take a chance. If something happens and we're not covered, I can lose the house."

"Some system."

"How does it work in The Netherlands?"

"It's pretty simple. Everybody pays about the same. Everybody's covered – for everything." "Doctor's visits?

"Yup."

"Prescriptions?"

"Yup."

"What about emergency room?"

"Everything, chiropractors, acupuncture, even some holistic treatments." (This is an exaggeration. There are limits. But nothing like the U.S. system.)

"Is there a deductible?"

"Yes, a few hundred Euros a year. It goes up a little every year. Everybody complains. What's your deductible?" I asked.

"A few thousand dollars each, but that doesn't include prescriptions or co-payments."

"Our system sounds better."

"That's socialized medicine. That wouldn't work here."

"It works in The Netherlands."

"They're socialists."

"America does it for education."

"We don't have socialist education."

"They call it universal education. Education in the U.S. is free for everyone through high school."

"So?"

"Why can't we do the same thing for medicine."

"Free health care doesn't exist."

"Free education doesn't exist either. We pay for it with property taxes."

"That's different."

Me: "How is it different?"

Mike: "Everybody doesn't pay property taxes. What about renters?"

"Everybody who lives in a building pays property taxes one way or another."

"Education is different."

"Isn't health as important as education? We pay for every child's education, not health. Don't you think there is something wrong with that?" I asked.

"I don't want my taxes raised to pay for someone else's cancer treatment," Mike answered.

"What if you get cancer?"

"That's my problem. No one else should have to pay for it."

"You pay for other kids' schools. When it's education, they call it universal education. When it's healthcare, they call it socialized medicine. Why don't they call it socialized education and universal healthcare?"

Mike ended the discussion with, "You're a communist."

It's an old argument.

After speaking with my brother, I called my son Mike in Tahoe. He said he was looking forward to my visit.

We had not spoken much over the last few months. Whenever we don't communicate, I worry something is wrong. I was anxious to visit and see how things are going.

Finally, I called Han. She told me that I had received a letter from an insurance company. She opened it. It was a threat to cancel the insurance on my house in Florida. She asked if there was something I needed to do. I explained that the letter was for the house in Pensacola. I've already sent that money. She asked me if I was sure.

"Maybe it's for the DeBary house."

"Read it. What address is the house?"

"You're right. It's for Pensacola."

"That's what I thought. We're OK on that. I paid for it before I left."

"What about the DeBary house? Is that OK?"

"I think that one is due at the end of August. I'll take care of that when I get back."

I've complained several times about insurance companies' Draconian business methods, so Hanneke is tuned in to U.S. correspondence, especially from insurance companies. I assured her I had this one under control. We hung up with fond farewells and no concerns. Which turned out to be a mistake I discovered two months later.

Journal entry in the motel:

"I rode 350 miles today, I'm tired. The worst was the ride through Kansas City. Did I know there were two? I've got to be more careful about picking my route."

I'd been sleeping comfortably in the tent on the ground. But it was a luxury to climb into a bed with a pillow and clean sheets. The motel shower was welcome, so was the air conditioning. I took advantage of the hotel electricity to charge my equipment. Time to turn off the light, nine o'clock.

I've always enjoyed an active dream experience. At home I keep a dream journal and have observed common themes and patterns. My dreams often add perspective to issues I deal with during the day. My dreams increase when my waking life is full and complex. My dreams during this trip were entertaining and I'm sure they were telling me something. I wrote a few of them in my day journal.

The previous night, I had dreamed Matt and Mike were hiking in the woods. I was camping with them, but they went off on their own. They are competent campers but for some reason I had a feeling they were in trouble. I left camp and walked through the forest looking for them. I found a rock formation and a cave. I knew they had gone in. I worried they didn't have a flashlight and would get lost or hurt. I walked into the cave to find them. It was wide and high at the entrance but narrowed and became darker as I walked further. I was following a rocky path with a cliff ledge on my right disappearing into a deep, black crevasse.

The path became a narrow walkway with a ledge at about shoulder height to my left and nothing on my right but a dark chasm, bottomless for all I knew. I inched forward, sure the boys had gone deeper into the cave. I worried they would not be able to find their way out. In the dim light I saw something lying on the ledge to my left. I realized I was staring at a sleeping snake, an albino boa constrictor. Its body dimensions were distorted. It was about seven feet long but very fat, like a slimy bulging telephone pole.

Sleeping on the ledge, its body was even with my head. As quietly as I could, I walked directly beside it, careful not to wake it up. I was desperate to go further into the cave to find my sons, but afraid of the snake. I inched forward, step by step along the narrow path beside the sleeping monster. My foot hit a pebble and knocked it over the cliff with an echoing clatter as it bounced off the stone walls below. I stopped, breathless. The snake raised its white head and turned toward me with yellow eyes. Shocked, I jumped away from the snake, into the air over the abyss. As I fell, my last thought was concern that my boys would not know the snake was waiting for them.

I snapped awake just before dawn with my heart pounding. I found myself on the floor beside my bed. I guess the physical and emotional stress of the trip was adding up. My dreams became my pressure valve.

Wednesday, June 12

I motored all day through flat, treeless farmland. U.S. Route 50 in Kansas is a high-speed interstate throughway for travelers, vacationers and a million truckers. An endless caravan of eighteen-wheelers blew by me at eighty miles per hour.

It was on this section of the ride that I developed my technique for approaching trucks, RVs and buses. I scanned the road ahead and the rear-view mirror for big rigs. Some created a powerful gust of wind, some didn't. Loaded as I was, with luggage and full saddlebags, I was vulnerable to wind from every direction.

I found it a puzzle. Why did some big rigs seem to slide by with little or no side wind, while others almost swept me off the road with a hurricane blast? This was true whether they approached from the front or from behind. Some passed smoothly, seamlessly, almost silently, while others huffed, puffed and blew tornados of wind that washed over me and pushed me sideways. On this stretch of road, it happened so often that I was determined to discover the pattern.

Everyone knows big, fast-moving vehicles cause turbulent air. The bigger the vehicle, the more air it moves. An oncoming truck, bus or RV pushes a wave of air ahead of it like a plow. It creates a vacuum behind filled by a following wind. A vehicle passing from behind, also pushes air and causes a vacuum behind it. Both situations cause a side wave of air to hit the vehicles it passes. Cars carry more weight on four wheels so they can withstand a lot of side wind. Sometimes even they are pushed off their travel line. Two-wheeled motorcycles are lighter and more vulnerable.

I learned to get low, get slow and get right when I saw a big rig coming my way – from ahead or behind. When I saw a truck approaching, I leaned forward with my belly close to the gas tank. This cut down my profile and presented the least amount of wind resistance. I slowed down: this allowed the vehicle to pass by me quicker and lessen my exposure. And I steered far over to the right side of the right lane, as far away from the passing truck as possible. Moving over a few feet to the right lessened the impact because it increased the distance between me and the big vehicle. Engineers can explain the turbulent air-distance equation but to summarize, "far is better."

I was on constant alert for passing big rigs. By looking closely at an approaching vehicle, I got pretty good at recognizing what to expect. Big dump trucks were the worst. The box shape and high bucket front is a perfect design for catching and pushing wind. On the positive side, they didn't usually travel as fast as a big cargo carrier. However, a big dump truck traveling at over sixty miles per hour can be a real distraction to motorcycles. Rack trucks, maybe carrying pipes, allow the wind to pass through. They don't offer a lot of wind resistance. They didn't blow me around much.

The eighty-thousand-pound eighteen-wheelers that cruise the highways at sixty to eighty miles per hour were the most common. These were the big rigs that helped me establish my truck-wind-motorcycle strategy. Later, I looked it up. These trucks push up to eighteen tons of air for each highway mile. Some trucks pushed me away as they approached, then sucked me back in as they sped away. I wanted to find out which ones didn't.

All day, I rolled by huge Kansas farms, yellow and green with summer wheat, sorghum, corn and soybeans, irrigated in quarter-mile circles by metal scaffolds on pneumatic wheels. I watched truck after truck roll toward me, pass and blow by. I got low, got slow, got right. Some blew my bike like a leaf in the wind. Some passed like a ninja in the night. After what seemed like forever, I discovered the reason. It was simple once I recognized the pattern. The newer trucks generated less wind. The late-model trucks and RVs were more streamlined, with big fairings on top and rounded corners. They are more fuel efficient and create less turbulence. I learned to look for big air foils over the cabs. My ride across Kansas farm country was a repeating exercise of low, slow and right.

On my ride west through Kansas, I passed thousands of wind turbines generating electricity. They stood in lonely formation, the tallest structures on the landscape for a hundred miles. Three-hundred-foot towers marched beyond sight to the horizon. The huge pinwheels rotated slowly in the breeze. For an hour I saw only corn stalks and windmills to where the yellow earth met the blue sky.

We don't hear much about U.S. wind turbines in Europe. In fact, windmills generate 337.5 terawatts, or 8.5 percent of U.S. electric power in a year. By comparison, The Netherlands generates 5,000 megawatts which is also about 8.5 percent of the country's electric power consumption. The huge Kansas wind farm was a surprise. I don't know if it was only one farm or more than one. There were more towers and blades than I could count. I stopped at a general store and filled up my tank in Syracuse. I asked the clerk about the wind farm. She was very helpful.

Me: "What are all those windmills I saw along the road?"

Helpful clerk: "Windmills."

"Who installed them?"

"Kansas Power."

"You mean the state installed windmills."

"I guess that's who's Kansas Power."

"I didn't know Kansas had windmills."

"Will that be all?"

I rode another twenty miles into Colorado and found a motel for the night in Holly.

CHAPTER 14: REFLECTION

We sell all our water to
Aurora and Denver.

Thursday, June 13

It was a simple thing, a split-second accident and totally unnecessary. My mobile phone shot out of my shirt pocket onto the parking lot. I glimpsed it as it flashed by. It hit the asphalt, CRACK! A spike of fear shot through my stomach like an electric shock.

I had slid my phone into my shirt pocket in the hotel room. It would have been a simple thing to button the pocket. The bike was parked in front of my ground-floor room. I carried both bags outside and set them on the pavement beside the bike. I had packed the bike so many mornings, I hardly thought about it anymore. Two nylon straps and five bungee cords secured my gear. Matt's system was fast, efficient and had become routine.

Tiny fragments of glass sparkled in the sun when I gathered the broken phone from the pavement. A spiderweb of diagonal cracks scarred the face of the phone from top to bottom, side to side. The worst damage was to the bottom, right corner where pieces of glass were missing from about a half-inch section. The top part of the screen was cracked but intact.

I held the phone in the palm of my hand to examine it. Little pieces of glass dripped from the corner and tinkled to the asphalt. I gently pressed the "on" button. The phone face brightened. I entered the access code and the home screen activated. Cradling the phone in my left hand, I opened the saddlebag to extract my tool kit. I stretched a piece of electrical tape over the broken corner.

I mounted the phone into the handlebar holder and plugged in the charger. The little lightning bolt indicated it was charging. I touched the screen to activate the map. Google was still with me. I typed Kyle's address in Aurora, Colorado. Next, I turned on my helmet Bluetooth receiver and the reassuring voice told me I was connected. The navigation system still worked. The phone was wounded but not fatally.

I was relieved, then almost immediately angry at myself, first for my carelessness letting the phone drop, then for my anxiety. I was disappointed in myself by my fear of losing the phone. As I rode away from Holly, I wondered if the phone would last the rest of the trip, the rest of the day. Would I have to buy a new phone? Did I need it at all? But mostly, why was I so worried?

In preparation for this trip I put a lot of thought, time and energy into selecting my route and equipment. It felt like my plans were unraveling as I rode west. The things I bought, packed and used for this trip were falling away one by one. And to my surprise my worries were fading away with them. I wondered if the things I brought with me, my stuff and my goals were the cause of my anxieties and fears.

Planning for the trip, I painstakingly and lovingly considered each piece of equipment, clothing, gadget, and goal, careful to avoid mistakes and omissions. I wrote notes, lists and created spreadsheets. I studied alternative routes, assembled first aid, toilet and tool kits. I selected and tested all my equipment and finally decided to rely on a mobile phone as my primary technology.

Before my departure, I practiced riding my motorcycle to sharpen my skills. I studied maps of national parks and forests to find the best campsites. I researched road maps and routes across the country, east to west and back. I estimated time between campsites, gas stops and rest areas. I checked gas prices, estimated mileage and developed a budget for food, lodging, fuel and maintenance.

On the ride out of Holly, I began to question my planning habits. I enjoyed the planning process. But was that really true? Maybe I was motivated by fear, trying to anticipate and avoid trouble, and control the trip. As each possession, piece of equipment, and goal failed, broke, or got lost I realized I could do without it. I didn't need it and maybe never did. The things I spent months collecting, organizing and planning were replaceable, redundant or unnecessary, even the motorcycle. I could have taken the bus.

Every day I inspected, folded, rolled, packed, protected and worried about all my stuff. How was I different from Bob in Pennsylvania who collected stoves, knives and pellet guns? It was not until something was gone that I realized I didn't need it in the first place. The first hint was when my navigation device almost dropped off the bike in Massachusetts. I obsessed about it for two hundred miles. I was frustrated and disappointed about the loss of my toilet kit in New York. In Virginia my phone-charging cable failed. I confronted a big fear in Pennsylvania when I dumped the bike. The bike accident caused me to doubt my skill, reflexes, my motives, even my judgment, but even that didn't end my trip. I abandoned my carefully planned itinerary in Missouri, consulted a map and readjusted.

All morning, as I rode northwest, I thought about what was really essential. I had meticulously assembled a camp kitchen. It was small and efficient. I had brought a compact, one-burner stove, plastic plates and cups, a set of stainless-steel pans, silverware, stove fuel, a repair kit for the stove and a little French press coffee-maker. The kitchen kit and a little food fit in one saddlebag. Yet I had seldom used it. I rarely ate breakfast. I bought lunch on the road and usually only ate half of it. I ate the other half for dinner at my campsite. I could have left the whole kitchen at home.

An enormous amount of planning time and thought went into selecting, buying and installing my technology. Was it necessary? While they might be useful, these things were a continuing source of anxiety. Was the anxiety worth the convenience? The technology was a bear in the planning and continued to growl as I rode west. I worried about each cable, connector, speaker and Bluetooth device. Would it work, would break, would fall off or get lost or stolen. But did I really need this stuff? Was it essential?

What was essential? What could I have done without?

I thought of my stealth camping trips, before cell phones and GPS navigation. I used paper maps, index cards, felt markers and pieces of paper with route numbers. New technology made navigating more convenient – when it worked. But technology also creates stress and sometimes confusion. And of course when I was out of range of a cell tower, the screen locked and my exact location and the road ahead were a mystery.

I figured navigation was about a wash, fifty-fifty, pro-con. I could do without it. In fact for the first forty years of motorcycle riding, I did. So why all the anxious worry now? I came to the conclusion that technology was a deceptive bear, scary but toothless, nothing to worry about.

I thought about the tool kit, carefully researched, assembled and packed. I even weighed it. I used it and it was a convenience. But was it really essential? I admitted I felt more comfortable knowing it was in the saddlebag, just in case. Not a bear, call it the precautionary principle, tied to the mechanical-failure bear.

I looked into the faces of my bears as I rode toward Denver. My toilet kit, long gone; my itinerary folded and forgotten; my kitchen kit clean, almost unused; and my mobile phone, cracked, taped and mounted on my handlebar. It occurred to me that, as my ride progressed west, little by little I was shedding my gear, plans and bears.

I rode twenty-five miles out of Holly and turned right onto U.S. Route 287. It was eight o'clock in the morning. There were no other vehicles on the road. I could see the horizon in all directions. I pulled over to take some photos of the bike on the empty road to show my Dutch friends. The Netherlands is a crowded country. A deserted stretch of road is a rarity. Not only were there no other vehicles, since leaving Holly I'd seen only a few trees. The land was a flat checkerboard of farms and fields bisected by quiet, lonely roads.

I wound my way north and west toward Eads, following farm roads and state highways, avoiding the one and two-digit interstates. After about a hundred miles, I was ready for some food and the bike could use some fuel. At Love's Travel Stop, I gassed up then rode into the gravel parking lot of JJ's Restaurant. It was a weathered wooden, single-story building with a rough railing around the farmer's porch. It looked like an inviting diner. I parked the bike and walked inside for a sit-down breakfast. I peeled off my jacket as I walked in and selected a booth by the window. There was a lively conversation going on between some customers and the waitress. She broke away, poured me a cup of coffee without asking and smiled.

"What would you like, hon?"

"How's the French toast?"

"It's our specialty."

"Sounds good. I'll have that and some bacon."

She walked away to place my order.

The other customers turned in their seats to look me over. They had watched me ride up on the bike loaded for travel. A man and a woman occupied the booth beside mine, the remains of their breakfast on the plates in front of them. They sipped coffee from porcelain mugs.

Man: "Looks like you're on a trip. Where you from?"

Me: "New Hampshire."

"New Hampshire, that's a long way from here. Where you headed?"

"To California to visit my son."

"I used to have a Harley. Thinking about buying another one next year."

"It's a great bike."

"I rode to Rapid City on mine a few years ago. Nothing like it."

"I'm headed to Tahoe."

"I drive big rigs now, long haul. I used to hate 'em when I was on the bike. Now I drive 'em. But I'm careful around a bike."

"Yah, they sure blow a lot of wind."

"You think it's bad here. Wait till you get to Utah and Nevada. You can get blowed right off the road. You watch out."

An image of a bear riding a motorcycle across the desert, shaggy fur blowing in the wind sprung to mind. I nodded and smiled.

"I'll be careful."

The waitress delivered my meal and refilled my cup then walked back to the kitchen. We continued our conversation while I ate and they drank coffee.

We talked about road travel in the U.S., about big rigs, RVs and motorcycles. Seems like everyone in the U.S. rides or has ridden a motorcycle and most of them Harleys. This couple, like many I met along the way, were seniors, sixty-plus years old. They were the people I saw when I stopped at diners in the mid-morning and afternoons. They were open and friendly, not at all put off by me or the motorcycle. That's another worry that evaporated.

Me: "Maybe you can tell me something."

Man: "If I can, I will. What do you want to know?"

"Well, I've been riding west out of Holly since this morning, maybe a hundred miles. And I've only seen four trees and one of them was dead. Where have all the trees gone?"

They both laughed.

"We sell all our water to Aurora and Denver. Look for our trees when you get there."

And sure enough, that's where they were.

I programmed my GPS to avoid highways. That worked well in the east, but the further west I rode, the non-highway routes became more primitive. Somewhere outside of Limon, Colorado, Google Maps took me onto a gravel road.

"OK, this is probably just a connector to get us to asphalt."

The bike and I don't like gravel roads. Gravel roads are bears.

"I don't like the looks of this."

"Me either. Go slow."

We rode under an overpass, past a ranch, around a turn. My phone screen showed a narrow, curly ribbon for a mile ahead.

"I'm willing to give it a try if you are."

"As long as it isn't too far. I wish we had a map."

"A map would come in handy. Wonder where this goes."

"I don't think it goes anywhere good. Don't forget my rear tire is getting thin."

We rode slowly for five miles on bumpy, slippery, loose gravel. Stones peppered the frame, fenders and fairing. The handlebars wobbled with the front tire. The back tire spun, slipped and skidded, sometimes sideways. I could hear Harley's asthmatic wheezing from dust clogging the air filter. The GPS instructed me to turn left from the gravel road to a smaller gravel road.

"OK buddy, that's enough. Let's find the highway."

"Finally. It's about fucking time."

We executed a slow, careful seven-point turn on the deserted narrow path. Even my boots slipped on the loose, rocky surface. We retraced our way back to the overpass and found route I-70. We stopped to check the GPS: we were about fifty miles from Aurora.

"OK, I can do an hour on the highway. How about you?"

"Anything's better than gravel."

We climbed the on-ramp and merged into the flow headed west. At noon, we stopped for fuel in Bennet. We were on our way to visit my sister's sons for a few days before heading to Utah and then Nevada. Two brothers, one wife, two kids and a

German Shepherd shared a rented house outside of Denver.

I had been riding for days through terrain so flat I could see to the horizon. I suppose that's why, thirty miles east of Denver, I mistook the Rocky Mountains for clouds. One hundred miles away, huge and snow-capped, they filled the western horizon, south to north. The thought of riding over those clouds sent a thrill of excitement through my heart.

At one-thirty, I pulled up and parked in front of Kyle and Sean's house in Aurora, 233 miles today, 2,828 miles from Paul's house.

CHAPTER 15: BUCKET OF CRABS

How do you like living next door to the marijuana store?

June 14 -15

My younger sister lives in Florida. My travels did not take me close enough to visit her but two of her sons share a house just outside of Denver. Kyle is single. He likes to travel and explore the world. He had visited us in The Netherlands a couple of years ago. Sean, his younger brother, is married with two small children. I had not seen Sean for about ten years. We agreed that I would visit them for a few days on my trip west.

It was about two o'clock in the afternoon when I rolled up and parked at the curb in front of the two-bedroom ranch in Aurora. Kyle and Buddy, their five-year-old German Shepherd, greeted me at the door. Kyle hugged and welcomed me into the shadowy living room. The dark curtains blocked the sunshine to keep the house cool. Buddy roared a deep-throated warning, sniffed curiously at my pants, then lumbered off and curled up in the corner, having done his duty. I followed Kyle into the kitchen.

Kyle is thirty-three years old. He moved to Denver from Seattle where he parked cars for a hotel. He's always worked two or three part-time jobs, usually in the hospitality industry. His shifts vary, sometimes weekdays, often weekends and evenings. When he's saved enough, Kyle uses his money to travel in the U.S. and Europe. In his spare time he creates pencil sketches. His trips always include visits to art museums. When Kyle was our guest in Holland, he visited the Rijksmuseum, the Van Gogh Museum in Amsterdam and the René Magritte Museum in Brussels.

I spent two-and-a-half days with the family. Courtney, Sean's wife, works at the franchised daycare facility that their two children attend. Even with Courtney's discount, the tuition amounted to half their monthly rent. Sean is a server at a restaurant. He works days; tips aren't as good, but he likes to be home with Courtney and their children at night. The family is enrolled in the medical insurance plan from Courtney's job. It's less expensive than Sean's and it covers the whole family – except Kyle.

Friday evening, Kyle barbecued thick steaks and savory rattlesnake sausage on the grill.

Me: "How long have you worked at the golf course?"

Kyle: "Six months. I worked at the restaurant before that. They cut my hours so I picked up the golf course job. I work at two golf courses."

"Two?"

"Yah, and I still have the restaurant job at night."

"All part-time?"

"Yes."

"Wouldn't you want something full time?"

"No, I like it this way. I can pick my own hours and take time off when I want."

"What about benefits; sick days, holidays, vacation time, health insurance, pension?"

"I don't get any of that."

"It doesn't worry you? I mean what if you get sick or injured?"

"If I get sick, I stay home till I'm better. If I get hurt, I go to the hospital."

"But with no sick days, you don't get paid."

"That's right."

"Doesn't your job offer insurance?"

"Not to part-time workers. It's the same with the pension plan."

"Do they offer full-time work?"

"Only to the managers."

"Seems pretty fragile."

"Uncle Bob, America is a bucket of crabs."

"What?"

"Everyone's crawling over each other to get to the top. America is a hard place and expensive. It's an 'a-la carte' society. If you want something, you pay for it. If you can't pay for it, you do without – or steal. Health care, a lawyer, car, house, food, sports, a university education are all here and there's plenty, but you gotta pay for it. If you don't have the money, you don't get it."

Sean and Courtney nodded in agreement.

"And you're OK with that?"

"We get by OK. Besides, what can we do about it?"

"Do you vote?" They all shook their heads, no.

"Why not?

"What's the point? All politicians are the same. They're rich. They don't care about us. We have to take care of ourselves."

In Kyle's bucket of crabs, everyone is scratching and clawing for a higher place. The competition is no less intense for those at the bottom of the bucket. My nephews agree that the system would benefit from some change, but how do you begin? How do you troubleshoot a country? They don't fear immigrants, God or kneeling during the National Anthem. They don't own guns, support a border wall or care about protective tariffs. They support national health insurance, universal education and environmental responsibility. But all these changes seem to be 'on hold' while the young people wait for their turn to make the decisions.

On Saturday morning while Kyle and Sean were working, I rode to the Harley dealership in Denver to replace my worn rear tire. On the return trip, I rode through the city on hot, crowded asphalt rivers where traffic flowed between concrete banks and neon sandbars. Billboards and bright flashing signs advertised services of every kind. A blinking red announcement eight feet high on a concrete island between streams of traffic caught my eye: "Smokin' Aces: Liquor in the front, Poker in the back."

Marijuana is legal for personal use in Colorado. I walked by a retail marijuana 'dispensary' in Aurora. Some neighbors were hosting a yard sale to dispose of some of their old stuff for cash. I walked up the driveway and said hello to the man sitting behind a table. He greeted me. Then I asked, "How do you like living next door to the marijuana store?"

"It's changed the neighborhood," he answered.

"What do you mean?"

"Well, for one thing, it's been here less than a year and it has increased traffic about three hundred percent. And look around. There's no place to park."

"They have a parking lot."

"Are you kidding? Look at it. It only holds about five cars. The rest are parked on the street. They block driveways and double park and jam up traffic. The police put up signs, but they don't do any good."

"Why not?

"There's nobody to enforce it. The police come by once in a while. But they can't keep a car here all day and night. That's what they'd need. And there are hundreds of these places all over the city. And a thousand permit requests are pending. Somebody is making a lot of money. They don't care if our neighborhood goes to hell."

After two days in the Denver suburb, I felt claustrophobic. Kyle, Sean and Courtney were kind hosts, but the house felt small and crowded and the city too intense. I preferred my tent to sleeping on Kyle's mattress in the basement. My allergy pills, necessary whenever I visit a home with an animal, dried out my nose and eyes. Most of all I was worried about Mike. My instincts told me not to delay any longer. I was anxious to get to Lake Tahoe.

Saturday afternoon while Kyle was at work, I sat in the shade behind their house and smoked my pipe. I felt a growing uneasiness that it was time to leave. Buddy looked on, calmly nestled in a dusty hole he had excavated under an overgrown evergreen.

I had planned to stay another day with my nephews. We had made plans to attend a Rockies ball game on Sunday. But I was itching to move west. I enjoyed my time with my nephews. I was happy to connect with them and become reacquainted. But I needed to be back on the road.

Kyle was understanding when I confessed it was time for me to leave. On Sunday morning we hugged and Kyle promised to visit us again in Holland.

CHAPTER 16: NO SERVICES

They used shovels and a fire hose to clean him off the road.

Sunday, June 16

Ahead, the ice-cream-cone peaks of the Rocky Mountains merged with the clouds. A great wall, a hundred miles wide, they stretch a thousand miles north and south, a barrier between east and west. Wild, cold, steep and craggy, they isolate the fertile eastern farmlands from a thousand miles of scorched western desert.

The highway climbed out of Denver toward the Continental Divide and the highest interstate tunnel in the country. The motorcycle roared with confident power, eager for the challenge. We snaked through the foothills rolling toward the towering mountains where pine forests surrendered to naked cliffs. The air cooled as we climbed. I pulled over to add fleece and nylon inner layers and close my jacket vents against the chill.

I left Idaho Springs behind and headed toward the Eisenhower tunnel. At eleven thousand feet it's a mile higher than Denver and about 20 degrees cooler. I marveled at the engineering genius and hard work that built this highway. The cliffs on both sides, carved by explosives, towered out of view. Chain link netting stretched across the rocky face to protect travelers from eroding earth and stones. The side of the road was littered with jagged rocks that penetrated the security net. The tunnel through the mountain stretched a mile and three quarters. I revved the engine to hear its throaty roar echo against the walls. Then we shot into the daylight.

I descended through the mountains and approached Vail at 8,100 feet. The air was cool and paper dry. Vail is a resort community, a holiday destination. Expensive hotels and gift shops lined the roadway. Luxury cars, imported SUVs and fat RVs rolled into the parking lots and discharged designer families.

Travel-worn, mud-stained and spattered with dead insects, my nineteen-year-old motorcycle and I were out-classed at the pump beside a pristine, palatial, family camper. The sparkling RV was forty feet long. An air-conditioning unit hummed on the roof. Four knobby-tired, multispeed bicycles were mounted and locked on the back. A compact car perched on a trailer behind.

Riding on two wheels, with my bags bungeed to the back of the bike, there couldn't have been a greater contrast between their

RECONNECTING WITH AMERICA

holiday and mine.

A woman with two teenagers trailing stepped out of a shop and strolled across the street. All three gripped the braided handles of glossy, printed shopping bags. They climbed into the RV without greeting the man wearing a yellow polo shirt, stoically feeding the thirsty camper. I bought my four gallons and was back on the bike in a few minutes. The man in the polo shirt, still pumping, turned to watch as I rolled out of the station and merged onto the highway headed west.

As I rode away from Vail, the image of the RV family stayed with me. A powerful, double-axle pick-up truck rolled by towing a silver bullet boat with two goliath, outboard engines mounted on the back. The equipment sparkled, clean, shiny and new. I watched it disappear around a turn through the bug-splattered windshield I had forgotten to clean at the gas station. I guess I was distracted by the RV family.

Many years ago, a fellow student wrote a paper on aircraft recycling. His research revealed that the major airlines in wealthy countries purchase new passenger airplanes. When the planes age, they sell them to smaller airlines in smaller countries. As the planes begin to deteriorate, it becomes more economical to cannibalize than repair them. Mechanics strip parts from some to keep others in service. Those planes are eventually sold to smaller airlines in poorer countries. They keep them running until they are no longer viable, then they scrap them, leaving them to collect weeds in airplane gravesites in third-world countries.

I think it's the same with American stuff. The people who vacation in Vail buy new mountain bikes, convertibles and speed boats. They transport them on new trailers behind glossy SUVs and two-bedroom recreational vehicles. They eventually tire of their toys and sell them to the not-so-rich and so on down the economic ladder. Eventually, we see the last phase of the life cycle in the front and back yards of single-family ranches and mobile homes. The cars and trucks rot in the weeds, rust and fall apart on flat tires with black holes instead of hoods. The same is true for the bikes, boats, skis and golf clubs. Another pick-up truck passed hauling matching bumblebee jet skis on a new trailer.

I recalled Bob in Pennsylvania proudly displaying his stuff; two cars and two campers, Christmas-lighted awnings, seventeen pellet guns, two hundred knives, two specialty stoves, another one on order. He recycled a camper to his daughter. He recycled a flashlight to me. He wanted me to have more stuff too. He owned stuff he could never use and jealously defended his right to collect more.

As I climbed through the winding mountain roads, I considered the obsession of collecting things. Bright, powerful vehicles rolled by towing expensive toys, plastic storage boxes strapped to their roofs with more stuff inside. Why do we need so much stuff?

I passed through Grand Junction, elevation 4,600 feet, almost to Utah. I didn't stop for gas again in Colorado. I had spent enough time and money in that state. It was illogical, but I felt if I bought anything else in Colorado, I would be contributing to the extravagant Vail lifestyle. I decided to wait and buy fuel at the first town in Utah. I stayed on U.S. Route 50 and rolled into Utah with the Rockies behind me. My trip odometer read one hundred and forty miles.

In Utah, the scenery changed dramatically. The mountains, pine trees and farms were gone. I was surrounded by low rolling hills, canyons and red cliffs. The land was dry, the vegetation prickly. Green turned to shades of brown. Yellow grass waved in the breeze. The open space was naked. There was no livestock or a tree as far as I could see in every direction. The wind was rising and dark storm clouds approached from the southwest. I wondered, "Where did all the traffic go?"

As I entered Utah the highway was as empty as the

land. I found the stark landscape strikingly beautiful. This environment was unfamiliar to me. I know the green forests of New England, where the land is wet and sweet. In the dry Utah desert, pungent sage was tangy, intoxicating. I breathed deeply to savor the taste on the hot wind.

The thrum of the Harley engine was reassuring. The powerful bike was performing perfectly. There were no towns in sight. I passed a sign: "No Services 44 miles." I looked down at my odometer: one hundred and seventy miles. Suddenly the scenery didn't seem so beautiful.

A quick calculation told me I would run out of gas before I reached the next exit with services. Alone on the deserted highway in the desert, it was easy to fall into conversation with the bike. The first stage was denial.

"That can't be right"

"That's what the sign said."

"You mean there's really no place to get fuel for forty-four miles?"

"You should have stopped in Grand Junction."

"How was I supposed to know that?"

"Don't yell at me."

"I didn't see a town even before we got to the 'No Services" sign. There must be someplace to get gas."

"Maybe we should turn around and go back."

"You know we don't have enough fuel to get back to a gas station."

I passed another exit announcing, "No Services". I began to believe it. There were no buildings in sight on either side of the road and as far as the distant mountain ranges. The off ramp led to a dirt road that cut north into a low mountain range, then out of sight.

"Where does that road go?"

"How can there be so much of nothing?"

I found myself hoping for the sight of a fuel station that I knew wasn't going to be there. I passed another deserted exit ramp posted with the annoying, "No Services" sign. The rising wind was driving low, purple storm clouds closer. They would cross the highway ahead from left to right, how soon or how far, I could only guess. I was riding in the bottom of a bowl. Mountains rose in the distance on all sides. The thirsty Harley purred, drinking gas, draining the tank minute by minute, mile by mile.

The beauty of the countryside scrolled by unseen. I became obsessed with my dilemma. I imagined myself marooned. I ran out of gas and stood beside my bike on the bottom of an ancient sea, stranded and adrift. The wind rose and the storm approached. Would a passing land yacht rescue me, carry me to safety?

I slowed to conserve fuel while I considered my options.

"I could run it dry on the highway and roll to a stop by the side of the road. Maybe hitchhike, walk, or camp."

"And where will you park?"

"By the side of the highway."

"Have you looked at the berm? It's steep and soft. I'll tip over."

"I'll use the kickstand plate."

"There is no shelter, not even a tree. "

"We could camp and wait till tomorrow."

"We'll still need gas in the morning."

"We're on the reserve tank now. That means we've got less than twenty miles to go."

"I know!"

A truck with a fat fuel tank and an air-conditioned cab blew past me. "Damn him."

I had no doubt about my situation. I didn't have enough fuel to get to the next exit with services, but I could decide where to stop before I ran out of gas.

"Where's the best place?"

"Don't leave me beside the highway."

"Right, I want to pull off somewhere sheltered."

The bike engine purred smoothly, just as though it had a full tank. The berm beside the highway was steep and sandy. I looked for a place where I could safely park the bike so it wouldn't fall over in the soft dirt by the side of the road. I also wanted to screen the bike from passing cars and trucks while I was away getting help. No sense in inviting theft.

I made a decision. At the next off ramp, I'd exit the highway and park the bike at the top of the ramp. Then I'd walk to the highway and hitch a ride. I was sure someone would stop. At sea, maritime law requires boats to stop and lend aid. I was sure there was something like that in the desert. I would stop for a stranded traveler in this desert.

There were a couple of advantages to stopping at an off ramp. There were few distinctive landmarks. The desert was beautiful but one location along the highway looked pretty much like every other. If the bike was parked near an exit, it would be easier to find. A service vehicle could turn around at an off ramp. As we continued to ride, I scanned the road ahead for the next exit sign.

I became conscious that I was no longer enjoying the scenery, in fact, had not looked at it except to find a place to pull over. Beauty was rushing by me on all sides, stunning, fragrant, spectacular, like the surface of an alien planet. But I was missing it. Once I brought it back into my awareness, it was almost overpowering. How had I let myself miss so much of it? I had allowed images of an empty fuel tank and the rising wind to steal away my enjoyment.

I thought of the Zen strawberry story. Instead of a tiger, the bear of an empty fuel tank chased me across the desert. In fear of the bear, I lost my appreciation for the beautiful scenery. I gazed in wonder, reawakened.

A few minutes later I spotted the sign for Frontage Road, "No Services". I steered right and climbed the exit ramp. A dirt road led off to the right, into the mountains but not to a fuel station. A silver-gray camper van was parked at the top of the ramp. As I coasted past it to park on the feeder road, I spied a gray-haired woman in the passenger seat, studying a map. The van license plate was narrow, rectangular with black letters on a white background. The left side was blue and marked with a white 'D' at the bottom.

I carefully set the kickstand plate and parked the bike on the side of the exit ramp, out of the way, if anyone drove by. I removed my helmet and secured it to the handlebar with the chin strap. I disconnected and removed my phone, picked up my gas tank pack and walked to the passenger side of the van.

A round-faced, sixty-something woman in the passenger seat was concentrating on the map she held in her lap. Through the window, I could see a gray-haired man wearing jeans and a polo shirt packing a bag at a small table in the back. I tapped on the window to get the woman's attention. Surprised, she looked up. I made a motion to ask her to roll down the window. I was a little surprised when she did.

"Hello. Are you from Germany?" I asked, trying to look harmless and friendly.

"Yes. How did you know?" She answered.

"I saw your license plate. I live in The Netherlands."

"We go to the Netherlands often. Where do you live?"

"Delft."

"Oh, we've been there. We like Delft very much."

"Where in Germany are you from?"

"Dusseldorf."

"I love Dusseldorf. I've been to the Christmas market. It is a great city. How long are you in the U.S.?"

"We're on a four-month trip."

"Well, I hope you enjoy your trip."

"Thank you. What about you? What are you doing?"

"I'm also on a cross-country trip. I started in Boston and am riding to California. I have a son in the Boston area and one who lives near Lake Tahoe. I am traveling to see the country and to visit them."

"That sounds like a nice trip."

"Yes, However, I ran into a little problem and I wonder if I could ask your help."

"What is it?"

"I've run out of gas and need a lift to the next service station. Can you give me a ride?"

Her husband had come forward and listened to our conversation. They discussed my request and agreed to give me a ride to the next exit with fuel services. They opened the side door and invited me into their camper van. We drove about twenty-five miles west to Thompson Springs.

During the ride, they told me they were retired. This was their second cross-country trip in the U.S. The first time they rented an RV. This time they brought their own from home. They still had three months left to this trip and were already planning the next one. America was just too big to see all at once. I agreed.

They pulled into the fuel station parking lot. I thanked them for their help. We said farewell and I waved goodbye as they drove off.

I walked into the service station wearing my motorcycle jacket and carrying my gas tank pack. I walked up to the young woman behind the service counter.

"How can I help you?"

"Guess."

"You ran out of gas."

"Yup."

"Let me call my mother."

Apparently, her mother usually handles this kind of thing. But as I waited at the counter, a big bellied, red-faced man in a dirty t-shirt approached. His bright smile broke through a forest of white beard. He wore a baseball cap over his bald head. I gratefully accepted his offer to give me a lift. He moved his rust-and-white pick-up truck to the gas pumps. We extricated a 5-gallon gas can from the clutter and construction debris in the back. I pumped about 3 gallons into the can and paid for it at the counter.

Tom was sixty-five years old. He talked as he drove for twenty-five miles and entertained me with his short stories one at a time.

"Big winds today, they're dangerous for a motorcycle. You'd better be careful.

"Last year a motorcycle was blown right into the side of a big rig. Killed him instantly. What a mess. Happened a few miles from here.

"One biker was blown right across the highway. Hit a truck all the way on the other side. They used shovels and a fire hose to clean him off the road. Hate to be that truck driver.

"A couple of years ago, two motorcycles blew into each other. That's the first time I ever heard of that. What a mess! One of 'em was a woman. Both killed. Closed the road for an hour to pick up all the pieces.

"Looks like a big storm is coming. When the thunderstorms hit, it's a white-out. Even cars with wipers on high can't see anything. Motorcycle got rammed from behind by an SUV, never saw him till it was too late.

"Pulling over's no good either. There's no shelter, cars and trucks can't see anything. A motorcycle got sideswiped last year – dead.

"I plan on buying a Harley next year, take a road trip. But I'm getting a trike, it's safer, more stable."

He continued his stories of death and destruction till we finally saw the sign for the Frontage Road off-ramp. My Harley waited patiently where I had left it, and my gear was still attached. The distant thunderstorm was rushing toward us and pushing an ocean of air ahead of it. The wind had increased. It was blowing a gale.

Tom pulled the pick-up truck beside the bike and stopped. I climbed out of the cab. I opened the fuel tank and leaned over to pour gas from the plastic spout. The wind was too strong. The gas sprayed from the spout, caught by the wind, flew away and disappeared. Tom saw the problem and moved the pick-up truck to serve as a windbreak. After that, I managed to pour most of the fuel into the tank.

Tom's monologue of mangled motorcycles had made an impression. I was hesitant to get back on the highway and challenge the gale winds of the approaching storm. I looked at big rigs rolling by at eighty miles per hour. The cars swayed in their wakes. I asked Tom about Frontage Road.

"Where does this road go?" I asked, pointing to my right.

"It runs directly back to the gas station at Thompson Springs. It's the old highway. Only locals use it now and not many of them."

"Is it paved?"

"Yes. Maybe not in the best shape but it's paved."

"I think that looks safer than the highway right now. I'll take that and see you back at the station."

I gave Tom twenty dollars for his trouble and thanked him for the ride. He turned west onto Frontage Road toward Thompson Springs. He waved from the cab and headed back, spinning his tires in a cloud of dust.

I spent a few minutes getting organized, then climbed on the bike and followed him. Two hundred yards down the road, the pavement ended. I rode west, navigating between potholes, chunks of broken asphalt, rocks and gravel. The wind blew hard from the south. I was grateful for my new rear tire.

"This sucks."

"I know it's bad, but it's better than getting blown away on the highway."

"I don't like it."

"I'll keep it slow."

We rode at fifteen to twenty-five miles an hour, kicking up sand and dust clouds that blew north ahead of the storm. I fought to control the steering and weave a safe route around the boulders and craters. Maybe long ago this road was paved but not anymore. It had deteriorated to dusty gravel and ragged sections of old asphalt. The handlebars bounced, my seat bumped, and the springs squealed in protest. I winced at every stone that twisted out from under the tires. My decision not to replace my front tire in Denver haunted me, not for the last time. The road was so rough, I was afraid my phone would vibrate loose, fall and crash to the ground. I meant it when I promised myself and the Harley out loud,

"No more dirt roads after we get out of this." Harley didn't respond.

We traveled for about twenty miles when I saw another, "No Services" ramp. We'd both had enough of this road. We were about five miles to the fuel stop, so I decided to risk a wind-blown death and got back on the highway. The storm had rumbled away to the northwest and the wind had diminished. I rode slowly in the right-hand lane, comfortable on the smooth pavement. We rolled off the highway into the station and parked by a pump to fill up. I didn't see Tom or his truck. I topped off the tank, thanked the friendly clerk then set off west, feeling pretty lucky.

Running out of gas had not developed into the catastrophe I feared.

Arches National Park is about forty miles from Thompson Springs. I rolled up to the gate just before five o'clock. The ranger informed me that all the campsites were occupied. He suggested I head toward Moab to find a place to stay for the night, then return in the morning.

In Moab I found a full-service, family campground. In addition to campsites it offered a gift shop, general store, swimming pool and playground for the kids; of which there were many. The campground was a hive of recreational vehicles, pick-up trucks, vans and trailers. The pool was full of laughing, splashing families. It was hot and I was tired, but I didn't look forward to setting up my little tent on a patch of gravel in the middle of all those families on wheels.

At the reception desk, I explained the place was perfect for families, but I was alone. It was a little too noisy and crowded for me. I wanted some peace and quiet to rest. The lady at the reception desk recommended a first-come, first-served, no reservations National Forest campground about ten miles away. She promised it would be quieter, but explained there were no services.

The Jaycee Campground was across the Colorado River about eight or ten miles down the road from Moab. The campground offered ten campsites and a restroom with a pit toilet. The back four campsites were flooded and swampy. High red cliffs boxed the campground on the west side. A narrow band of trees screened the Colorado River that flowed brown across the street. The campground was quiet and I was alone.

At six o'clock, I sat at my picnic table, eating the second half of my cold-cuts sandwich. I considered if I should have stayed at the crowded RV park. After all, my purpose was to talk to people. There were lots of families at the park. A swim in the pool would have been refreshing in the heat. But not today. I was tired and just wanted rest. 392 miles today.

CHAPTER 17: COLD SHELTER

He served up a veterinarian pizza.

Monday, June 17

I woke from a dream at five in the morning. Faceless suits in a corporate conference room offered me a job for a lot of money. They wanted me to steal onto an island and move wetlands markers into the jungle. I agreed. Then I discussed it with someone, Hanneke, maybe my conscience. Moving the markers would mean the corporation could burn and bulldoze the jungle to develop a vastly profitable beach-front real estate project. I needed the money for my family but couldn't reconcile the destruction it would cause to the environment. I decided not to do it. Later, I learned they hired someone else and the project moved forward anyway.

I sat at the picnic table exhausted, aimlessly tracing the little diamond patterns in the metal top with my index finger. I was slow to gather energy for the ride ahead. I stalled over my breakfast of hot coffee and oatmeal with raisins and honey. I was worn out, drained. My body and mind felt thick and stupid. I stared at the cover of the atlas in front of me and considered the effort it would take to lift my arm, open the map and turn the page. Instead, I sipped my coffee, dull-eyed and weak. The intensity of the trip was wearing me down. Even my sleep was busy with complex dreams.

A family of four had arrived at the campground last night, just before dark. They made several trips back and forth carrying gear from their car. I waved to the kids as they passed in the dusk. They looked but did not wave or smile. I was too tired; they were busy and it was already dark by the time they settled down so I didn't walk over to visit. I guess that's another camping courtesy. Don't meet your neighbors in the dark. If you've already met, it's OK to visit in the dark, but not for the first time. I don't know why. Maybe it's just me.

I was awake before my neighbors. I delayed my departure with a second cup of coffee, still tired from yesterday's long, windy ride. I told myself I was being courteous, waiting for them to start moving around. I was reluctant to disturb their quiet morning with a motorcycle engine echoing off the red cliffs like cannon. The real truth was that I was bone tired, gathering energy and motivation for my journey into the Utah desert.

I guess the caffeine finally had its effect because my arm found the strength to open the map and I began to plan my route. My first stop was Arches National Park. The Visitors' Center opened at seven-thirty. If my neighbors didn't wake up soon on their own, I'd help.

In the quiet morning, their tent zipper broke the silence. A man and woman in their thirties climbed out and started preparing breakfast. They set up their stove, rattled out pots, pans, plates and cups. They dug into bags and coolers for food and drinks. Their activity was my signal to start cleaning up and packing. My weary muscles managed to lift my body off the bench. I cleaned and put away my kitchen gear, packed my bags and carried them to the motorcycle.

The roads were almost deserted. The five-mile ride to Arches National Park took only a few minutes. My pass gained me free entry. Purple clouds cast shifting shadows over the striking landscape inside the park. I was not alone, but the few other vehicles neither slowed me down nor pushed me along.

This was John Wayne country or a Star Trek alien planet. I found it stark and strange, like another world. The reds and browns shone when the sun broke through the clouds. A dust devil rose in the distance, scrambled across the flat dry land, then disappeared, evaporated into nothing; another rose and ran for a mile.

I pulled over to snap some photos, but my pocket camera wasn't up to the task. The panorama was spectacular. I committed my trust to my eyes and memory to record the breathtaking views. I wanted to capture and hold this beauty within me. The air, the land, the rocks stole the moisture from my body. How can anything survive out there? The rusty gravel crunched beneath my boots.

Cars and campers carrying couples and kids rolled through the park gazing out the windows. People of all ages stopped, reverently inspecting, touching and gazing at the rock formations, arches and towers with awe and respect. They followed paths into the red desert, kicking up tiny dust clouds that floated away in the early morning breeze. They posed for pictures, pointed at the rock formations, hugged and gazed at the horizon.

Like them, I was grateful that someone, a long time ago, had had the foresight to preserve and protect this land to share it with everyone. I worried about the growing pressure to lease and sell national parks, forests, conservation and wildlife refuge areas for profit. The protected federal lands are rich with natural resources. Investors want to harvest lumber, extract minerals and drill for gas and oil.

We who visited Arches that day were privileged to enjoy and share this stark, strange countryside. I prayed these lands were never dug, blasted, bulldozed or drilled. It was painful to imagine the beauty of this park destroyed for money, or a government willing to let it happen.

I stopped at Papa Joe's psychedelic general store and gas station in Crescent Junction. The green and purple building with its outer space motif was reminiscent of Timothy Leary and Jack Kerouac. I imagined a Twilight Zone episode. A van broke down sixty years ago and the passengers got locked into a time warp. In this installment, Rod Sterling's hippies were not vegetarians, they were carnivorous capitalists. Papa Joe's offers gas, coffee, cold drinks, and several species of jerky. They charged the highest prices for fuel I'd seen since the start of my ride. I filled my tank with one gallon of premium fuel. A female cast member in a flowered tent dress with a gravel voice advised me to top up.

"It's 126 miles to the next station in Salina."

"How far is the next gas after Salina?"

"You have to check in Salina about Nevada."

I paid cash, thanked her, turned right, out of the Twilight Zone and headed west.

I was riding across a dry Martian seabed. The Utah landscape was a study in reds, browns and yellows. The earth was dust and rock with low prickly bushes. Visibility was crystal clear, fifty miles in all directions. Ahead rose the San Rafael Swell and the La Sal mountains. I knew little about the topography of this region but imagined I was riding across the bottom of a dried, post-apocalyptic ocean floor.

As I approached the mountain range, a line of clouds migrated across the sky from the south. The rising land was blanketed beneath a purple/gray sky that blocked the sun and chilled the air. A light rain greeted me in the foothills and increased as I climbed the winding road into the clouds. The landscape offered no trees, no buildings, no bridges, no shelter of any kind. The rocky shoulder beside the road dropped off into a gully, perhaps a seasonal water course. There was no place to pull the motorcycle off the road to wait out a storm. The rain seemed to be deciding what to do. The band of fat clouds floated slowly following the mountain range north. The showers intensified and the temperature dropped as I climbed.

The road wound up and up adjacent to Salina Creek, but I seldom saw the creek, or much of anything because the rain swelled to a downpour. I passed Dead Horse, Maple Spring and Cottonwood Canyons unseen through the sheeting rain.

Finally, with the rain streaming across my windshield, washing over my helmet and dripping down my neck, I glimpsed the sign I was afraid to hope for: "Rest stop ahead." I turned into the Ivie Creek Rest Area, dripping wet. I parked the bike, set the kickstand, climbed off and trudged up a flight of steps carrying my gas tank pack to the nearest shelter.

Fat drops fell in sheets from a slate gray sky. I huddled in a corner on a cold steel bench watching the rain drench my bike and soak everything I owned. The wind rattled and rain pounded the metal roof of the open-sided shelter. Water pooled on the hard-packed dirt, on the concrete walkways, and little rivers trickled under my boots while I shivered.

Thunder rumbled close by. Flashes of lightning cracked the

southern sky. My unprotected ears were chilled, my hands trembled. The cold, damp air seeped through my clothes. I shivered under three layers of clothing and three more layers of motorcycle jacket. My Harley waited, lonely and dripping in the pouring gray rain. I waited shivering in the shelter. Other travelers drove in, stopped, then drove out in heated, four-wheeled vehicles. Families and couples hurried to the restrooms with shoulders hunched, then ran back to their warm, dry campers and cars.

When the downpour stopped, thunder in the distance warned that it was only a pause. Waves of wind-driven rain cycled over the rest area, following the mountains on their way to Canada. Between deluges, I walked around my little shelter, slogging through the puddles for a glimpse of the sky, hoping for a gap in the marching clouds. There was none. The band of thunderstorms extended to the south as far as I could see. When the rainfall began again, I scurried to my shelter, munched a candy bar, sipped some water and considered my options.

"Rain isn't the fun part of a motorcycle ride."

"You always want sun."

"This is the part that makes the other parts feel good."

"You're rationalizing."

"I'm cold."

"I bet it's warm in that camper."

"Wish I had a camper."

"No you don't."

"If this rain doesn't stop, I may have to sleep here tonight."

"It's stopped raining. Let's take a look."

It took enormous effort to force my stiff, cold muscles up off the bench and walk behind the shelter. To the south more clouds fat with rain pushed north.

"Damn."

"This sucks."

"Stop complaining."

"What if I get back on the bike, rain or not?"

"What if the rain gets worse? What if there isn't another rest stop ahead?"

"Let's look at the map."

My 1:3,000,000 scale Utah map didn't show enough detail to include rest stops and there was no cell service, so Google was useless.

"If I get on the road and the storm increases, I won't be able to see. And if there is nowhere to pull off the road I'll be trapped."

"Are we feeling sorry for ourselves?"

"No! Maybe."

I was afraid to go on, but I couldn't stay where I was much longer. I was getting colder; I was shivering, and the cold rain was dripping down my neck and seeping into my clothes. The rain had no doubt soaked my gear and clothes still strapped to the bike. I suspected darkness would fall before the rain stopped. Thunder in the distance reinforced that fear.

"Well, here we are, afraid to move and afraid to stay."

"That pretty much covers it."

"Then, it is time for a change."

"Rain or no rain, we can't stay here forever."

"Safe as it might be, it's doing me no good."

"The cold is adding up and there's no food."

"Then we agree."

"Yup."

During the next pause in the downpour, I zipped up, packed up, climbed on the bike and got moving. The showers returned as I climbed the mountain road, determined to press on in spite of the bad weather. Twenty-five miles on, I climbed through Emigrant Pass, elevation 7,900 feet. The rain stopped. I was shivering and wet, but as I rode down the mountain, the clouds parted and the sun broke out. The Ivie Creek Rest Area was situated near the top of the mountain. The downslope started a few miles to the west. I had unknowingly stopped in the worst part of the weather pattern. The storms washed the eastern slope of the mountain range, but the western slope was dry.

As I rode west down the mountain and the warm sunshine dried my clothes, I reflected on the last few hours. I had sheltered from the storm under the open-frame refuge, while the damp cold infiltrated my clothes and skin and seemed to penetrate my bones by inches. I was afraid to move. Cold, inertia and fear all but paralyzed me. My situation continued to deteriorate till I reached a tipping point. Only after I committed to move forward did my circumstances improve. Had I made the decision earlier, I could have spared myself hours of shivering cold. At about four o'clock in the afternoon, I rolled into the parking lot of the Rancher Motel-Cafe on Main Street in Delta, UT.

The diner looked like an old Western saloon with rough, dark wooden shingles, a low roof, plate-glass front windows and a gravel parking lot. Inside, the rustic wood-frame building was warm and welcoming. The people were friendly and unhurried. They seemed to have time for each other and time to welcome visitors. It was a place where people were more important than the food and the food was good and there was plenty of it. It was a place where the staff knew the customers by name and the customers refilled their own coffee and stacked their dirty dishes in the plastic tub when the waitress was busy.

The waitress multi-tasked as the motel clerk. She delivered a heaping tray of food to a group of men at a booth, then approached me.

"What can I do for you, hon?"

"I'd like a room for the night."

"Did you make a reservation?"

"No I didn't. Do you have a room available?"

"We have one left."

"Great."

"Let me check if it is cleaned out and ready."

She walked off to speak with another woman. I scanned the cozy diner. There were six or seven men drinking coffee at the counter. The easy flow of conversation made it clear they all knew each other and this was their afternoon routine.

Man 1: "He's doin' pretty good for himself. He runs that pizza place outside of town."

Man at the end of the bar wearing a neck brace: "Have you been there?"

"Sure. He served up a veterinarian pizza. It was pretty good. Crust was thin and crisp. He's had the place for about three years. Really making a go of it."

There was a pause. For a minute no one spoke. Finally, the man at the end of the bar cleared his throat and asked:

"Veterinarian pizza?"

"You know what I mean."

"Yah, I know, but we got a stranger here and he might think we're cannibals."

He turned to me. "Where you from?"

"I come from Boston."

"That your bike out there?"

"Yah."

"Come on over and have a cup of coffee. She'll find you OK when she gets back."

I sat down at an empty stool at the curve in the middle of the counter. All the men were seniors, wearing casual work clothes, not dirty, but well-worn and comfortable. A couple of men wore wide-brimmed, sweat-stained Stetsons. The social group included some men and women sitting in booths, nearby.

The waitress had moved to the back of the restaurant and was talking with a table of customers. The man who asked about the pizza walked around the counter to get me a cup of coffee.

"Milk and sugar?"

"Just black, thanks."

He poured a glass of water and placed the glass beside the coffee mug on the counter in front of me. The other men all sat with coffee cups and water glasses on the counter in front of them. The conversation circled around work, driving trucks, farming, ranching and a kids' softball game. One of the men had watched his granddaughter play that afternoon. Then it returned to me.

They listened to a brief account of my trip. They asked about the range of the motorcycle on a tank of gas. Pete was a tall, thin, wiry seventy-five-year-old regular at the diner with a craggy face lined by a lifetime of outdoor work under the Utah sun. He volunteered some information about the road ahead, so I didn't run dry again:

"Fill up here. Then it's one hundred and fifty miles to Ely,

Nevada. There's nothing in between but desert.

"Fill up in Ely. It's seventy-five miles from Ely to Eureka.

"Then it's seventy miles from Eureka to Austin.

"You can probably make Austin from Ely, but if I was you, I'd fill up in Eureka anyway."

Just about then the waitress returned with a key for my motel room. I said farewell to my new friends and walked across the parking lot to my room.

I emptied the Harley bag and laid my damp clothes on every horizontal surface in the room and the bathroom. I spread my socks, underwear, pants and shirts over the chairs and curtain rods and wherever I could to air them out to dry. I emptied the wet duffel bag and repacked it with the dripping nylon tent, soaked sleeping bag, liner and my wet sneakers. I carried it all across the street to the laundromat. I spent the evening with my e-reader in a molded plastic chair, listening to my gear tumble and bang in the clothes dryer.

CHAPTER 18: TV AND BEER

Washington is Oz.

Tuesday, June 18

I woke from a dream at five-thirty. Sunshine beamed through the gap between the dark curtains of my motel room. My two brothers and I were constructing a house. We each took responsibility for our own section, refining the drawings, sizing the rooms, building the walls, wiring, plumbing, carpentry. We worked on our own and helped each other when needed. It was a cooperative, flexible process. We were enjoying the work.

My father (who died in 2017) called us together. He said we need to be more disciplined and organized. Somebody has to be in charge, decide who does what and schedule the tasks. He criticized the plan, saying it would not get the permits and inspection approvals. He said the plan was vague and incomplete. We should redraw it. We were making too many changes.

They were costing time and money. We shouldn't make changes or the work would never get done. He warned us that winter was coming and the house wouldn't be finished. We'd have no place to live.

By seven o'clock, I had packed my gear and loaded the bike. I walked across the parking lot to the diner for breakfast. Pete was sitting at the counter with his coffee. I took the stool next to him and we talked about travels. He reminded me:

"Fuel up at Ely, that's a hundred and fifty miles. Then it's seventy-five miles to Eureka, then seventy to Austin. Fill up at each town, you'll be OK.

"If you come through here on your way back, stop in again. There's a lot to see in Delta. And I want to hear how your son is doing."

I said farewell to Pete and walked out into the cool, bright sunshine. I climbed into my riding jacket, strapped on my helmet and slipped on my gloves. I fired up the engine and rolled onto Main Street with the sun at my back. It was seven-thirty.

The Rockies are the tallest mountains between Colorado and California but not the only ones. U.S. Route 50 through Nevada crosses the Great Basin Desert, the hottest and emptiest stretch of land between Denver and Tahoe. I anticipated a thousand miles of scorched deserted highway surrounded by flat, hard-packed sand and cacti. With Delta in my rear-view mirror. I was excited and anxious about the Utah-Nevada desert crossing

Siever Lake is forty miles west of Delta. It's a shallow alkali lake twenty-five miles long. Wind-blown chalky white dust rose in mini tornados across the surface. The dry, warm air tasted gritty and alkali. It sucked the moisture from my exposed skin. I was a lone astronaut exploring a desert planet.

About fifty miles outside of Delta, the road climbed into the foothills of remote mountains with terrain so bewildering it's called the Confusion Range. The highway wound into the mountains, through barren, treeless cliffs, mottled in yellow, brown and red. The motorcycle glided through the turns, pressing forward and up. The throaty rumble of the engine echoed off the cliffs. The Harley was a powerful, tireless animal, running into the wilderness.

The path flowed in long, rolling curves climbing toward Kings Canyon. At the summit I eased off the throttle and coasted down the western slope, down-shifting to spare the brakes.

The desert wind, rolling turns and the rumbling engine filled my senses. I never tired of the stark scenery, terra-cotta stones, skeleton sagebrush, saltbush, snakeweed, prickly pear, Mormon tea and yellow-green tufts of spikey grass. The desert was not lifeless. What survives is tough, wiry and efficient. Water felt a thousand years away.

A line of telephone poles stretched across the bare earth; laser straight, they disappeared in the hazy foothills of the distant mountains. I was riding along the bottom of a valley between ranges. The land was open, barren and thorny. The wind scooped up sand and created dust devils that leaped to life, raced along the ground, then collapsed, exhausted. The spicy, bitter-sweet odor of sage was everywhere, subtle, heady and fragrant.

The rising sun baked my black motorcycle jacket. I pulled over, careful not to flip the bike on the soft, sandy berm. I circled in the gravel pull-out, using the engine, not muscle, to point the heavy bike, nose toward the road. I tossed the kickstand plate into the dust beside me and inched it under the kickstand with my boot, then climbed off.

It was early but the day was already hot. I peeled off my jacket and removed the fleece, and nylon liners. I stuffed them into my saddlebag and removed my water bottle. I sipped and tracked the road ahead as far as the next mountain range. I turned and squinted into the sun to view the range behind me and savored the desert perfume.

I snapped some photos. The packed motorcycle leaned on its stand, beside the deserted highway with the mountains in the distance. A clear blue, cloudless sky hovered over the yellow-brown earth. I hoped my memory would save and store the feel of the wind, the echoing silence and desert fragrances.

My boots crunched on baked earth in the silence. I scanned sunbaked earth to the horizon. Rocky dunes, tufted mounds and crevasses cut by dry riverbeds infused the land with character and depth. There was no sign of life as far as the distant mountains. A dead, dry, empty snakeskin withered in the dust at my feet. Rail and wire fences fifty feet from the highway stretched east and west beyond sight. To the left and right dirt roads cut meandering routes into the mountains where they disappeared.

A flash of sunlight reflected off a windshield approaching from the west. A dusty SUV, towing a camper, materialized out of the hazy sunshine. The driver gave me a thumbs-up as he passed. I waved in return. Everything was OK.

The car faded away leaving only the rattle of dry grass on the breeze. I returned the water bottle to the saddlebag. A car flashed by headed west – no wave. I climbed on the bike, fired it up and rolled thirty miles west into the mountains.

The narrow black asphalt stretched flat across the Great Basin

Desert. Forty miles east of Ely, Nevada, the road climbed into the Egan Range. Utah was behind me. A series of signs greeted me when I entered Nevada. The first simply welcomed me. It was followed quickly by: "Road construction ahead."

It called up images of trucks, excavating equipment, workers in yellow hard hats and traffic delays.

"Road work, great."

"Just be careful. There's no hurry."

As the road climbed the warnings became more ominous. "Loose gravel on the road."

"You promised no dirt roads."

"I've got no control over gravel on paved roads."

The next sign warned, "New oil."

"You've got to be kidding me."

The next sign added a touch of dark comedy. "Falling rocks,"

"I guess If the loose gravel and oil doesn't finish us, they'll throw rocks at us."

As if to reinforce the message, the sides of the road were littered with sharp-edged boulders, stone chips and red dirt.

The next sign was comically redundant, "Dangerous turn."

"This whole road is a dangerous turn."

The final insult was the sign that warned, "No services next thirty miles."

"They must mean medical help."

I inched my way into Nevada, keeping as far to the right as I dared after the "Soft berm" and "No turn-out" signs. I dropped the bike into low gear, gripped the handlebar tighter and held on while my wheels slipped, squeaked, squirmed and wobbled. I was determined to get out of those mountains alive. And it seemed Nevada was determined I wouldn't. I didn't abandon all hope, but I was careful as hell. I never saw any construction workers.

Cautiously navigating dangerous turns on loose gravel, lubricated with new oil, I skidded down out of the mountains into Spring Valley. The grade dipped into a bowl about thirty miles east of Ely into a seventy-seven acre windmill farm. Row upon row of wind turbines turned gently in the breeze as if in greeting. The highway looped around the farm then climbed on dry, smooth pavement into the Egan Range.

At the end of the descent, I rolled into Ely, NV, which sleeps behind a twenty-five mile per hour speed trap at the bottom of the mountains. It was the first, but not the last strategic traffic control I would pass. I stopped in Ely for fuel and a meal.

Since the descent from the Rockies, the road drifted over sleepy, baked, blistered land, empty and old. The pavement was smooth and flat, marked only by weeping asphalt repair snakes. I cruised, relaxed in the saddle with an unimpeded view to the next mountain range. The few other travelers passed with a wave. The bike felt strong, tireless, eager to run.

On the horizon, mountain ranges appeared in the distance, brown walls forced up from the desert floor by ancient cataclysms. Craggy, sometimes snow-capped, they rose and barred the way. The road ahead turned into the hills and was lost in the haze. The mercury on the flat reached the mid-nineties but it cooled in the foothills. Mountain ranges manufacture their own weather. The highest peaks were cold, bright with snow and often cloud covered. The low mountains were cool, brown and red with sun-dried and wind-blown dust. The peaks were bald and treeless. The engine thrummed powerfully up each steep grade, never failing or faltering. As we climbed, the air cooled, the road switched back and we leaned into the turns. Up, up and up we rode till it seemed our path must drop off a cliff. At the summit, the road turned on itself again and descended like a snake between the boulders, and the air warmed.

On the western route from Delta, the road climbed through the Hot Creek, Monitor and Toiyabe Ranges, then down into their basins. On the western side of the mountains, the road flowed through sun-bleached clusters of buildings, remote towns that offered fuel, food and rest. From Delta to Ely, Nevada, on to Eureka then Austin, only fences and telephone poles hinted at civilization. There were no services, no homes, and few vehicles between the towns, just desert. The desert-mountain-town sequence echoed for a thousand miles from Denver to Tahoe.

Each town hosted a twenty-five mile per hour speed control toll booth at the base of the mountain. After my first lucky escape, I was careful to slow my final descent out of the foothills. I stopped at the widely spaced towns. I parked, set the kickstand plate and climbed off the bike to stretch my legs. I filled the tank, checked and topped off the oil and paused for a drink or a meal. The day was fiery hot, with temperatures exceeding a hundred degrees. Few people walked along the cracked sidewalks. Padlocked shops, "For Sale" signs, soaped and newspapered windows lined the Main Streets. A few restaurants, bars and budget motels survived. The old towns were drying up and the desert was creeping back in.

Late in the afternoon, I stopped in Austin, Nevada. A few likely restaurants and a fairly well-maintained, Western-style bar looked inviting. I turned off the main road into a parking lot surrounded by a rambling, single-story motel. A tall, dark-haired young woman wearing jeans and a snug, white t-shirt walked out of the building to greet me as I dismounted and removed my helmet.

"Hi, I'm Lily. Welcome to Austin."

"Hi, thanks. Do you have any rooms available for tonight?"

"Do you have a reservation?"

"No, I don't."

"Sorry, we're full. You should have called ahead."

I looked around. A single-story, weathered, white-washed wood-frame building surrounded the asphalt parking lot. Paint peeled from every window and door frame.

"No rooms, really?"

"Yes, we're full-up pretty much every night all summer. This is the tourist season.

"Tourist season?"

She recognized my skepticism. "Yah, it doesn't look like much but we're the only town till Fallon."

"Can you recommend someplace to stay? I'm beat and I'd like a place to crash for the night."

"We're the only motel in town. The other one closed down. There's a campground a few miles east of here. It's a family camping place for RVs."

"I've got a tent."

"I have a place you can camp for free across the street."

We walked over together to take a look. She talked as we walked. She asked and I told her where I was from.

"I'd like to live in Europe; Spain or Portugal. You can live there pretty inexpensively – or Asia," she said.

We walked up a hill, across the street from the motel to a grass plot under the shade of a big tree. Ten noisy chickens and one bold, red rooster greeted us at the top of the hill. The site overlooked the motel and the highway, no doubt quiet at night. As we talked, chickens pecked contentedly in the grass and the rooster circled suspiciously. Vegetable scraps littered the grass at my feet.

"Watch out for the rooster. He's mean," she warned.

On cue, the rooster leaped in and pecked at my ankle, then jumped away. "Ouch."

"See what I mean. You've got to watch him."

The hens pecked at the ground. The rooster circled closer.

"You can set up your tent here for the night if you want."

It was four o'clock, sunny and hot. It was cool under the shade tree. I was tired, hot and ready for a meal and rest. But this place didn't have good vibes. As if to seal my decision the rooster attacked again. I kicked at him and missed.

"He's quick," she said.

"Too quick for me. There's no other motel around?"

"Not in town. But there is one at Cold Springs Station."

"Where is that?"

"It's about an hour west. Then there is nothing till you reach Fallon. That's a hundred miles from here."

"Do you think there's a room at Cold Springs?"

"Do you want me to call and check?"

"That would be great."

She called and we reserved the last single room.

We walked back down the hill and across the street to the motel. She explained that her boyfriend had just arrived from Oregon. She wasn't sure how things would work out. He worked from home so he could work from here. But there wasn't much to do in town and nothing nearby. There wasn't even a movie theater.

I looked around at the bleached and deserted main street. Mountains to the east, desert for a hundred miles to the west.

"Fallon's a long way to go for a movie."

She paused, looked up and down the street, then toward the corner of the motel as if deciding how much to say.

"Yah. That's not the only thing."

I waited while she made up her mind whether or not to continue.

"His politics don't really fit in here, mine either. I guess that's the real reason I want to travel. This is a remote town. People are kind of set in their ways. They don't like change and don't welcome strangers, especially brown strangers. If you don't hunt or fish, there's not much to do."

I nodded, waiting for her to continue. But she just took a breath and shrugged. Maybe she had said more than she intended.

"So, how do I find Cold Springs?"

"It's fifty or sixty miles west on Route 50. It's on the left."

"How big is the town? Can I get fuel there?"

"It's only one building. It's mostly a trailer park."

"It's just one building?"

"You can't miss it. It's the only thing between here and Fallon. There's a restaurant and a store but no gas station."

I would have liked to spend more time with Lily and her boyfriend. To talk to them and share stories. But I was tired and still had an hour to ride. I thanked her for her help. I wished her good luck, waved good-bye and rode west.

An hour later I turned left, wheeling across the cattle guard into Cold Springs Station. Lily was right: it wasn't a town; it didn't even appear on my road atlas. It's the only sign of life between Austin and Fallon. It was a welcome oasis after 350 miles of desert. I rolled into the deep gravel parking lot of the restaurant/gift shop/RV park and motel.

This was a pure desert environment, treeless as far as I could see. Hills in the distance were bleached, barren and golden in the sun. The still air was infused with the perfume of creosote and sage. Waterless, hard-packed, cracked earth surrounded the gravel drive and parking lot as far as the mountains. The RV park offered no shade except the bleached canvas awnings of the mobile homes. I stood in the dust beside the restaurant steps and read the Cowboy's Prayer, etched into a copper plate mounted on a post.

May your horse never stumble
Your cinch never break
Your belly never grumble
Your heart never ache.

I clumped up the wooden stairs and pushed open the door. A welcome wall of cool air washed over me. Four customers sat at the bar and a few more at high tables in the restaurant. I sensed high energy in the place, excitement. The customers were animated, like they were waiting for something. The feeling of anticipation was thick in the air. I asked the young blond woman tending the bar.

"Is there something going on today? Everyone seems pretty excited."

"The Pony Express is riding through tonight. We're expecting a big crowd."

Apparently, my confusion showed on my face.

She explained, "This is an historic Pony Express relay station. Every year they re-enact the ride. A mail carrier will ride in tonight. A whole bunch of people will be here to celebrate. It's a big party."

"How many riders will there be?"

"Only one in and one out."

"What time?"

"Probably about eight o'clock but we can't be sure exactly."

She checked me in at the bar then I rode slowly across the parking lot to the four-room motel. An hour later, showered and changed, I walked outside where the sun still burned white out of a breathless pale sky. My boots crunched and puffed dust mushrooms as I walked through the dry gravel to the restaurant. Several horse trailers lined the perimeter of the lot. There were no horses in sight.

I ordered a hamburger, fries and a coke. The restaurant was doing a brisk business at the tap serving cowboys outfitted in silver belt buckles, jeans, tooled boots and Stetson hats. The TV over the bar broadcast Fox News with the sound muted.

At a table across from me, sat a fit, square-shouldered man, maybe sixty years old dressed in dockers and a clean polo shirt.

He was sharing a meal with a slim, middle-aged woman wearing jeans fastened with a big silver belt buckle and a red, long-sleeved shirt. I guessed they were probably part of the group waiting for the Pony Express rider.

I finished my meal, bucked up my courage and walked over to their table. I'd been meeting people at campsites, but hadn't yet been forward enough to sit down at someone else's table in a restaurant. I introduced myself and asked if I could join them. I was really stepping out of my comfort zone. They weren't excited to meet me but too polite to turn me away.

Dick was a retired fireman from Carson City, Nevada. His wife's name was Emily. They had trailered her horse to Cold Springs so she could participate in the Pony Express Re-ride.

Emily left the table to see to the horse. Dick explained.

"Later tonight, we will drive west about ten miles with the horse in the trailer. My wife will take the mail sack and ride on till she meets the next rider who is waiting further along the route. They relay the mail non-stop, just like the Pony Express."

The original Pony Express operated for about a year and a

half, from April 1860 to October 1861. It ran mail from Saint Joseph, Missouri over the Rocky Mountains to Sacramento, California. They used mainly small, fast, tough horses that looked like ponies. In 1861, the transcontinental telegraph reached Salt Lake City and made the Pony Express obsolete.

Emily is a volunteer rider for the National Pony Express Association. It organizes west to east rides on the even-numbered years and east to west on the odd-numbered years. Riders in 1860 traveled about seventy-five miles per day. Riders now carry the mail in short sections of five or ten miles.

This year, the riders started in St Joseph on June 10. They ride twenty-four hours a day, for ten days and deliver the mail two thousand miles away in Sacramento to commemorate the Pony Express.

"Do they carry real mail?"

"Absolutely. They're official. They carry a mail sack, just like the old Pony Express. And today they stop here."

It was just dumb luck and a bad-tempered rooster in Austin that delivered me to Cold Springs Station on the right day.

Dick picked at the remainder of his stuffed mushrooms with his fingers. I briefly told him about my trip and that I wanted his opinion.

"OK, shoot," he invited.

"Well, I guess I just want to know what you think about what is going on in America."

"What do you mean?"

"Well, I've been away for quite a few years. And it seems like things have changed."

"Nothing has changed. Things are pretty much the same as they've always been."

"I'm not sure I follow you."

Dick explained: "Twenty years ago, when I got home from work, I had my TV and beer. I'm retired now and I still have my TV and beer. It doesn't matter who's in the White House or which party is in power."

Dick picked up the last stuffed mushroom, popped it in his mouth.

"In fact a lot has gotten better in twenty years; cars, TV, telephones, medicine, internet. There have been lots of lifestyle improvements. That is not to say that everything is perfect. But as long as everyone has their TV and beer (whatever that is for them), nobody cares what the politicians say or do.

"Politicians are in Washington. That's a long way away. Washington is Oz. Or maybe it's Hollywood. Either way, it's not real. Real people don't care about Washington. The politicians know they can do whatever they want, just so long as they keep making sure we get our TV and beer. It's like our social contract. When that stops, then there will be changes. So they do whatever they have to, so we all have our TV and beer and we leave them alone."

"Do you think things will change?" I asked.

"When people can't get their TV and beer, that's when there'll be trouble. Like water, there'll be water riots someday. Oil is running out. The number of poor people is increasing. There are homeless people living in tent cities all over America. The police are keeping them under control now, but they can't do that forever. And climate change will need to be addressed. We've got to do something about the environment. Medical insurance is a big problem. We don't have an answer, but we need one. These things are expensive to fix. Somebody's got to pay for it. It's going to take away TV and beer money.

"We don't have to worry about it, we'll be dead by then. It will be our kid's problems, or more likely our grandchildren. We don't have to change but they will. They'll have to make big changes."

"Wouldn't it be better if we made little changes now? Then our children won't have to make big changes." I suggested.

"Sure, but it doesn't work that way does it? Nobody changes unless they have to. Change only happens when it is necessary. And it's not necessary now. Most of us still have our TV and beer. The politicians aren't stupid. They know this. They make sure we, or most of us anyway, have our TV and beer. Then we don't care what they do, they keep their jobs, get rich and we don't riot.

"There's a machine running that keeps running no matter who's in the White House. It won't let things get out of control and we can't affect it."

"Doesn't voting affect it?"

"Like I said, it doesn't matter who's in office."

The restaurant was filling up and there were more people outside. The Pony Express rider was approaching. Emily returned to collect Dick. They loaded their horse trailer onto their SUV. I wished them luck and said a quick goodbye. I paid my bill and walked out to watch for the mail.

Thirty or forty people gathered outside the building, scattered around the parking lot and entry drives, most looking east to catch an early glimpse of the incoming rider. Some had brought their own horses and about a dozen were wearing jeans and red shirts.

The excitement grew while we waited for the rider to appear. Mobile phones and walkie-talkies kept us apprised of the rider's approach. The sun dipped behind the western hills and took the heat of the day with it. The air became chill, and the shadows lengthened before the rider approached.

The horse and rider materialized out of the darkness and

galloped into the parking lot. He jammed the leather mail sack into the hands of the waiting rider, a young woman who galloped west. I imagined it was done much the same in 1860 – except for the camera flashes and applause.

After the rider disappeared into the darkness, the spectators made their way back to the restaurant, the RV park or to drive off to meet the riders at the next stop. I returned to my motel room to plan my next day's ride. My mobile phone greeted me with the now familiar "no bars" icon. I was invisible.

I made some entries in my journal and looked over my maps before climbing into bed. I drifted off to sleep thinking about TV and beer and the changes since the Pony Express connected east to west.

CHAPTER 19: TAHOE

Tattoos are stupid

Wednesday, June 19

It's sixty miles from Cold Springs Station to Fallon, Nevada, and about a hundred more to Tahoe City. Fallon is an agricultural community that is famous for its military base. Fallon hosts the Top Gun fighter pilot training facility. In 1963, the Department of Defense detonated a 12.5-kiloton nuclear bomb 12,000 feet (about 2.3 miles) below the desert surface at Los Alamos National Laboratory, about thirty miles southwest of Fallon.

My route to Mike's passed through Carson City then along the northern coast of Lake Tahoe. The road congealed with mobile plaque: Fourth of July vacationers, SUVs, double-axle pick-up trucks and recreational vehicles. They hauled mountain bikes, snowboards, jet skis and rocket motorboats. The convoy lumbered over the narrow, tree-lined roads that circled the lake. It was a civilian army outfitted with a full complement of state-of-the-art recreation equipment. They advanced en masse and decamped around the city.

The road through Tahoe City center funnels through a main street of shops, restaurants and service stations. It extends about a mile along the lakefront. You can glimpse the sparkling water through gaps between the buildings. I joined the parade crawling through a gauntlet of crosswalks and traffic lights. We idled and grumbled, boxed among commuters, inching toward the last stop light. Finally, we broke free and cruised west on River Road.

Mike was waiting for me on his porch steps when I pulled into his driveway. It was three o'clock. He stood to greet me. I had been riding for almost three weeks, and had traveled 3,990 miles across 16 states. It was an exciting thrill to see his smiling face.

Mike and Leah share a walnut-stained, wooden A-frame, three-bedroom chalet. Double-paned windows look out on the forest, a winding river below and snow-capped mountains in the distance. We stood on the deck, above the river sparkling in the afternoon sunshine, while Mike explained their situation.

"So you rent two places?" I asked.

"For now, his girlfriend wants us to get our own place."

"What's the matter with this place?"

"The landlord told his girlfriend she has to move out by July 15th."

"I thought you said you have it for a year?"

"The landlord's an attorney. He's getting a divorce. He decided to sell the house. The real estate broker told him it would sell easier if it was empty. So he's kicking us out."

"What are you going to do?"

"We're looking for a place."

"What will you do if you don't find one by the fifteenth?"

"Our fallback plan is to move into the room at my apartment."

"The one you share with two other guys?"

"It's not ideal, but for now it might be all there is."

"Two people and two dogs in one room?"

"I know, but there's nothing available. We have to live someplace."

"Is it really that bad?"

"Dad, there is nothing available. This couldn't have happened at a worse time. The summer season is in full swing. Whatever was for rent is gone and there won't be much available till the summer crowd leaves. We're looking every day. Let's leave this alone for a while. How 'bout a beer?"

The houses in and around Tahoe are built along mountain roads. For the most part, they are wood-framed, stained dark brown with sharply slanted roofs, designed to shed the twenty feet of snow that falls in the winter. They blend into the alpine environment. You almost don't notice them nestled under the trees. We sipped beer leaning against the deck railing shaded by towering Ponderosa pines.

Mike's girlfriend is a vegetarian, so we cut and grilled lots of vegetables and mushrooms. Mike and I barbecued marinated steaks. It was only later I realized the barbecue and beer were exorbitant luxuries they could little afford.

Thursday, 20 June:

I woke from a dream at five o'clock. I was attending a family party. The family was made up of two or three mature families, so there were multiple sets of boys and girls about the same ages. We were sitting outside at a big table formed in the shape of a square. There was a lot of furniture set up on the grass and we were surrounded by pine forest. Mike sat in a spindly, folding chair at one corner of the table. Its legs were resting on an uneven surface and it was very unstable. One leg was sinking into the soft earth.

Everyone at the table sat in front of a heaping plate of food except Mike. He had no plate, cup or utensils. There were big platters of different kinds of food on the table, meats, vegetables, fruits, and a tray of colorful pastries. It was all out of Mike's reach. Everyone at the table talked together, animated and friendly to each other. Mike sat alone, an outsider, ignored.

There were a lot of dogs roaming around; big ones, little ones, old, young and a variety of breeds. They lounged on the furniture and ranged around and under the table nibbling scraps the family dropped and fed them. I was sitting opposite Mike. I had plenty of food in front of me. When I tried to slide some across the table to Mike, someone intercepted it. Each time I tried, someone took the food before I could get it across the table. I could not get food to Mike.

I was trying to figure out how to make a polite exit with Mike. Then I wondered why I cared about courtesy. No one paid any attention to us. I woke before I could get Mike out of there.

Mike and his girlfriend love the outdoor lifestyle, biking, hiking and snowboarding. They love the lake and the mountains of the Tahoe region, the clean air, three hundred days of sunshine and the high-altitude snowfall. By relocating they sacrificed the more diverse, big city job markets. In Tahoe, they find what work they can while they try to break into the economy.

The magnitude of their dilemma weighed on me as I came

to understand it. There are more opportunities in Reno, even in Truckee. His girlfriend explained that they do not want to abandon the mountains for either of those cities. "Then you might as well live anywhere."

We attended an outdoor concert by the lake where his girlfriend hosted a fundraiser for the local science camp. Mercedes, BMWs, Lexi, Audis, Range Rovers and Escalades filled the parking lots.

The grassy lawn in front of the stage was packed with the Tahoe holiday crowd. They turned out in casual elegance, sporting leather boat shoes, synthetic cargo shorts, designer tops, hideously expensive signature jewelry and Maui Jim sunglasses. Yeti coolers cradled craft beer and Chardonnay beside folding teak deck chairs and woolen blankets. The concert goers spent their money at the microbrew tent, not for education raffle tickets.

During my stay, we visited local tourist sites, restaurants, ski slopes and even played some golf. One day, Mike's girlfriend and I drove to nearby Donner Pass where unfortunate American pioneers on their way to California in 1846 were trapped by winter blizzards. More unfortunate were the pioneers in their party who were eaten so the others could survive. I gained some insight into Mike and his girlfriend's struggle in the Tahoe bucket of crabs.

On the next day, Mike and I drove fifteen miles to Truckee. An historic marker caught my attention. We stood in front of the old Truckee jail. I read the story of a visit by Baby Face Nelson in the early 1930's. He was fleeing from a Reno bank robbery and found himself in Truckee. Drinking at a local tavern, he met the off-duty sheriff. Baby Face challenged the sheriff that there wasn't a jail he couldn't break out of. He bet the sheriff breakfast that he could break out of the Truckee jail before morning. The rowdy group marched the stranger to the jail and confidently locked him in. Nelson went to sleep. In the morning he paid his bet and went on his way. It wasn't until the next day that the sheriff discovered who had used his jail for a hideout while the Reno police searched all the hotels in the area.

In Truckee, I spoke with an agent about local real estate. I told a white lie to get the conversation started.

"I'm considering a move to this area. My son lives here. He loves it. I am selling a house in Florida and want to look at real estate."

"This whole area is a holiday destination. Homes are priced three to five times what they would cost anywhere else," the agent told me.

"What kind of prices are we talking about?"

"There is no top limit to house prices. These are second and third homes purchased by rich people who use them for a few months or weekends a year."

"OK. What if I want to rent something till I find a house to buy?"

"There's nothing."

"You mean there is *nothing* for rent?"

"There is not enough housing for the hospital staff. That is the biggest employer in the city. People have to go to Reno to find something they can afford. They commute an hour, sometimes two if the traffic is bad."

She looked at the computer. "Here's one. It's the only rental in the area with a one-year lease. A month's rent costs more than four nurses make in a month."

"That is the only house available? What about apartments?"

"This is the worst time to look. When a rental comes available, it becomes a bidding war. In October, the market will open up a little when people leave for the season. Even then it will still be tough. Rentals are snapped up as soon as they are offered – at any price."

She continued to explain the Tahoe area housing market and the news kept getting worse.

"Most places rent before they are advertised. There is an active network of property managers, landlords and prospective tenants. When somebody's leaving the area, they tell their friends.

The friends contact the landlord or manager and make the deal before the place is ever advertised. Outsiders never hear about it.

"And some of the rentals are terrible. Homeowners put a toilet and shower in the corner of a garage. They rent it as a studio or one-bedroom apartment. Even then tenants are lucky to get a five or six-month lease. The real estate market is all in favor of the owner. It's too expensive for young people.

"People who can afford to buy around Lake Tahoe then own property that continues to increase in value. They fly in from Sacramento or San Francisco for a long weekend during ski season. When they are away, they rent it to somebody who will watch the property for them. The electricity and the heat have to be turned on anyway, so the pipes don't freeze, and they collect enough rent to pay for the utilities and it's a tax deduction. For the owners, it's a win-win-win."

I left the real estate office with a better understanding of Mike and his girlfriend's dilemma and a new perspective on Lake Tahoe. I began to view Lake Tahoe as a third-world country, isolated by mountains. There are only two roads in and out. It has a simple, small economy with limited employment opportunities. It is populated by the very rich and the very poor. The rich come for the scenery; skiing and snowboarding in the winter, swimming and boating in the summer.

Tahoe offers hiking, climbing, mountain biking, camping,

kayaking and sailing. There are lots of restaurants, gift shops, and historic sites.

The rich build multi-million-dollar cottages perched on the sides of mountains. They drive or fly in for their holidays and attend art fairs, sailing regattas and concerts. In the summer they enjoy the spectacular mountains, forests and lakes. In the winter, they ski and snowboard in designer recreation gear.

The Tahoe area is also home to the non-rich. They are the labor force for the privileged. A recreation community can't survive without a fully functioning service industry. They teach skiing and snowboarding; sell, rent and repair the equipment. They tend the yachts, mow lawns, rake leaves, shovel snow, pump gas, wait tables, babysit, and sell hand-made beads, art and souvenirs.

The rich and poor meet every day. They share the congested roads. They buy their food and gas from the same supermarkets and service stations. But mostly they meet when the rich need services.

Prices in Tahoe reflect its resort community status. Products and services cost an average of 30-50 percent more than in the real world. In fact, the state of the housing is a telling example of how dysfunctional the system is.

Only the rich can afford to buy land and build houses in the Lake Tahoe area. Many occupy the houses for holidays, for a few long weekends, maybe a month or two in the summer or winter. Sometimes they offer their houses for rent. But these are short-term leases of five or six months, at prices not quite within reach of the service staff. So a waiter teams up with a ski instructor and maybe a landscaper. They pool their resources to rent a small condominium. And because of the scarcity, they are happy to find any cabin, shack or converted garage with a roof.

But any solution is only temporary. The season changes

every six months. Then they'll need to find their next house. The poor compete for housing. They comb newspapers and internet websites, speak with networks of contacts and bid against each other. There is a continuous shifting, moving and changing of housing and roommate combinations. The Tahoe service staff leads a nomadic existence.

Why? Because they love the spectacular beauty of the area. Lake Tahoe is a stunning, breathtaking third-world island in a first-world country. The hospitality, recreation and retail industries make up more than 50 percent of Tahoe's economy. Manufacturing, IT, finance and agriculture together make up less than 10 percent. Visitors travel to this exotic location, use the resources, spend their money, play, drink, and eat, but not much is actually produced here. Real estate, taxes, food, gas, water all cost more in Tahoe than in nearby Carson City and Reno.

The choice for the non-rich in Tahoe is the same as the choice for all third-world citizens. They can live a fragile existence with no security, at subsistence level, or they can migrate to a geographic location with better opportunities.

One evening during my stay, Mike and I were dining at an over-priced restaurant by the lake. A wealthy yacht owner was hosting a dinner with some crew and friends at a table for ten. The drinks were flowing and the conversation was loud. They were a boisterous, noisy group. The guests at the party competed for attention. From my seat at a nearby table, I observed Tahoe's elite at leisure. Everyone at the table was attentive toward their host, keying on him for approval, waiting for him to drink first, eat first, speak, laugh. He was playing king and they were his court.

A pretty, young waitress hurried back and forth attending to the demanding table. She refilled water glasses, delivered drinks and collected dropped silverware. She worked quickly and efficiently, always with a smile. The sleeves of her blouse rolled up exposing a three-color tattoo of a lotus blossom on her forearm. One member of the party group saw the tattoo as an opportunity to ingratiate himself to his host. While the waitress filled his water glass, he offered an observation, loud enough for all to hear:

"Tattoos are stupid. I don't get it. Why would anyone disfigure their body with ink?"

The host did not hear, or if he did, did not acknowledge the comment. The waitress did. She didn't look up. But her smile lost its shine, her step its spring and her shoulders slumped. She finished filling the glasses, then moved away, a little slower than when she started. The conversation at the table remained animated, unaware of the pretty young girl who carried the pitcher back to the kitchen, stone faced.

The term 'third world' originated as a political designation during the Cold War. It described countries not aligned with the first world (capitalist) or the second world (communist, socialist). The rest constituted the third world, regardless of their economic or political systems. The term 'third world' has since evolved to refer to poor, underdeveloped countries with unstable economic and political systems. These countries are the source of a wave of immigrants.

It only makes sense that people living under oppressive systems will flee economic hardship, instability and insecurity to seek someplace safe. From the Middle East and Africa, they migrate to Europe. From Central and South America they flee to the U.S. Economic and political instability and unequal division of resources forces people to make the same choices everywhere. They can continue to live a marginal existence with little or no hope. They can continue to support a system designed to keep them poor. Or they can flee into the unknown for the hope of something better.

The economic system works for the people in Tahoe who have their TV and beer, yachts and jet skis, restaurant dinners for ten, million-dollar vacation homes overlooking the mountains, SUVs, and jobs in Sacramento. But it doesn't work for the people who mow their lawns, serve their food, fix their boats and gas their cars.

The life cycle of the Tahoe service population is predictable. After a season or two of subservient life with little or no hope for improvement, and tired of working three part-time jobs at low pay with no health insurance, vacation time or holidays, they lose hope. They want more than temporary housing, menial work and tattoo insults. They emigrate to a more sustainable environment.

Mike confided to me that they were considering a move away from Tahoe. They agreed that if they could not find housing by October, they would migrate to a more balanced economy. My hope was that their relationship could endure the stress.

As I began preparations for my return trip, I became increasingly concerned about Mike and his girlfriend. These are two beautiful, smart, talented young people who love each other. They were experiencing enormous stress about jobs, housing and financing. Mike's job was decomposing out from under him. He was working fewer days each week. He had no savings, an old car and no medical insurance. There was little hope on the housing issue. They were in a tough spot.

I struggled with conflicting emotions. I'm his dad. There must be something I could do. I wanted to help them solve their problems, buy them a house, give them a bunch of money, and offer advice. As much as I wanted to help, I knew it was wrong. In spite of my feelings, I have to admit the truth of Vasudeva's advice to Siddhartha, shared by the author Hermann Hess. "But even if you died ten times for him you would not succeed in relieving him of even the smallest fraction of his destiny."

Mike and his girlfriend have to find their own way. My answers aren't theirs. They can no more do things my way than I could do it my father's way.

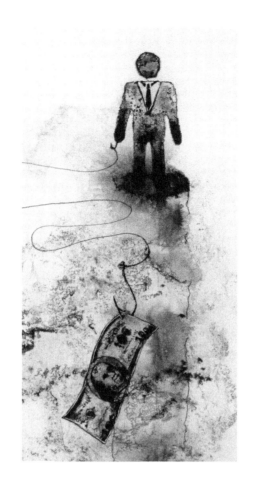

CHAPTER 20: LOLA

Mierda de toro!

Friday, June 28

It was a melancholy departure from Mike and his girlfriend on Friday morning. Foremost in my mind was the frustration that I could not help with the difficulties they faced. If I could write the script, I'd move them from Tahoe to any place with more opportunities. But it wasn't my decision. They needed to discover their own answers.

Our farewell was bittersweet. They invited me to stay longer. My heart would not permit it. They needed time together to work through their challenges. I felt I would only get in the way. I departed Tahoe, in low gear, mired in traffic, low spirits and gray thoughts. I mechanically filled the tank and topped off the oil in Carson City then rode east into the blazing sun of the Nevada desert.

While planning for the trip I loaded Lucas Davenport's one hundred "Best Songs of the Rock Era" plus a few of my own favorites into my mobile phone. I imagined myself as Peter Fonda, cruising across the country with Steppenwolf blasting in my helmet. During my early struggles with the Harley, music was an unthinkable distraction. However, over the last few weeks the Harley and I had developed a mutual understanding, in fact a fondness for each other. Maybe some music would lighten my mood. Outside of Carson City, I stopped by the side of the road and programmed the music to transmit to my helmet via the Bluetooth connection.

When I touched "Start", rock and roll pounded out of the speakers and filled my helmet. I was alone on the highway with an unimpeded view of the desert for fifty miles in every direction. I lifted my feet onto the cruising pegs, leaned back and stretched my arms to rest my hands lightly on the handlebar grips. I relaxed. In time with the music, I weaved the bike in big "S" curves from curb to curb along the deserted road at seventy miles an hour. Eric Clapton, George Thorogood, Bruce Springsteen, Creedence and Aerosmith merged me, the bike and the road. We floated, weightless and glided through the dunes in the hot morning sunshine. For an hour I was transported, weightless, timeless, with rhythm of the road and the music in my head. Not a single car passed. Nothing disturbed that rock-and-roll ride through the wasteland.

The sun burned like a laser out of a white sky. It baked the road gray and the land brown. It heated the air that burned my face. I stopped at a pharmacy outside of Fallon to buy sunscreen and painted my nose and cheeks with white grease. I peeled off my inner layers to my t-shirt and opened the vents on my jacket arms, shoulders and back. Still it got hotter. The air was infused with the fragrance of scorched ash, sage and mesquite. I rolled past a white salt lake and a dry riverbed, their blistered and cracked surfaces baking in the sun. It was a miracle the yellow, dry grass didn't burst into flames. The soles of my boots absorbed heat from the blazing asphalt. My knees were air fried by the burning wind.

I stopped for fuel and parked the bike in the shade by the pump. I checked and topped off the engine oil and rested in the shade to cool me and the bike.

I rode into the sun, three hundred miles across scorched earth, through the burning alkali wind. I crossed the desert basins and climbed through low, brown mountain ranges into Eureka. Then I turned off the music. I wanted to feel my environment, to smell it, taste it, see it and hear it. The music was great, but I wanted the ride. I was content to experience the ride without music for the next four thousand miles. I'm listening to the music as I write this and thinking of the desert.

At five o'clock in the afternoon, I was sitting on a plastic chair in front of my room at the Ruby Hill Motel beside Lola.

Lola was one of those women with classic features that don't seem to age. She was short and lithe, with dark hair and eyes and a ready sense of humor. I guessed she was somewhere between forty and sixty years old. She moved with the grace and agility of a young woman. She offered me a bottle of water and sipped hers as we talked. We sat in the shade with the sun behind the building. The late afternoon air was still hot. Lola managed the motel. She also cooked at a bar and grill down the street.

Lola was a Mexican immigrant, who relocated to Eureka from Tijuana twenty-five years ago. Before that she lived outside Mexico City, a single mother, deserted by her husband, left to support and care for her four children.

I asked about her life in Mexico.

"I was a cook in Mexico City. I worked two jobs, eighty hours a week. It was a two-hour commute each way. I left home at four-thirty in the morning. I walked to the bus then took a train into the city. Then I walked to my job from the station.

"My shift started at seven o'clock. I worked till three. Then I waited an hour to start my second job. I worked till midnight. Some people drove me home in their van. I paid them for gas. I slept on the ride home."

"What was your second job?"

"Also cook. I worked in Mexico City for three years. Then I got a job in Tijuana for better money with a shorter commute.

"I wanted to move to Tijuana but my kids didn't. They were teenagers. You know how they can be. They didn't want to leave their friends."

"How did you get here?"

"While I was working in Tijuana, I got a job offer from a man who owned a restaurant in Eureka. It was a better offer than my job in Tijuana, fewer hours, more money, still a cook."

"So you took it?"

"I didn't even know where Nevada was. My kids refused to move. I tried to tell them it would be better here, but they had friends, school – teenagers."

"So you went anyway?"

"*Si*, my kids stayed with my sister. I got on a bus and went without them. I had no passport, no school, no money and no English."

"How did that work? I mean there must have been some legal stuff to do."

"*Si*, my boss, he did all the paperwork so I could stay in America. But I had no English. So I learned."

"How did you learn?"

"By watching TV. A lady gave me a dictionary. I read the newspaper with an English-Spanish dictionary. That's how I learned. I got my high school diploma on the internet.

"I couldn't believe it when I got my first paycheck. It was as much as I made in Mexico for eighty hours. After ten years I applied for a green card and five years after that I said the oath and became a U.S. citizen."

"So you like it here?"

"It's tough here. Nobody gives you anything. You have to work and keep working. The President, he says Mexican immigrants are criminals, drug addicts, rapists, lazy, poor people looking for a free and easy life. I say, *Mierda de toro!*"

"Mierda de toro?" I don't speak Spanish.

Lola explained, "Bullshit. Those people are already here. They are everywhere, in every country. A coyote charges seven thousand dollars to bring a Mexican over the U.S. border. Then what? They bring them over the line and then say, 'Here you are'. They just leave them there. They have nothing, no job, no place to live, not even transportation to someplace with water. It's all desert. They have to find their own way. If you want someone to bring you someplace, like out of Mexico to an address, like in a city it costs fifty thousand dollars."

"How do they pay for that?"

"They save for years, empty their bank account, sell everything, their house, car, jewelry if they have any – everything. If they have a family, it costs more. When they get here, they have to start over. They have nothing."

"Why do they do it?"

"Being poor in America is better than being poor in Mexico. The city is the only place there are jobs. In Mexico you have to work eighty hours – two jobs – to live. And how do you live? You live two hours from your job because you can't afford a room in the city. So you have to commute. You are away from your family all day and most of the night. You can only afford a tiny apartment, sometimes it has electricity. You spend all your money on food and housing. And what about your kids? What are they doing all day? You don't know, you can only hope they're OK. What kind of life is that?

"In America you have to work hard too, but you can have a life. America has a President who is a businessman. There are people like that everywhere. They use you as long as you can make money for them. Then they throw you away like a Kleenex. The rich get rich. The poor stay poor. But it's better to be poor in America."

While we were talking, two young Hispanic men driving a dusty pick-up truck with a smoking tailpipe and mud-covered all-terrain tires rolled into the parking lot. They stopped in front of us. Their faces, clothes and hands were streaked with dirt, sweat and black grease. They appeared to be in their twenties, short, dark and rail thin. They wore exhaustion like a cloak. Lola stood up and walked over to speak with them in Spanish.

She returned to her chair beside me and explained.

"They are from Guatemala. The county hires them to cut mesquite in the desert. They leave for work at four o'clock in the morning and don't get back here till evening. Their visa is good for three months. They work like slaves then go home."

"What did they want?"

"I do their laundry. They wanted to know if it was ready."

"Why do you do their laundry?"

"They are nice boys. They work hard. I can help. So I do."

CHAPTER 21: TOPAZ CITY

*. . .keeping America's stock up
to the highest standards...*

Saturday, June 29

I rode out of Eureka at seven o'clock in the morning. The bank thermometer read 37 degrees Fahrenheit. Seventy-five miles later I spotted a Denny's sign in Ely. I backed into an open space on the curb among a crowd of other motorcycles on main street. Half the shops were closed and padlocked, with "For Sale" signs posted in their windows. I walked in and out of several open shops searching for the Denny's. I finally found the restaurant in the back corner of the casino.

At nine o'clock in the morning, more than half the town was closed but the casino was crowded, noisy and brightly lit. Floor to ceiling mirrors lined the walls. The room was packed with dull-eyed men and women who sipped frosty beverages from plastic cups. They fed coins into video poker and slot machines. A cacophony of bells, sirens, flashing lights jangled my nerves.

I found a booth as far from the gaming floor as possible. A lethargic waitress, too tired to communicate verbally, recorded my order. She delivered a tasteless breakfast of over-cooked eggs, bacon, toast and burned coffee. I ate as much of the uninspiring fare as I could swallow and decided to say farewell to Eureka. I left cash and my unfinished breakfast on the table. I found my way out of the building into the sunshine to rejoin the world. I was eager to return into the peaceful desert. The thrum of the powerful Harley engine was soothing after the chaos of the casino.

I rode east. The landscape evolved from stark white, to pale yellow, faded beige and then darker hues of brown, gray and green. The bare dunes covered in grassy fur softened as they rolled away from the road. I was tempted to stop and run my hands over their contours. Barren land stretched as far as I could see. Only a wire fence separated me from the downy hills.

By mid-afternoon, when I rolled by the bank on Main Street in Delta, UT, the mercury had risen sixty degrees. The little city is an oasis resting in a barren flat bowl, surrounded by mountain ranges on all sides. I pulled into the parking lot of the Rancher Diner and walked into the restaurant. I recognized Pete, sitting on a stool with a cup of coffee and a glass of water. I sat down at the counter beside him and ordered an iced tea. Pete greeted me and asked about my trip and visit with my son. I told him about the beauty of Tahoe and the bipolar economy. Then I expressed my fascination with the desert. I loved riding through the hyper-reality of the glaring sun, bleached sand and spiny vegetation. I never tired of the scenery and especially enjoyed the baking heat. He wasn't surprised.

"Some people don't see it. But it's beautiful country," Pete said.

"I love it. I just wish I knew more about the geology of this area."

"This whole valley was under water 10,000 years ago," Pete said.

"I knew it was an ancient ocean."

"Not an ocean, a huge prehistoric lake. If you're interested, you should visit the museums in town. They're just down the street."

While riding across Utah and Nevada, I was overcome by the beauty of the landscape and struck by my ignorance of how it was formed. The land, undulating from horizon to horizon in every direction, gave me the impression I was riding across the bottom of a drained ocean. Something about the shape of the hills, cliffs and valleys, the rise and fall of the ground inspired a vision of an ancient inland sea.

The Great Basin Museum in Delta is a good place to learn about the geological history of the western desert. The friendly hosts welcomed me at the entrance and asked what part of their museum interested me. Though I'm a history buff, always curious about the people and events that shape a community, in Delta I wanted to learn about the events that shaped the land. They were happy to help.

My guides directed me to the collection of maps, drawings and photos that illustrated the geological history of the area. I learned that the current site of the town was under three hundred and fifty feet of water ten thousand years ago. The Snake River, the Siever River, Siever Lake and the Great Salt Lake were all part of a vast prehistoric watershed that extended over most of what is now the state of Utah.

Almost the entire state of Utah was under a thousand feet of water eighteen thousand years ago. The giant lake extended into Idaho and parts of Nevada. It was dammed by the surrounding mountain ranges. Glacier melt and centuries of rainfall caused the lake to swell and fill the bowl formed by the ring of mountains. When the lake surface reached the lowest mountain passes, water began to flow over the natural walls that formed the reservoir. Heavy rains caused the flow to increase.

Over time, the earth holding back the lake eroded and the dam crumbled. A deluge of water erupted out of the closed lake and flooded through the surrounding lowland. Eventually, it washed almost the entire lake system into Idaho, down the Snake River into the Columbia River and from there into the Pacific Ocean. For five thousand years the flood drained Utah, and what was once a vast, deep lake changed to a desert. Only the Great Salt Lake, Siever Lake and a few small bodies of water remain. The Bonneville Salt Flats were named for the prehistoric lake that covered the region. I left the Great Basin Museum and saw the surrounding desert with new eyes.

I walked a few steps along the sidewalk and entered the Topaz Museum. As a student I had read about Japanese-American internment during World War II. The Topaz Museum depicts how that internment impacted the lives of thousands of people. It shows how fear, bigotry, greed and filthy politics can manipulate a society to commit acts of injustice and cruelty.

The museum offers visitors a glimpse into the lives of the people who were confined in the Topaz War Relocation Center, also known as Topaz City, named for a nearby mountain. It was not called a concentration camp because America didn't build and operate concentration camps, the Nazis did.

Topaz City was constructed under a 1942 order of Franklin D. Roosevelt. It was a prison for eleven thousand people forcibly relocated from their homes on the West Coast. The 20,000-

acre town officially opened on September 11, 1942, and operated for three years.

Prior to World War I, the United States had an open border policy that allowed immigrants from anywhere to enter liberally. The recession following World War I led to a rising tide of anti-immigrant prejudice. White Americans feared Asian immigrants were an economic threat. A widely publicized suspicion was that immigrants held radical beliefs that threatened the American way of life.

After World War I, a series of federal laws and informal international agreements restricted immigration into the United States. The 1924 Asian Exclusion Act and a series of federal laws slowed immigration from Asian countries, specifically Japan. The laws also applied to China, Eastern and Southern European countries. The United States Border Patrol was established at this time with deportation powers. The Ku Klux Klan and the American Federation of Labor supported the 1924 anti-immigration legislation.

U.S. borders were tightly closed for thirty years by the Johnson and Reed Act. David Reed proposed the bill with the stated purpose of "...keeping America's stock up to the highest standards..."

Fear and prejudice against the "Yellow Peril" were especially strong on the West Coast. The bombing of Pearl Harbor at the start of World War II ignited the already deep-seated bigotry against the Japanese. Anti-Japanese animosity was further fueled by the American press. Through a campaign of inflammatory "news" stories and editorials they challenged the loyalty of Japanese Americans, capitalizing on widespread fear and bigotry. The Press sensationalized an imagined threat and incited fear. They accused Japanese Americans of assisting in planning the Pearl Harbor attack. They accused them of serving as spies in America. They speculated without proof that Japanese Americans were waiting for orders from Japan to mobilize as a fifth column for an invasion of America. It was all untrue.

In the face of rising anti-Japanese sentiment and fear among West Coast citizens, and despite a complete lack of evidence, Japanese Americans became war victims. One hundred and twenty thousand Japanese Americans were herded into trains, trucks and buses, transported from their homes and relocated to ten detention camps in remote parts of the interior of the country. One of these camps was sixteen miles outside Delta, Utah.

The prisoners in Topaz City were citizens and permanent residents of California. They were forced to sell, place into storage or abandon their personal property, real estate, businesses, homes, farms and automobiles. They were transported to stadiums and racetracks until their relocation camp was ready. Some detainees were moved directly to the camp and used as construction labor to build their own prisons.

The residents lived in barracks. They grew their own food, and raised chickens, pigs and cattle. They managed the internal politics while the U.S. military managed security from outside. The detainees formed self-governing organizations and established schools for children of all ages and adults. The army guarded the perimeter, enforced order, good behavior and mandatory oaths of loyalty.

There was no instance of a Japanese American performing any act of sabotage, treason or disloyalty against America, before, during or after the attack on Pearl Harbor.

In 1942, the country turned against its own people. Japanese Americans lost everything they owned, including their freedom. Their homes and businesses were vandalized, painted with racial slurs, and their windows broken. Parents, grandparents and children were seized, confined, guarded and threatened with death if they approached the prison wall. All this occurred while Americans were fighting a war against the same injustice on another continent. But we called that injustice fascism.

The newspapers that published the inflammatory lies for profit paid no damages. The neighbors who vandalized and destroyed Japanese homes paid no damages. The guard who shot James Wakasa for walking too close to the fence was tried and found innocent. The politicians who bartered bigotry for votes were re-elected. The prisoners were released from Topaz in 1945 after three years of confinement. Most returned to their old neighborhoods to rebuild their lives from the ashes.

Nearly fifty years later, President Ronald Regan signed the Civil Liberties Act. He apologized to the Japanese Americans. Each internee still alive was awarded a payment of twenty thousand dollars. The United States government admitted that the relocation and detention of Japanese Americans was based on "race prejudice, war hysteria and a failure of leadership."

Many people I spoke with during my trip expressed concerns about immigrants entering the U.S. from the south. Public media is full of stories that incite strong emotions. The Topaz Museum offered an historical perspective on Lola's immigration experiences. The Japanese, almost a hundred years ago, like all the immigrants who populated America, had given up their old life to find a new life in a new home. When they arrived, they fought for survival against fear, bigotry, political opportunism and irresponsible journalism. Could it happen again? To Lola, to me?

I returned to the diner for an early dinner. My melancholy thoughts were interrupted when Pete sat down next to me at the counter.

"Gooden taag!" Pete's craggy, lined face was smiling.

"What?"

"I said, *'Gooden taag.'* I learned that from some Danish tourists that passed through here a few years ago. Means hello," Pete explained.

I smiled back.

"Well, *Gooden taag* to you too."

"That's right, isn't it? *Gooden taag.*"

"I don't speak Danish but it's pretty close to Dutch and German. Sounds right to me."

"How did you like our town? Did you get to the museum?"

"I visited both of them. I always felt like I was riding at the bottom of a dried-up ocean. Now I know why."

"Yup, this whole town was under water. Did you go into the Topaz Museum?"

"I did. It was really impressive. I didn't know there was a detention camp near here."

"You can go out and see it if you want, it's not far. They do tours. There isn't much left. They pulled down all the buildings and there's only a marker there now. But the foundations are still there. You can see the layout even if it's overgrown."

"No, I saw all I needed in the museum. It was pretty hard on the people there."

"Some of them came into town to work. The commandant or whatever he was called gave them permission if they got a job. They could come here for the day to work, then go back at night."

"What did they do?" I asked.

"Well, with the war on, we needed labor for the farms and construction. They were good workers. One fellow came to my ranch. He liked to ride horses."

"I was thinking about those people being taken away from

their homes and brought here. It must have been hard on them," I said.

"That was a bad time. Everyone was afraid. They weren't bad people once you got to know them," Pete agreed.

"Yah, I guess nobody is."

"When are you leaving town?"

"Tomorrow morning."

"What time?"

"Oh, about seven-thirty. I don't like to fire up that Harley too early and wake everybody up."

"Well," Pete said, "if you're around at about seven o'clock you can stop in here for coffee before you go."

"I thought the diner was closed on Sunday."

"It is, but a few of us meet here every Sunday morning for coffee. The lights will be off and the door is locked but we'll be in here. Just knock on the door. Somebody will let you in."

"I think I'll do that. Thanks."

I finished my burger and coke and paid my bill. I shook hands and said goodbye to Pete. He sat at the counter and focused on his chicken-fried steak and French fries. I walked across the parking lot to my room.

Early Sunday morning, I walked to the front door of the diner. Just as Pete described, the restaurant looked closed. I could see no lights and from the outside, it looked dark and deserted. I cupped my hands and peeked in the glass front door. I thought I could make out a form moving near the counter. I knocked on the door and waited. After a few seconds someone opened it from the inside. I looked into the dark restaurant and saw seven or eight men sitting on stools at the counter.

I didn't recognize the man who opened the door. He didn't recognize me. "Yes?"

"Umm, I was looking for Pete. He said there was coffee."

From the inside I heard, "Sure, come on in. That's Bob. I told you about him."

He opened the door and stepped aside to let me pass. Then he closed and locked the door.

The men sitting at the counter turned to watch me enter. One man offered me the stool beside him.

"Howdy, I'm Jim. How 'bout some coffee?"

"Sure."

I sat down at the corner of the counter. Four men sat to my right, three to my left.

Jim was a big man with broad shoulders, a narrow waist and thick arms. He gave such an impression of strength that I almost didn't notice the white, plastic neck brace that extended to his shoulders. He walked around the back of the bar to pour my coffee. He filled a glass with water and set both in front of me.

"Just black, right?"

"Yes, just black." I was surprised he remembered from my brief visit almost two weeks ago.

From the easy flow of the conversation I knew that each Sunday at the diner was a comfortable repeat of the one before. Old friends met and told and retold old stories and jokes. That Sunday morning we shared coffee, stories, and jokes and laughed at each other and ourselves. No politics, no race, no religion and only local economics. They talked about the price of a load of lime, well pump maintenance and driving trucks.

"When you gonna get rid of that dog collar?" said a man seated in the corner stool.

Jim: "Doc says another couple of weeks."

A man to my left asked, "Your truck fixed yet?"

Jim: "Nope, still lookin' for parts. Oughta be ready 'bout the same time I get this contraption off."

"Shouda been lookin' where you was goin'."

Jim: "That gate wasn't there the last twenty times I drove down that road."

Corner stool offered, "That gate was built in 1987."

"Well, it was never closed," Jim griped.

The conversation rolled around the room without segues, touching on familiar topics and old stories.

"Is that old truck of yours still runnin'?"

"Yup, but I'm sellin' it."

"Why, you just got it fixed."

"Don't need it anymore. Bought a new one."

"I'll tell you this, when you sell your truck, you better take your name off it."

"That old dump of yours still runnin'? Who's got it now?"

"I sold it to the Blakes. Then a couple of years ago they sold it. I don't know who to."

"So what's the problem?"

"I got calls complaining about my driving five years after I sold that truck."

"You shoulda painted over your name."

"He said he was gonna repaint it."

"He never repainted a truck in his life. He kept my old one eight years, with my name on it. You shoulda known."

Jim to me: "How do you like it here? Ever been to this part of the country before?

Me: "I've been to Salt Lake City and Las Vegas, but I flew there. I never rode through the desert. There just aren't any trees."

Jim: "I drove in New England once. All those trees, I felt like I was driving through a tunnel. I couldn't wait to get back. I like to see the horizon."

I spent about forty-five minutes over coffee with strangers who could be friends. These men enjoyed each other's company and I felt privileged to share it. I was sorry to leave but it was time for me to be on my way. I bid farewell to the men of the Rancher Diner, climbed on my bike and rode into the desert.

As I rode, I was working through conflicting concepts about my country. America is a country of immigrants, a land of opportunity. But each new wave of immigrants has been feared, resented and resisted. They struggled and gambled to get there, worked hard to gain a foothold, then fought to keep it. Lola's story is one of determination, endurance and perseverance. Does everyone fear losing what they have or that someone might take it away from them? And does that make us less tolerant, less willing to accept and welcome new people? Do we all come to fear newcomers as a threat to our beer and TV?

I thought of Kyle's "bucket of crabs."

My son and his girlfriend struggling at the bottom of the Tahoe bucket darkened my spirits. Two bright, talented young people had immigrated to the resort community and struggled to gain a foothold. They were American immigrants fighting for survival with the odds and laws against them. The American economic system is not kind. Mike and his girlfriend don't want a free ride. They want to build a life and are willing to work for it. Yet instead of opportunities they were met with rejection and tattoo insults.

I reflected on my experience in the Rancher Diner. What was it about the place that made it so special? Everybody seemed comfortable in their skin, at ease with themselves, content with life and the people around them. The waitresses were busy, but not rushed. They took time to look at and listen to the people around them. Customers patiently waited their turn and helped out when they saw the need. Everyone was relaxed. They relaxed me.

What was different in Delta? Why were the people there so open and comfortable, friendly and welcoming? Why did they invite me into their group, share their coffee and stories? They didn't seem afraid.

CHAPTER 22:
DOMINGUEZ ESCALANTE

I collect skulls.

Sunday, June 30

Three hundred miles of ancient lake bottom lie between Delta, UT and Dominguez Escalante National Conservation Area. I traveled through and around Fishlake and Manti-La Sal National Forest, Devil's Canyon and San Rafael Swell. The hours of heat, solitude, boundless undulating hardpack under a blazing blue sky were tranquil, almost hypnotic. In contrast, a battle for survival was written on the mottled bark, spiny needles and brittle branches of every dehydrated plant. The craggy terrain evoked ice-age visions of geologic upheavals, prehistoric tribal struggles and climatic catastrophes.

This was a land that time had used up. If it once enjoyed a rich past, it was eons ago and long forgotten. Now it is old, dry and silent; asleep except for the wind which has cried protest, howling unchecked across the miles and years. I love the desert. I never tired of the heat, the mesquite and sage perfume and the raw elegance of iron red cliffs and jagged canyons. Dominguez Escalante was my farewell evening in the west.

I filled the gas and oil at Green River, rode past the Moab and Arches National Park turnoff and rolled by Thompson Springs, awash with hot desert wind. I saluted the Frontage Road "No Services" turn off where I had parked before I ran out of gas, and I continued east. At Fruita, CO, I filled the tank again and checked the oil. I sweltered in the shade on a warm concrete bench searching the internet for an evening campsite.

The Dominguez-Escalante National Conservation Area is a strikingly beautiful, austere desert wilderness. Camping is free. The entrance, off U.S. Route 50, is about thirty-five miles southeast of Fruita. I'm sure there is a marker along the road, but I didn't see it. I spotted a tiny dirt road, one of those that seemingly leads nowhere and disappears into the desert. I pulled in, careful not to skid or drop the bike on the loose, rocky sand. The weathered dirt road cut up a rise and around a turn. I pulled into an empty gravel parking area, large enough for several RVs. I sat on the bike and looked around. The highway was deserted. The dirt road was primitive. The land was peaceful, dry and desolate.

"What do you think?"

"No dirt roads."

"This is supposed to be a camping area."

"I don't see a ranger station."

"Me either."

"I don't see any cars."

"That's true."

"I don't see a sign."

"OK."

"I don't see a picnic table."

"Maybe it's around that turn."

"Why don't you walk up there. I'll wait here."

I stepped off the bike, removed my gloves and helmet, peeled off my jacket and laid all three on top of the Harley bag behind my seat. I crunched up the dusty road on stiff legs. The rough surface was scarred by water runoff and erosion, strewn with jagged, red-brown rocks, as big as cinder blocks. I followed the grade, spied ahead and glimpsed an RV almost hidden beside a thorny bush. An open space at the top of the rise offered a rocky, flat open space large enough to accommodate several vehicles and tents. Beyond the open area, the dirt road traced the contour of the land west, rising, then dropping and vanishing in the distance.

This was primitive camping. No people, tents or buildings, no picnic tables, fire pits, toilets or any source of water disturbed the landscape. I searched the rocky ground for a likely spot to set up a tent. A few anemic, thorny bushes and some dry grass littered the space. I counted four bushes, all dehydrated, one dead. As I walked back down the road to retrieve the bike, I scanned the road surface for the safest route from the parking area. It was a slow, wobbly ride over and around the rubble-covered path to the campsite. I positioned the bike in the soft, dusty earth to point toward the exit. I pulled the plate from my gas tank pack, tossed it to the ground and adjusted its position under the kickstand with my boot. I set the bike carefully on the kickstand and dismounted. I surveyed the site. There was no hope of shade. The temperature was well over 90 degrees.

Through experience accumulated from years of Allagash camping, my first action at a new camp is to set up my tent. The northern Maine rainstorms are the stuff of legends and miserable wet nights. I learned new camping skills in the desert. Instead of tent first, then me, in the desert it was the other way around. My greatest need was to cool down. The ride had been broiling and at four o'clock in the afternoon I was cooked. I opened my bags, pulled out my shorts and sandals, perched on a boulder and changed clothes in the open air. I think a car may have passed by on the highway in the distance, but maybe not. My camp was remote and deserted.

I extracted my water bottle from my saddlebag and discovered only about half a liter of water remained. I took one small sip and set out to explore the area around my camp. I could see fifty miles in every direction. I was surrounded by red cliffs and rocky tufts of brown/yellow grass.

The highway to my north was a thin, black ribbon, too far for me to hear the sound of a passing vehicle. The rising wind blew across the vast desert, rattling the skeleton bushes and wiry grass. Violet storm clouds, flecked with lightning, darkened the sky to the south. Thunder grumbled in the distance.

I stood on a south-facing plateau peering at a wide expanse of barren, rocky hills. At my feet, a steep cliff dropped to flat land below. To my right, the road cut like a scar between rock walls. It weaved following the rise and fall of the terrain until it shrank to a narrow thread, tiny and remote. The RV seemed deserted. It was an old model and well traveled. A trailer, constructed from the bed of an old pick-up truck, was attached to the rear end. An idle gas-powered generator and a bank of 5-gallon fuel tanks filled the trailer. The sound of dogs barking drifted out through the open windows.

I walked back to my campsite and assembled my tent. I packed and stored my gear safely inside. The wind continued to rise. Towering, dark storm clouds sparkling with lightning approached from the south. The intervening land was naked. No tree or hill rose within fifty miles to divert the rising wind. My tent bucked and flapped. I double-staked the corners to secure it against the storm. Then I settled down listening to the approaching thunder.

I was reclining on the hard ground with a rock for a pillow, reading, when someone moving around outside the RV caught my attention. I tossed my e-reader into the tent and walked over to say hello.

I met Mike O., retired. He lived with his wife and seven dogs. His colorless, worn, baggy clothes did little to hide his bulk. He was a big man, tall, wide and hulking, He limped in his unlaced hiking boots as his dogs weaved between us and around his feet.

"That rig looks like it has everything," I said.

Mike: "Yah, it's old but it still gets us around."

Me: "Where are you from?"

"Right there."

"What do you mean?"

"I'm homeless. Or, not homeless, that's my home."

"So you live here?"

"Not here all the time. We move every fourteen days."

"Why fourteen days?"

"We can't stay longer or the rangers will kick us out."

"Then what?"

"Then we have to move at least twenty-five miles away."

"So you move to another campsite, then back here."

"We have a few campsites around the area we like. As long as we keep moving it's free."

"Is your wife in the camper?"

"No, she's visiting her sister in town. She can visit her family, clean up, take a shower."

"So, how do you spend your time?"

Mike: "I like the wilderness. I go on hikes. I collect skulls. Do you know what 'geocaching' is?"

Me: "Skulls?"

"You'd be surprised how many you find out here. All kinds of animals, picked clean. Never found a human. Let me show you something. Follow me."

We walked toward the plateau.

"I was hiking around this cliff. Down below I saw some bones. I thought it might be a skull. It turned out to be a deer, all bleached white, chewed, broken. Bones was all that was left, no skull."

He led me down the rocky hill. My footing was unstable in my sandals. The thorny underbrush and rocks scratched my feet and ankles. We scrambled up the rocky hill and found the bones.

"See, this is where I was looking. Then I noticed an odd rock pile. So I went to look at it. See, it's over there. You can just see it under that rock overhang behind the bush. Go take a look."

He stood behind me while I walked up the hill to peer into the shadow of the overhanging rocks. To be honest, I was a bit nervous about turning my back on a stranger who collected skulls. I pushed away Hanneke's warning against the gang of hijacking, kidnapping, murdering truckers.

A green army ammo box rested in a hollow behind the pile of rocks, against the side of the hill. I reached in, pulled the box out into the open and carried it down the hill. Inside we found note paper with signatures and dates. The box was filled with odd trinkets; a foam drink koozie, a plastic toy deer, a glass marble. Mike explained geocaching.

"People who find the box take or leave something, nothing expensive, just for fun."

"How do you know where to look?"

"There's an app for your phone. If you put in your location, you can see the location of the caches near you. You hunt by the GPS co-ordinates. When you find a box, you record it, take something out, put something in, leave a note, then put it all back for somebody else to find."

"They're all over. There are four more down that road if you want to look for them."

He pointed to the rocky dirt road that led into the hills.

"I better put this one back." I closed the box and returned it to its hiding place.

Mike waited on the side of the hill. We walked back to his trailer. His seven dogs roamed around friendly and free, sniffing the ground and my legs. I decided to broach a concern that had been on my mind since I unpacked. I asked for Mike's help.

"Mike, I rode into this camp unprepared. I don't have enough water. I could really use some if you can spare it."

"Sure, I can help you out with that. I have plenty."

About fifteen minutes later, he walked over to my camp carrying a gallon milk jug filled with water. "Just leave me the jug before you go."

"Thanks, this is a great help. I'll make sure to return the jug."

Mike and his wife have been homeless for two years.

"We have seven dogs; nobody wants to rent to us. So we do this.

We move every couple of weeks. We've got another place about thirty miles east. We'll go there next week. The ranger takes license plates."

The campsite was bare, desolate and windy, so windy I worried the tent would blow away. A storm was rising in the southeast and moving in my direction. Low ominous clouds, flashes of lightning and long, slow booming thunder rolled northwest behind the rush of wind. Dry, dusty sand peppered my skin, tent and bike.

The warm wind increased to a gale that rattled my tent, flapped the fly like a sail and caused the guy lines to snap and sing. The gusts blew the fly and ripped tent pegs from the earth. They shot out of the ground and flew in the air, whipped in the wind at the end of the thin nylon twine. I grabbed the flying line, pulled it back into position and used a rock to pound the pegs into the hard-packed earth. I used all the extra pegs in my bag and double-staked the four corners, sides and ends of the tent and fly to hold it to the earth. I piled all my gear around the inside perimeter and sat in the middle to anchor it against the rising gale.

The storm darkened the sky. Dusk fell and impossibly, the wind increased. There wasn't a single tree to break the wind's charge across the expanse of desert. A sudden blast pushed the tent flat on top of me. It sprang back on graphite poles when the gale paused, then collapsed again like the hand of God had slapped it flat. I scampered out of the tent and removed the fly to let the air pass through the netting. I gathered up the fly, rolled it up and threw it into the tent. I followed it in and laid on my back, gazing through the netting at the clouds racing across the sky. I glimpsed stars twinkling between passing clouds. Thunder approached. The wind howled. Spits of rain collected in the netting of the tent roof and spattered on me and my gear.

I sat on my sleeping bag, surrounded by my gear waiting for

the storm to strike. I thought, "What else can I do to prepare?" I packed my sleeping bag into its waterproof sack. The flashlight hanging from the tent roof swung in the breeze, whirling its beam like an unhinged spotlight. I unhooked it and held it in my mouth.

I closed and covered my clothes bag and prepared my gear for the approaching rainstorm. I expected a downpour. The wind diminished as the lightning and thunder approached. I counted the seconds between flashes and booms, fifteen... eleven... then five seconds. The storm was a mile away and moving fast.

I donned my rain gear and waited for the storm to break. I covered my gear and wrapped the fly around my body like a blanket. I stretched out on the tent floor and listened to the gusts, watched the lightning, and counted the seconds waiting for the deluge. For two hours the sky darkened while the angry tempest howled, flashed and rumbled threats. My world turned black and white; black clouds, black sky, black horizon and jagged white lightning. Blasts of air, booming thunder and fat drops battered the fragile tent pinned to the ground by string, tiny bits of steel and me.

Sometime late that night, the rain stopped and the storm wandered north west. The wind continued to gust and blow but the worst was over. I climbed out of the tent to assess the damage. In New England this storm would have felled trees, broken branches and littered the ground with ripped leaves. Houses would lose shingles. Telephone poles would topple, drop wires and cause power failures.

Here, there were no trees, no houses, no telephone poles and no power failures. The rocks didn't move. Only the rain-pockmarked dust on my motorcycle testified to the passing of the storm. A few stars winked through the breaking black cloud cover. I remounted the fly and secured it with two pegs in every grommet. It continued to flap and blow all night.

Monday, July 1

The clouds sprinted north and the sky became an amazing black curtain, sparkling with eternity. At five o'clock I gave up on sleep and decided to get an early start on the day. What a beautiful, barren, inhospitable wonderful wilderness, free to anyone who chooses to visit.

My motorcycle was shrouded in dust, a moonscape of little rain craters. I used a cloth dampened with some of Mike's precious water to wipe the worst of it off the seat, fenders, handlebars and gas tank. Then I loaded my gear. Mike and his seven dogs slept in their vintage recreational vehicle. His electric generator was silent which told me he didn't use his air conditioning at night. It was not running yesterday even though the temperature approached one hundred. Mike didn't waste his resources.

An hour later I was climbing the passes over the Rocky Mountains about one hundred miles south of Denver. The narrow switchbacks spiraled into cold, misty clouds that obscured my vision, chilled my bones and streaked my windshield with droplets. The road glistened. The towering cliffs leaked foamy tears and my jacket ran with moisture till I descended through the clouds and emerged into the sun on the east side of the mountains.

South of Black Canyon, I rode through ten thousand years of history. Gunnison National Park is a wilderness of tall cliffs, pine woods and rushing white rivers. Mirror lakes fill the valleys reflecting snow-capped peaks, marshmallow clouds and craggy cliffs. There's a prehistoric beauty here, boundless forests, game trails and sheer mountain cliffs. The terrain inspires visions of an old life, campfires, game roaming through ancient forests and trout jumping in frigid, deep, ice age lakes. This is harsh and magnificent country. Winter blizzards howl through the canyons and across the slopes. Snow blankets the freezing earth and cracks trees.

Avalanches roar down the slopes like thunderous tidal waves. Spring rains spawn torrential waterfalls and wild rivers that tumble boulders, uproot trees and sweep for miles.

I cruised through this pristine country in the benign summer. I glimpsed only a hint of the cataclysms that shaped the land. In July, snow-capped peaks top black cliffs above the tree line. In December, it's all freezing white. It was cool on the road in the shade of the overhanging cliffs. Three layers of modern synthetics kept my shivers at bay. How did people survive here before GoreTex, Thinsulate and fleece? On the other side of the clouds, the sun was a glowing bright basketball, close and hot. I warmed fast and dried, steaming into the azure sky.

By nine o'clock I reached Gunnison, CO, about one hundred miles from my start. I stopped for breakfast and fuel then continued through the mountains, into the foothills on the eastern slope of the Rockies. At Canon City the landscape flattened. I continued east into the tropical sunshine of the Colorado plains. The cool mountain air, with its mist, shade, winding mountain roads and towering trees were behind me.

I stopped for the day in Fowler, still in Colorado. Two motorcycle riders from Tennessee were sitting outside their room, relaxing in the shade, drinking beer from cans. They invited me to join them. They were headed for California on a five-week road trip. I admired their powerful, new bikes. They were polite and complimented me on my antique. Theirs sported digital readouts for speed, mileage, even temperature and gear numbers. I envied their modern innovations like in-dash GPS, cruise-control functions and especially their beverage holder on the handlebar. We talked outside their room for an hour, sitting on a small, wooden bench with a cooler of beer at our feet.

Jim was sixty-five years old. He grew up working on a farm and joined the Navy out of high school. He rode a late-model full-dress Harley with hard luggage bags.

"I used to have a Triumph. My ex-girlfriend poured sugar in the gas tank. When the engine quit it almost killed me. I pulled over and got clipped by a passing car. I broke an arm and tore up my clothes. I woke up in the ambulance on the way to the hospital."

He described it as a bad break-up.

His traveling buddy Junior was seventy-two years old.

"If you ever get in a bar fight you want Junior on your side of the table." They told traveling stories and shared hair-raising ATV experiences.

I finished my beer and said goodbye to Jim and Junior. They rode into town for dinner, while I walked to a nearby sandwich shop. They returned at about eight o'clock and sat on the bench talking and drinking beer long after I closed my eyes for the night.

For once somebody else's motorcycle woke me up. At three o'clock in the morning, Jim and Junior started their motorcycles and rode off. At seven o'clock I packed my bike for my departure. They left a dozen empty beer cans piled on the concrete pad outside their door. I silently wished them good luck.

CHAPTER 23: RICHARD

*Oxy killed more people
than the Vietnam War.*

Tuesday, July 2

It was a cool Tuesday morning on the Colorado plains, east of the Rockies. I rode into the sun for an hour. I passed several fast-food restaurants, then spotted a local restaurant with a name I did not recognize. The dozen or so cars in the parking lot hinted that the food was pretty good and the prices reasonable. I got it half right. The restaurant was not a mom-and-pop diner. It was a local franchise, a McDonalds knock-off furnished in molded plastic. They served greasy sausages, eggs and biscuits under glaring fluorescents.

It occurred to me that my breakfast track record in the U.S. was about the same as my meal selection success had been in Asia. My unaccompanied batting average, good to bad meals in China, Japan and South Korea was about .500. When I dined with a local, I was always happy with the meal choices. If I dined alone, half the time I left the table hungry with my inedible food still on the plate. Even the photo menus offered in the larger restaurants were not much help. In the U.S. I experienced about the same success record, except at local, owner-operated diners. They served tasty breakfasts every time.

My second cup of coffee turned out to be better than my first, so I sipped it slowly and scanned my atlas. The map showed straight lines and open spaces heading east. I had no plan, distance or goal for today's ride. My itinerary had long since fallen away. This trip had evolved into a day-by-day ride and I had plenty of days left. It was sunny and warming up fast. I had more than half the country in front of me but no schedule, nowhere special to go and no place to be. I was comfortable with that. Yesterday's ride through the Rocky Mountains had been breathtaking, intense, cold in the morning and hot in the afternoon. I was exhausted at the end of it. The deserts and mountains were behind me. I already missed them.

I finished my coffee, still not sure where the end of the day would find me. I paid the cashier and mechanically answered her mechanical questions. "Yes, everything was fine." She returned my change and completed her checklist without making eye contact. I walked out slowly, relaxed, soaking up the warming sunshine. The little town was sleepy with few cars on the road and fewer people on the sidewalks. The shops on Main Street were not yet awake.

Across the street, I saw a motorcycle standing at the curb in front of a shop. It was an old black Harley Heritage

Softail almost exactly like mine with black leather saddlebags, chrome crash bars and a sport windshield. I noticed the bike before the man. He was thin, wearing jeans and black t-shirt. Sitting on a wooden bench, he was enjoying the morning sun, smoking a cigarette.

The window sign advertised, "Bikes for sale." The sign on the building announced the County Day Care Center. He watched me as I detoured to cross the street and say hello.

I reflected on the changing times. In this little Colorado town, a sixty-year-old Harley rider was responsible for opening the day care center and another senior Harley rider was ambling across the street to sit on a bench and talk to him.

I've been riding a motorcycle since 1968, when drugs, violence and gangs branded all American motorcycle riders with skull and crossbones. Forty years ago we were society's rebels, bad boy bikers, worse – Harley riders. Did we change or did our culture expand to include us? Neither of us looked very dangerous now.

In my early riding days, I knew most of the other riders in Quincy. There weren't many of us. We waved to each other as we passed on the road. Non-motorcycle riders were not so friendly. I learned to keep my eyes open for other drivers who either didn't see me or saw me as a target. I learned to always plan an "escape route" in traffic. I always kept a close eye on the mirrors, especially when braking. Back in those days, motorcycle riders were not popular. The notorious biker gangs of the sixties tainted all of us with pit bull reputations.

I was concerned that a negative bias against motorcycle riders would impact my trip. Would a black-jacketed rider on a Harley intimidate people? Put them off? Inhibit communication? The answer I found was absolutely not! I discovered my Harley was like a puppy. Instead of pushing people away it drew people to me. It seemed everyone I met owned one, used to own one, knew someone with a Harley or wanted one. They were eager to talk about their Harley or the Harley they planned to buy. They talked about their rides, past, or future. People stopped to talk to me at filling stations, campsites and in restaurants. It was a surprise and a great relief. I wonder when we changed from pit bulls to puppies.

I walked across the street and we met; two strangers, with only motorcycle riding in common, and greeted each other in friendship. Rail thin and weather-worn, it was hard to estimate Richard's age. From across the street I thought, sixty years old. His skin was sallow, his face wrinkled and his thin, gray, hair cut short. As we spoke, I thought maybe he was younger. I could only guess somewhere between forty and sixty. Richard spoke fast, chain-smoked and paced while he talked. He spoke of serving in Iraq, Afghanistan and the Gulf War. I had thought he was closer to my generation, more like a Vietnam War veteran. He told me he was discharged from the Navy after being wounded in Iraq. He lifted his worn, baggy jeans to show me the shrapnel scar on his calf. He still remembers the pain.

"Navy doctors prescribed Oxycontin. I wanted physical therapy, acupuncture or chiropractic, but insurance didn't pay for that. They just kept writing prescriptions. I became an addict. It went downhill. Eventually I couldn't work, lost my job. But I was still hooked so I sold everything I had to buy drugs. The doctors kept writing prescriptions, but it wasn't enough anymore. I couldn't pay my bills. I lost my apartment, my girlfriend, everything."

Richard spoke without a pause while we sat on the bench in front of his store.

"Oxy killed more people than the Vietnam War. Do you know there were more deaths from Oxy overdoses in the last three years than from ten years of the Vietnam War? You don't see riots in the streets about that. And that doesn't include people who don't die, the ones who just ruined their lives. There are millions. Look around this town."

He waved his arm and I looked up and down the street.

"Look at all the closed stores. What do you think that's about? Drugs. There's a bad drug problem around here. You get hooked. But that's OK because the doctors keep writing the scripts. But you need more and more. You think you need it for the pain. But that's not it anymore, you just need it. Then you lose your job and the insurance stops. They stop writing the scripts. You get sick. So you turn to something else like meth, or heroin or pretty much anything you can get. And you'll do anything to get it. Don't leave your motorcycle unlocked around here.

"I was a mess for five years. Then I heard about this place down the road from here, a special rehab facility that uses an unconventional system – there is no system. They believe that everyone, even if they are an addict, knows the right thing to do. They give them a place to find it for themselves. So they let you stay and do your own thing, whatever that is. Like some people do pottery, some paint, some try music, make jewelry, whatever you want. And they provide what you need to do it. They have everything there or you can bring what you want to do. Like if you bring your own guitar, that's cool. You rest and do your thing and get well. And there's none of that Kumbaya bullshit, pardon my French. They don't make you do the twelve steps, meditate or pray or anything you don't want to do. There's no counseling, no mandatory group therapy. Course, there are people there to talk to if you need it. But basically, they give you a place to stay, feed you and leave you alone and let you heal. There's only one rule, no drugs or alcohol – none."

Richard stood up, stretched and lit another cigarette, then sat back down and continued.

"It sounded perfect. I don't go for the bare-your-soul kind of crap, or the boot camp shit. I had enough of that in the Navy. At that time I was living in a town about fifty miles west. I was ready to sign up, so I contacted the VA. They will pay for about a month of rehab. So I closed up my apartment and moved here.

"Then I found out the program was for three months and it cost ninety thousand dollars. I didn't have that kind of money and the VA wasn't paying for it. I was stuck: I was still using, I had no job and no place to stay. So I started asking around. Trying to figure out something else to do. I met someone here in town who told me I was wasting my time. That place is for movie stars and athletes. They sign up to detox, clean out before their next movie deal or go back to playing whatever sport it is that earns them the big money. They don't go there to rehabilitate. They go because they need a clean piss test. Sometimes it's in the plea bargain. Then they just go back in before the next season starts or the next movie. That wasn't the place for me. I wanted to get off the junk."

Richard paused, took a drag from his cigarette and stared off into space as if reliving the disappointment. I waited.

"He told me about a different place, a real place. Like a rehab halfway house. I got in right away because I was a veteran. I spent two years in this residential rehab clinic. They provide jobs for people in and around the town. They do volunteer work, work for the town, public works, build stuff, anything to keep people busy while they get clean. Then they connect them so they can get a job and stay off the shit.

"Do you want to see what I'm doing now?" Richard offered.

"Sure," I said.

He stood up. I followed him to the door of the shop behind us. He unlocked it and we walked in.

"I bought this from the town five years ago. I opened it as a bike shop and evolved into what it is today."

The building was about eighty years old with a wooden floor

and white, sheetrock walls. Wall shelves, display cases and racks crowded with collectibles, video discs, used and hand-made jewelry, clothes and tools lined the front of the store. The bikes were in the back. Richard operated a consignment shop, like a flea market. He rented space to local people who had things to sell. They paid Richard a monthly fee for the space and 20 percent of sales. If sales were good, he gave them a pass on the rent. He explained he was helping out people trying to make ends meet.

"There are no jobs. People need to sell their stuff to make money. I just want to help."

In the back of the shop, wall shelves and tables displayed a selection of used bicycles and equipment; tires, pumps and tools.

"I get the bikes from a local police evidence room. They have to get rid of them to make room for the marijuana."

"I thought marijuana was legal in Colorado," I said.

"It is, but only in small quantities. You can grow five plants for personal use. But people break into abandoned houses, strip out the walls and fill them with plants. They steal the electricity and water and put their own padlocks on the doors. It's not their property so the police don't know who it is unless they catch them there. They hire lookouts to tell them if the police show up. Sometimes they rent places and clean them out to fill them up with marijuana plants. The police fly over with heat sensors in helicopters; they check electricity and water use to find out where the illegal farms are. The police confiscate so much shit, the evidence room is full. Not just marijuana; methamphetamines, heroin and oxy are everywhere. It's bad."

We walked further back in the store and behind a curtained-off area was another large room. It was set up as a meeting room with rows of folding tables and chairs. On the left side of the room was a refrigerator, a sink and a long counter with a coffee machine and a stack of porcelain cups.

"This is where I host the local AA/NA meetings. There is no place in town with a room like this so I do it."

He was animated and seemed nervous but enthusiastic and proud. He was thinner than I first thought, almost gaunt. His addiction had taken a heavy toll.

"Let me show you this."

He pulled a curtain aside and led me up a dark, narrow staircase on the left side of the meeting room. The creaky wooden stairs emptied into a single attic room above the shop. The narrow floor planks were rough and unfinished but clean and sanded. The dingy, sheetrock walls and ceiling had last been painted before Nixon was President. The room was bare, with no furniture, wall decorations or curtains. The only light filtered in through a dust-streaked skylight in the middle of the peaked ceiling.

Richard became more animated as he told me his plan. He pointed at the blank wall to his right and waved his arms around the room.

"A dispensary is going to open next door. They offered to buy this building. They offered me four times what it is worth. But I won't sell. I'm going to open a head shop here. I'll put in some display cases. Sell everything you need to smoke marijuana; pipes, papers, everything but the marijuana."

"Don't they sell all that in a dispensary?" I asked.

"Yes, but they will be expensive. They charge for one-stop shopping. I'm going to sell everything at a discount and 10 percent off for veterans. But no meth or crack or heroin paraphernalia. You know, those crazy pipes they use. I hate that shit. I won't have anything to do with it. I won't support it. I'll only sell stuff to smoke marijuana – and hash."

As I listened to Richard describe his plan, it struck me that he didn't recognize a conflict between his head shop plan and his recovery from substance abuse. He didn't worry that his customers might themselves be struggling with addiction. He also didn't consider that his head shop or the dispensary next door would pose a temptation to the alcoholics and narcotics users at his AA/NA meetings. He only expressed enthusiasm for the business opportunity.

We walked back down to his shop and out the front door into the bright sunshine. It gave me an opportunity to admire his 1999 Harley Softail. We complimented each other on our good taste in bikes, both of us happy with our choices.

Then he asked me about my plans. "Where are you heading today?"

"East on fifty."

"How far?"

"As far as I feel like. I've got plenty of time."

"Well, you want to check out John Martin Reservoir. It's about twenty miles east of here. It's worth a look."

"What is it?"

"It's a state park. You can camp there if you want. Or you can just ride around and have a look. It's beautiful."

"Are there any trees?"

"Sure, it's a campground. It's nice there. There's a dam and a swimming beach. Lots of people go there for the fishing."

We said good-bye and I headed out of town, still with no plan. When I saw the sign for the turn off to John Martin Reservoir, I turned in to look it over.

The massive concrete dam is the most distinctive feature of JMR State Park. It is visible from a mile away. Visitors can circle the lake via a paved road over the dam or launch their fishing boats north of the dam. This monolith towers over the campsite nestled below. Arkansas River water pours over the spillway and forms Lake Hasty and the surrounding wetlands. Behind the dam, the river rises to form a lake that reflects the sunshine like a mirror in the grass.

I decided to camp overnight at JMR. By noon, my riding day was done. I picked a campsite on the water's edge shaded by a powerful elm tree. The dam rose and roared to the west.

I backed my motorcycle onto the pavement by my campsite. The campground was flat and bleak, barren except for the few wooden structures and massive elm trees scattered between campsites. This campsite provided a four-post roofed shelter that offered cover from the rain and shade from the sun. I took my time setting up my tent and organizing my gear in what had by now become a familiar routine.

I opened my duffel bag and extracted my tent, sleeping bag and sleeping pad. I pulled out the tent, ground cloth, stakes, poles and fly sheet and spread them out on the grass in the sunshine. The tent was damp from the DENCA storm two days before but a few minutes in the sunshine dried it out.

Warm sunshine, a hot day, water rushing over the dam, pooling and swirling a few yards from my seat, were all too much to resist. I donned my bathing suit, exchanged my hot boots for open sandals, picked up my towel and walked to the beach.

James Martin Reservoir is a fishing, not swimming destination. All the other vehicles in the campground trailered boats. The other campers were off on the lake side of the dam, hunting sea monsters with monofilament. I was alone on the swimming beach. I walked into the cool water up to my knees, then dove in and paddled in the cool water. It was a shallow pool with a mild slope. I swam to the middle of the lagoon and found the muddy bottom with my toes. I floated, paddled and dipped into the clear water with the sun shining hot above me. I splashed out and sat on the towel with my feet in the sand. The sun dried my wet skin in minutes. My eyes wandered around the sand. I followed the coast and watched the tall grass wave in the gentle breeze. I enjoyed the laziness, relaxed.

Back at my campsite by late afternoon, I strung a line between two trees. Even in the shade, my suit and towel were dry in an hour. I looked over my maps and saw that my next day's ride would take me to Kansas. More than that I didn't need to know. I spent a lazy afternoon reading, smoking my pipe and updating my journal. The wind began to rise and dark, purple clouds approached from behind the dam. Thunder boomed in the distance. The tent leaned and twisted on fragile legs. I pounded extra tent stakes into place with a brick, then removed the fly to let the air flow through the screens. Still the poles shifted and strained in the gusting wind before the storm. Under purple storm clouds, wind-whipped, angry waves battered and washed over the concrete abutment.

I collected all my gear from the picnic table and stowed it in the tent before the rain hit. I reattached the fly, checked the lines and climbed into the tent to wait out the storm. It was brief, but ferocious. Darkness descended like a curtain. Wind gusts twisted the tent, pushing it left and right, bending the poles and whistling through the netting. Rain hammered the fly and pounded the ground. Lightning flashed and thunder cracked, closer by the minute.

The storm approached from the northwest and took all afternoon to arrive. The tempest hit my camp like a freight train and sped off just as quickly. It breached the dam, hammered the campground, then drove away. It left behind pock-marked sand, pools of water in the gravel roads, soaked grass flowing with rivulets and downed tree branches. The surface of little Lake Hasty behind my campsite was dark and restless. Waves lapped the shore, splashing in the tall grass laid flat by the wind. The gusts slowly died down and the evening breathed a peaceful sigh of relief.

I crawled out of my tent and reset my sleeping pad, bungee cord and luggage bag lounge on the picnic table bench and watched the storm move off to the southeast. The breeze was still fresh and pushing clouds behind the storm. The early evening brightened as the cloud cover receded. I lit my pipe, opened my journal and with pen in hand reflected on my experiences of the last month or so. Sitting at the picnic table at John Martin Reservoir as the storm thundered in the distance, I reflected on whether I had done what I came to do.

In the last month, I had experienced a vast diversity of the American landscape. I was stunned by beauty everywhere I traveled, from the water-rich, verdant eastern forests to the dusty, dry Nevada desert. The Appalachian Mountains and Shenandoah Valley glowed with a hundred shades of green, beautiful and wild. I had crossed the flooded Mississippi awed by the magnitude of the River's quiet power. I had scaled the Rocky Mountains twice and each time was a stunning thrill. The Martian landscape of the Utah and Nevada deserts inspired visions of ice age cataclysms. And I had experienced the breathtaking beauty of Lake Tahoe cupped within towering white-capped mountains. I had gained a new appreciation and respect for the vastness and raw beauty of America.

What did I hear from the people who lived here?

Dan worried about protecting his business from Democratic give-away programs like socialized medical insurance. Paul favored building a wall around America against a thousand immigrants per day. Bob was prepared to use his seventeen pellet guns to protect what was his. They feared the hordes of uneducated criminals, rapists and drug addicts that were swarming into the country from the south.

Rose and her brother talked in Shenandoah about municipal budgets strained by increasing costs for police, emergency technicians and hospitals; medical resources expended on those who can't pay like immigrants and drug addicts. Pat worried because decreasing tax revenue threatened her teaching job. Rose was concerned for her safety. Her neighbor was beaten and robbed by drug addicts.

John was a union worker. Immigration and cheap labor threatened his job. He was afraid the Democrats would increase taxes to pay for social services for illegal immigrants. He asked the question I heard many times, "Why should I have to pay for what they receive for free?"

Dick, the retired fireman from Reno, was fatalistic. "As long as I have my TV and beer, I don't care what happens."

I recalled my conversation with Lola, the Mexican immigrant who held two jobs twenty-five years ago in Mexico and holds two jobs now.

"Every country already has criminals, rapists and drug addicts. You can't build a wall to keep them out. They are already here. *Mierda de toro!*"

She said that the people trying to enter America want to work. They are used to working hard in their own country. They hope that they can work hard here and have a better life. That's what they want, a better life.

I reflected on the presentations in the Topaz Museum. The Japanese migrated to America in the early 1900's for a better life too. They worked hard but were feared by the people who got here first. How was the Yellow Peril different from the Brown Wave?

I thought, "Is that why everyone seems obsessed with collecting stuff?"

I sat at the picnic table in the diminishing daylight, as the wind died down and the storm faded into memory. It occurred to me that most of the people I spoke with were well established, between the ages of forty-five and seventy-five years old, baby boomers. In the sixties and seventies, they were the revolutionaries demanding change. Now, many have retired. Most own homes, cars, recreational vehicles. They have accumulated savings and retirement pension plans. They have worked or are still working, paying taxes and collecting stuff. They view change as dangerous.

Many of the people I spoke with were afraid that change would threaten what they had worked for all their lives. They resist change in demographics, social structure and politics. They resist publicly financed social programs like national healthcare, which they call socialized medicine. Some recognize changes are needed, but those changes can wait for their children or grandchildren. They like things the way they are. It seems to me that the older generation (my generation) wants to keep America from changing. The wall is more than a barrier against immigrants. It is symbolic protection against change.

It was getting dark and the mosquitos arrived. It was time for me to retreat to my tent for the night.

CHAPTER 24: DODGE CITY

They stole the jail.

Wednesday, July 3

I didn't wake up at five-thirty, I simply gave up trying to sleep. By daybreak, the storm was just a memory. The air was calm and the campground was silent. I stretched and turned in my bag, wide awake but much too early. I shifted my position and sat up. Since the start of the trip, I had enjoyed restful, uninterrupted sleep and suffered no morning aches or pains from lying on the ground. Last night had been the exception. I was uncomfortable all night. No matter how I shifted, twisted and turned, the ground under me felt hard and bumpy.

I am always careful about where I place my tent. I look for a flat space, big enough to fit the tent. If the ground is inclined, I place my feet toward the downward angle, my head up. I avoid bedrock boulders that rise out of the earth like icebergs and can't be moved. Before I raise my tent, I sweep and harvest little rocks, even pebbles. I clear away branches, pinecones and acorns and I avoid tree roots that poke up through the ground. Last night was the first night my sleeping pad failed to cushion my body. I slept fitfully, my back ached and I felt bruised.

I speculated that the roots of the shade tree above me were poking up through the ground under my tent. Maybe there were fallen branches or rocks under me. I thought I had cleared the ground before I set up the tent. Maybe I missed something. Whatever the reason, my night's sleep was almost a total loss. It was time to give up and get going. I climbed out of my sleeping bag.

As I moved around inside the tent to gather my clothes and start the day, I discovered a hard lump directly under my hip. I reached down and pulled out the nylon bag that held my tent stakes. Somehow it had found its way into my sleeping bag. All night I had been lying on my extra metal tent stakes. No matter how I moved the sleeping pad, shifted the bag or moved it around the tent, I had not found a soft spot. It was because the bumps were inside my bag. Every time I moved, I carried the bag of tent stakes with me, and they lodged under my back, side or hip when I shifted position. I lifted my t-shirt, lowered my pants and saw a dark bruise on my right hip – my stupidity tattoo.

When I emerged from the tent, the weather was already warm and the sky was clear. By six-thirty I was restless to move on. I fired up the Harley, sure I was waking everyone within a mile. I whispered a silent apology to my neighbors as I rode off.

Dodge City was about two hundred miles east. U.S. Route 50 through Kansas is straight, flat and treeless. Huge mega-farms lined both sides of the road with irrigation equipment so huge it can be measured in mile fractions. The moist, green circles they create are visible from an airplane window at forty thousand feet. I counted horizontal scaffold-like segments beside the road and estimated their size with my odometer.

This is the magnitude of farming it takes to feed America. The labor must be mechanized because along the way I saw no people in the fields and few buildings on the land, just oceans of crops and trainloads of equipment. The Arkansas River was somewhere to my right, concealed by miles of waving fields of yellow grain.

I stopped for breakfast at Casey's in Lakin. Over coffee I checked my free campsite app for something near Dodge City. Sure enough, there was a free campground on the outskirts of the city, along my route. I entered the address into my GPS.

As I approached the city, the horizon closed in. Traffic increased, cars jockeyed for position, trucks belched, creeped and squealed and the air burned my throat. The black asphalt radiated heat that intensified by the mile. I had long since removed all the linings and my long-sleeved shirt and opened the air vents in my jacket. It didn't seem to help; I was steaming under my Kevlar like a poached egg.

On the long ride around Dodge City, I discovered another side of Kansas' industrial food production. It was not limited to miles of fragrant green soy, wheat and corn fields. I climbed a rise and came upon an unfamiliar sight. The musky, pungent odor of ammonia, raw fertilizer and steaming methane assaulted my senses. I rolled over a rise and descended into the dead air that surrounds a stockyard. Thousands of cattle wandered aimlessly, stood alone or in small groups under the brutal sun. They were confined within hundreds of fenced segments.

Spread across the naked rolling hills to my right was a square mile of bare, black dirt. Thousands of cattle hooves had stripped the land of vegetation. No shade tree or blade of grass greened that bald wasteland. No plant survived the stark landscape, only steel rail fences, galvanized feed tanks and water pipes. Thousands of four-footed prisoners waited to be "processed." Huge silos stood sentinel beside great metal-roofed barns adjacent to the fenced stalls. I rode toward this open-air livestock detention center and whispered a grateful prayer to the universe that fate did not cast me as a cow. For surely this was animal hell on earth. The sight and smell inspired a vegetarian lifestyle, even religion.

My phone guided me past the stockyard to a parking lot. The free camping area was a triangle of grass bordered by three busy roads. An abandoned gas station occupied the site across the street. Constant traffic streamed past. The background noise reminded me of the lowing of the doomed animals on the barren hills a few miles west. A few trees lined the eastern border of the parking area. A four-posted shelter and picnic table rested on a patch of grass the size of a baseball infield. A sign offered free camping provided by the city council. It invited campers to use the site, park responsibly and place trash in an uncovered green 55-gallon drum beside the picnic table.

It was like a campsite in the middle of a Walmart parking lot. This was not a campground; it was a rest stop at a highway interchange. I wanted a camping bargain but there were quality of life issues to factor in. This site had bad mojo. I couldn't feel relaxed. It was not a safe place to leave all my tent and gear while I played tourist. I might as well post a "free stuff" sign. It was sweltering hot. I peeled off my motorcycle jacket. I pulled out my water bottle, phone and map. I found a motel that advertised a pool and free breakfast a few miles down the road, closer to the city. A single room was offered on their internet site for forty dollars. I called.

Me: "I'd like to rent a room for the night. Do you have one available?"

Motel clerk: "Yes."

"I see a price of forty dollars on the internet site. Is that the price?"

"The price is $52.99."

"Why is it forty dollars on the internet?"

"I don't know. Maybe it's an old price. Do you want it or not?"

"It says you have a pool and free breakfast. Is that still correct?"

"Yes."

"OK, will you reserve it for me? I'm just a couple of miles away. I can be there in ten minutes."

"We need a credit card to reserve a room."

"OK, I have a Visa Card."

"What's the number?"

I read the number from the card.

"What is the name on the card?" I gave him my name.

"Expiration date?"

That's easy. But I know it will get tricky from here.

"What's the billing address?"

I answered his question, knowing I was in trouble.

"I live in Europe. It's a Dutch billing address."

"We don't take European money."

"It's an American credit card, from an American bank," I answered.

"Then what's your billing address?"

"It's in Europe."

"Then you are a foreigner."

"I'm an American. I just live in Europe."

"I need the billing address to verify the credit card."

I told him my European address. I spelled it slowly. I could hear him repeating it. I knew he was writing it. Then I waited. I could hear him entering the information by keyboard.

"What is your street address?"

I repeated it and spelled my street address. I could hear him typing.

"What is your zip code?"

"We don't use zip codes. We have post codes."

"Then give me your postcode."

I repeated my postcode.

"It is supposed to have five numbers. What are the letters for?"

"It is a European postcode. It's got two letters."

"Well that doesn't work. I need a zip code."

After several attempts, he couldn't input my address into his computer. The zip code and state fields don't recognize European addresses. He couldn't verify the credit card. Finally he gave up.

"I can't make a reservation without credit card verification. I can't reserve you a room."

"How many rooms are available for tonight?"

"What do you mean? How many rooms do you want."

"I mean, what are the chances they'll all be booked in the next ten minutes?"

"I don't know. But I can't guarantee you a room without a credit card."

"I'm ten minutes away. Do you think all your available rooms will be gone by the time I get there?"

"If you want to reserve a room, I need your address."

"I'll ride over to you and book a room in person."

"I cannot guarantee there'll be any rooms left."

"You know what? I'll take my chances. I'll see you in about ten minutes."

I collected my gear and rode to the motel. I stood face to face with the clerk and was lucky to book one of the last twelve rooms available. From $40 on the internet to $52.99 on the phone, with tax the single room cost $61.88. The pool was out of service for repairs. In the morning I found the free breakfast was corn flakes and powdered orange juice.

Similar conversations occurred in fueling stations. The process started at the pump when I inserted my credit card into the slot. I never knew if my transaction would go smoothly. If a pump did not require a zip code, I'd pump my gas and ride away. Some pumps required a zip code or some other U.S. identification. When I did not provide it, the pump locked up. There was never a 'Cancel', 'Back' or 'Delete' button. Without the required input, the pump would shut down. Then I'd walk into the store to speak with a clerk. The conversation quickly became circular:

"I'd like to fill up my tank and pay by credit card. The pump wants a zip code. I don't have one."

"What do you mean you don't have a zip code? Everybody has a zip code."

"I live in Europe. We use post codes."

"Then put in your post code."

"The machine doesn't recognize postcodes. They have letters in them."

"We don't take European credit cards."

"It's an American credit card."

"Then put in the zip code it's billed to."

"It's billed to me in Europe."

"We don't take European credit cards."

Around and around it went. The results varied, depending on the clerk, or store policy; they might authorize my credit card at the counter. Sometimes I paid cash, sometimes I left a deposit then came back for my change. Sometimes they charged my credit card prior to filling, then gave me a rebate for the unused amount. Once I gave up and rode to the station across the street. I stopped to buy gas about fifty times during the course of my trip. Each visit to the gas station was a new adventure with a tinge of insecurity. One attendant in New York yelled at me for underestimating my gas purchase. This required him to step into the office, open the cash drawer and give me change.

My motel hosts in Dodge City were a family of immigrants from India. I met the father when I checked in and saw his wife when I checked out. I didn't see any children, but I heard them behind the wall of the reception area. I presume it was the grandfather who I spoke with about the city.

"It's my first time in Dodge City. Where should I go to see some tourist stuff?"

"Dodge City is that way." He pointed.

It was July 3, the evening before Independence Day in the U.S. Usually there are fireworks to celebrate and sometimes concerts and parties.

"Are there fireworks tonight?"

"I don't know."

He did not know why I thought there might be fireworks. He didn't know about Independence Day.

"Do you have a map of the city?"

"No."

"Where can I find some tourist information?"

He pointed down the road then exited the reception area through the door behind the counter.

I walked from the reception area to my room. Heat rose in waves from the black asphalt of the parking lot. It was a dreary room. The air conditioner strained, rattled and hummed. The cheap furnishings were worn, stained and scarred. Even the bed linen was frayed. Heavy drapes, closed against the glare and heat of the bright sunshine, darkened the room. Even in the dim light cast by the low-watt bulb, I could make out the stains in the faded, worn carpet. The room smelled of mold and stale cigarette smoke.

The front door opened directly onto the black asphalt parking lot, radiating heat in the glaring sunshine. My neighbors stood in the shade under the second-floor balcony, wearing jeans and sleeveless t-shirts drinking beer. I braved the heat to look at the pool. I found a huge, green petri dish, thick with old algae. A superfluous "No swimming" sign hung on the gate at the top of the stairs. Back in my room, I sat on a squeaky wooden chair at a rickety desk and wrote in my journal.

On this revisit to my homeland, I came to appreciate some of the reasons why Americans live in a constant state of insecurity. The motel room pricing strategy is just one example that extends to almost all facets of American life. I had become accustomed to European price tags that include the sales tax. I learned not to trust any price or offer for any product or service in the U.S. When you inquire about a product or service you are a fish. The advertised price, for example for a hotel room, is the bait to get you on the hook. I experienced this with everything I bought in the U.S. – except gasoline at the pump. For some reason, the gas pump is the only reliable offer in America. You pay the price that is advertised at the gas pump. But this happens nowhere else, not at restaurants, service stations, or retail stores and not at motels.

There is always some kind of additional charge. There are fifty states and each one levies its own hidden charges. Sales taxes are the most common. They range from about 3 percent to over 7 percent. The tax rate is seldom displayed. In addition to the state sales taxes, many local government bodies levy other taxes. City taxes raise the sales tax rate, in some cases to over 10 percent. There are over eleven thousand sales tax jurisdictions in the U.S. None of the taxes appear on the product or service price tag.

Sales tax is not the only add-on charge that keeps Americans off balance. Motels add other fees to bump up prices, so your economical room is really no bargain. Some add cleaning fees.

There are "resort" fees that don't appear on the internet offer. I'm told these help to pay for the extras like the pool, health club and sometimes the coffee and Wi-Fi. Sometimes you pay fees for parking, early check-in or late check-out. I've seen fees for use of the room safe and the coffee maker. There are pet fees, extra person fees and environmental fees. None of them are listed anywhere on the price offer. They add up quickly and as I traveled across the country, I was never sure what I would be charged, no matter what the price tag or advertisement promised

Tipping in a restaurant is another example of a fee that doesn't appear on the product offer. I've become accustomed to the European perspective about meal prices. Isn't tipping just a way to deceive customers with a lower menu price? Why do Americans put up with the "tip tax"? The meal costs twenty dollars but you are expected to tip 15 or 20 percent. Why don't restaurants advertise the price as twenty-four dollars and pay the servers more?

Throughout my trip, focusing new eyes on my country, I discovered many examples of hidden charges for almost all products and services. The Americans I spoke with along the way, young and old, were surprised that I found this practice deceptive. They did not consider any of these price add-ons deceptive. They didn't consider it at all. They were fatalistic. What can you do? This is just the way it is. They didn't think it was necessary to include the sales tax or tip on a price offer. They are used to this sales system. They think it is a normal way to do business.

For the European me, never knowing the actual price for anything left me insecure. I never was able to comparison-shop because each vendor included different add-on fees. And the add-on fees covered varying services. For example, one motel charged a service fee, another a cleaning fee. Some of the service was cleaning. Both rooms left a tip envelope, one included a recommended tip amount, the other a range of percentages.

My only oasis in this wasteland of price confusion was the gas pump. Each gasoline vendor in every state, across the country and back, on highways and back roads, all posted accurate prices. Those were the prices they charged. There were no hidden, added taxes, no service fees, no environmental fees. I knew exactly what I would pay to fill up my tank. However, the process of accepting payment varied from vendor to vendor. At the gas pump, my insecurity took another form: identification. Each fuel vendor used its own method to verify credit card validity. I used my U.S. bank debit card for as many purchases as possible to avoid carrying a lot of cash. It also helped me keep accurate records.

For most face-to-face purchases, the debit card served me well. I used it in motels, restaurants, retail stores and gas stations. My credit card caused anxiety in two situations: at the gas pump and reserving a motel room by phone. American gas stations are calibrated for American credit cards with U.S. addresses and zip codes. I suffered from the lack of an American address for two months at the gas pump.

Without exception, I found it impossible to communicate my

European address to motel desk clerks by phone. They just didn't get it. In person, it works fine, I carried a business card with the info printed clearly. Over the phone something goes wrong. I tried giving an American address, but it doesn't work. They need an address that matches the billing address on the credit card. It gets even more complicated when I tell them my address is in Europe. They did not understand how a foreigner can have an American credit card.

I developed a split-image view of American life. One view was from my American background. This is the country I think of as home. It's where I grew up, attended school, worked and raised a family. The other view was by someone who has been living in a different county for a long time and traveling around the world. Since leaving America, I've come to know people from many countries and cultures. I realize my experience has changed my view of the world and of America. I reflected on Shakespeare's observation on our inability to be objective about ourselves. "The eye can't see itself, except by reflection in other surfaces." This summarized my evolving perspective.

I lived in America for most of my life. I did not recognize its cultural characteristics as unusual or special. I didn't even know they were different from other places in the world. But during my two-month road trip, I saw components of American culture that were distinctly different from other countries and cultures. Little things like how Americans use a knife and fork and tipping in restaurants and big things like how our concept of universal education does not translate to universal healthcare where in other countries the two go hand in hand.

One of the things my return has shown me is something of the insecurity that is woven into American culture. Product and service price practices are one example. In spite of how significant this aspect was to me, no one I spoke with during my visit home gave it any concern. It's just a way of life. It is so much part of the culture that it is all but invisible to the people who live with it.

I started to think about the American concepts of independence, freedom and self-sufficiency. These characteristics helped build a nation that spanned a continent. Pioneers spent months traveling at great risk across the vast lands that I rode over in just a few weeks. They packed all their worldly goods, risking their lives and those of their loved ones to seek their fortunes.

Rugged independence built a rich and prosperous country, family by family. Those who are willing to take risks reap the rewards. It's part of American culture to reward the bold, the brave and the successful. They climb to the top by their own sweat, brains and strength of character.

But during this trip I saw that this rugged independence is a two-edged sword. By lionizing the successful, we "sheepize" everyone else. The successful fight their way to the top. Everyone agrees they are entitled to the benefits. However, those who don't make it to the top are on their own. They are not entitled to the benefits of a rich country, no matter how hard they work or the sacrifices they make. The culture of success is also a culture of selfishness and fear. What are the options for people who become victims of a system that rewards only the rich? They become sheep, afraid to lose their little plot of ground. I began to think of America as a country of wolves and sheep with a few lions who run things.

* * *

The temperature was ninety-five degrees when I climbed on the motorcycle. I wore jeans, boots and a motorcycle jacket over a t-shirt for the ride to Boot Hill Museum. Shorts, sneakers and no jacket would have been infinitely more comfortable. But in spite of the heat, I kept my promise. It had become a promise to myself as much as to Hanneke. It represented my commitment to the precautionary principle, upside versus downside. The upside of dressing light was comfort in the heat. The downside was injury in a possible accident. Also, I promised Han I'd be responsible. I couldn't break that promise. But wow, was it hot!

The Boot Hill Museum was a straight shot three miles down Wyatt Earp Boulevard from my dump of a motel. I parked the bike near the front entrance, rolled up my jacket and bungeed it to the rear rack. It was heavy and hot. Even after the short ride, I was happy to be free of it. I climbed the wooden steps to the museum entrance. I glanced over my shoulder at the jacket on the back of the bike, gambling it would still be there when I returned. I rationalized;

"It was July, over 90 degrees. Who would want a used motorcycle jacket? Who would dare to steal it from the back of a Harley, even in Dodge City?"

I took the chance. The precautionary principle had loopholes.

The Boot Hill Museum comprises a small group of buildings, designed and decorated to portray an old Western town. The Boot Hill cemetery isn't really a cemetery. It's a replica of something that existed only in legend. But it's fun to walk through, imagine what once was, and read the tombstones describing how people died in the Old West. The people were real. Their deaths were real. The bodies are just not buried in the earth under Boot Hill. They are gone but at Boot Hill Museum they are not forgotten.

Walking through the historical collection and displays, visitors get an impression of life in the Old West. The museum displays more than sixty thousand pieces of Old West memorabilia; including tools, clothes, photos, letters, and an impressive collection of antique firearms.

Dodge City during the late 1800's to early 1900's was a dynamic, exciting and sometimes dangerous place. The Santa

Fe Trail carried thousands of immigrants from Missouri to New Mexico through Dodge. Native Americans and buffalo were among the casualties. Fort Dodge was the real center of old Dodge City. The army provided the only protection and legal redress for hundreds of miles. Museum displays recreate native life, wildlife, cowboys, cattlemen, and daily life in the Dodge City of 1880. A Hollywood display depicts photos of movie stars and television shows that imitated life in old Dodge City.

A small wooden building stands on the left side as you climb the boardwalk to the cemetery. It's the size of a free-standing walk-in closet. You can easily walk by without noticing. It is not distinctive. Its rough wood frame and walls are faded and worn. The sign reads Fort Dodge Jail. It was moved to the museum from Fort Dodge. That is the short version of the story. The longer version is more interesting.

The jail was owned by the federal government. It was unused and falling apart in old Fort Dodge. In 1953, the Dodge City Jaycees offered to buy the building. They wanted to display it as part of the new museum. However, because it was owned by the government, a technicality in the law prevented it from being donated or purchased. But sale or donation were not the only options.

An imaginative official assured the Jaycees that if the building were stolen, nobody would come looking for it. Therefore, one evening in November 1953, a group of masked cowboys on horseback raided Fort Dodge. They stole the jail. With log rollers, they picked up and dragged the old building about five and a half miles from Fort Dodge to the Boot Hill Museum. And there it still stands.

I smiled as I read the description of how the jail came to be part of the Boot Hill Museum collection. What fun it must have been for the men and women involved that night in November. They dressed up as cowboys, rode horses, used ropes and even wore bandannas over their faces like outlaws. They must have laughed and joked as they worked. The authorities smiled and looked the other way. Anonymous photos appeared in the local newspaper. Everyone involved was breaking the law. Everyone was having fun and saving a little piece of local history. It all worked out to the good. They showed that when people get together, they can overcome obstacles that governments cannot.

I didn't buy souvenirs; no space for those on this trip. I was relieved to find my jacket still attached to the back of my bike. In spite of the heat, I redonned my portable sauna and zipped up. On the way back to my motel, I bought a sandwich for dinner. It was still light when I returned. I spent the evening organizing my gear and my thoughts. Loud TV, crashing furniture and arguing upstairs neighbors kept me awake until after midnight.

CHAPTER 25: JAMES AND BART

Mars is causing climate change.

Fourth of July

Thursday morning, no red, white and blue streamers flew in the deserted motel breakfast nook. A sign on the wall instructed paying guests to serve themselves. I filled a Styrofoam bowl with corn flakes from a foggy plastic dispenser. I extracted a carton of milk and a pitcher of pale orange juice from the scratched, brown refrigerator. I carried my breakfast to a Formica-topped table. My yellow, plastic chair wobbled on spindly legs. The instant coffee and powdered OJ were too anemic to drink.

Exotic aromas drifted under the door behind the front desk. Presumably it led to the residence. My hosts were cooking breakfast. Hinges squeaked behind me. A woman with caramel skin and almond eyes peeked at me. She quickly closed the door before I could say hello. I ate in silence and considered my hosts. I thought about the son who refused to reserve the room without an address. The old man who didn't know or care that it was the Fourth of July. And the exotic woman who spied and hid. These people shimmered with a dingy aura of unhappiness. It seeped through the closed door and darkened my mood.

I turned to scan the reception area. The table tops were chipped and scratched. The information rack was sparsely furnished with faded, frayed and dog-eared tourist brochures. It was obvious, my hosts didn't like it here and didn't enjoy their job. I wondered about their story. What brought them from Asia to Dodge City and why did they stay? Why does anyone stay when they don't like their job, their life? Do people recognize their own unhappiness?

Two Hispanic men wearing jeans and work shirts crossed the parking lot and entered the office. One man appeared to be about fifty years old, gray haired and stocky. The other man was younger and thinner, so perhaps they were father and son. We nodded to each other. They busied themselves preparing their meals, selected a table and began to eat.

I discovered that their rented truck was parked outside the office. They were on their way to Los Angeles from Chicago with a load of furniture. They expected to arrive tomorrow and pick up a load in LA before driving back. That way they got paid both ways.

"You are driving today, on the Fourth of July?" I asked.

"Holiday don't matter. We get a flat rate for the load. Don't matter what day it is." The older of the two said.

"You came from Chicago yesterday? How long did that take?"

"We had a problem, had to switch trucks. We got here last night at three in the morning."

"It's seven o'clock. You mean you got four hours of sleep and you're driving to LA today?"

The older man pointed at the other. "He's the driver. I sleep."

The other man smiled. He pointed with his thumb. "He's the boss."

"And you're going to LA today?"

"If the truck don't break down," the younger man said. They both laughed.

My ride from Tahoe was leisurely in comparison. They'd ride further today than I did in a week. "How long will you spend in LA?"

Older man: "Just long enough to pick up a load. We save money if we don't spend it all on hotel rooms. Sometimes we sleep in the truck."

"And you're driving right back to Chicago?

"No, first we go to Dallas, drop that load, pick up another, then Chicago."

"That's a lot of driving."

"It's our job. We're glad to have the work."

The younger man added, "We'll be back in Chicago by next weekend. We can spend it with our family."

"You two are related?"

"My uncle," said the younger man, nodding.

The older man slapped the other on the shoulder. "Call me boss." They both laughed.

The younger man got up to leave. The older man sipped his black coffee. "*Adios,*" said the younger man as he headed out the door.

"He's a good boy." The older man smiled.

"I help him drive sometimes if it's a long way." He pointed across the parking lot.

"That your bike?"

"Yes."

"Nice. Where you headed?" He asked.

"I'm going east. I'm on my way back from California."

"You going a long way too."

"But I'm taking my time, enjoying the ride."

"We enjoy the ride. We talk, listen to music, read. It's OK."

"Do you miss your family?"

"It's OK too. They happy when we get back. We're happy too." He smiled. "Gotta go. Lotta miles to cover today. You too, I expect."

I nodded. We shook hands. His nephew was behind the wheel. The uncle walked around the front, opened the passenger door and climbed in. I watched as they drove off.

I didn't care if they were U.S. citizens. It didn't seem to matter. They worked as freelancers, on consignment for an independent trucking company. They were paid a flat rate to take a load from one part of America to another. Furniture, car parts, fruit, they carried whatever they were told. They could pocket the money they saved on expenses. There were no luxuries on the road and few motels and food stops. They snacked on junk food in the cab. Unlike me, they traveled the highways to save time. When there was trucking work, they made as many trips as they could. When there wasn't, they did landscape or construction, whatever they could to feed their families. In spite of their hard life, these men were happy. Without realizing it, my melancholy had evaporated, and I had absorbed their energy.

I dropped my room key into the box on the counter. My hosts never made an appearance. I donned my jacket as I walked to my waiting bike. I felt heat rising from the pavement through my boots. It was seven-thirty and already warm. I felt no guilt when I revved the beast out of the parking lot and onto the highway. I was happy to see this motel shrink in my rear-view mirror. This place needed a little waking up. I rolled east, with the question of happiness on my mind; the motel family's, the truckers' and mine.

Route 50 in Kansas is a major highway for fast cars and faster eighteen wheelers. I chose U.S. Route 400 east out of Dodge, hoping for a respite from the traffic, wind and noise. The road was straight and flat, with no natural barrier to block the wind. A sign beside the road announced Pratt Sandhills to the north. The land was flat to the horizon. I could see no hills.

Wind swept across the road, buffeting my bike. Purple thunderstorms crossed the highway ahead from north to south. About thirty-five miles east of Wichita, I stopped at a Subway sandwich shop.

I sipped coffee at a table by the window to keep one eye on my bike. I looked over my map. My eyes wandered around the restaurant. Sometimes you recognize someone with a special spark of life. They exude a child-like quality, a joy of living, a wonder at the world. Every day is an adventure. They love life and it's contagious. They bring smiles to others just by being themselves. The motel family in Dodge darkens the world around them. Other people brighten the world and spread joy. The Mexican truckers did that for me at breakfast.

I felt that happiness emanating from a young girl behind the counter at the Subway sandwich shop in El Dorado, Kansas. For some reason, she caught my attention, and I watched her from my seat by the window. Her bright eyes saw everything. They never stopped moving except when she was talking to someone, then they were intensely focused. From across the room I could feel her energy, enthusiasm and joy. She was precocious with a lively sense of humor.

She talked and joked with her colleagues behind the counter. She smiled easily and was relaxed with customers. I gathered she was new to the job, receptive to instructions and eager to learn. Maybe this was her first job. She was young enough: early high school age, old enough for some people to have become cynical. But in my imagination, she would always be a child of wonder bringing joy to the people she meets. I wondered what her future held. What gives people that special spark? What extinguishes it? I silently wished her good fortune on my way out the door.

I arrived at Cross Timbers State Park in the early afternoon with half a cold-cuts sandwich in my saddlebag and three bottles of water. I stopped at the entrance to the park and spoke to the ranger through the glass. Here, I encountered another American cultural oddity.

Ranger: "What's your social security number?"

Me: "Why do you need my social security number to register for a campsite?"

"Because the State of Kansas will not let you use a state facility if you owe child support."

"What if I'm OK with child support, but I'm a felon?"

"We don't have access to that database." The ranger answered, without a smile.

I provided the number.

The humidity was so thick, I could feel it on my face. The smell of wet mud permeated the air. I selected a campsite on high ground, well away from the lake in case of more rain. This was a dramatic climate change from the dry western deserts.

I backed my bike into the campsite and set it on the kickstand. I quickly completed the routine of unpacking and setting up my tent on the grassy lawn. I spread out my gear and sleeping bag on the grass to dry in the sun. Then I changed into shorts and sandals and walked down the hill to explore the park by foot.

I followed the campground road to the Toronto Reservoir. Heavy spring rains and summer thunderstorms had flooded the south section of the campground. The tops of oak trees sprouted like mangroves from flood water. The shore roads were washed out and submerged, inaccessible. Superfluous "Road Closed" barriers blocked gravel roads under three feet of water. Picnic tables with only the tops visible were the only sign of the drowned campsites. The lake shore was scattered with tree trunks, branches and piles of rubble from the flood. Dead tree stumps and logs blocked the road and driftwood littered campsites that had drained but not dried.

Recent heavy rains discouraged park use. I explored the campground as far as the submerged boat ramp, then walked back to my campsite. The waterfront sites bordering the reservoir were flooded so visitors congregated at the campsites on high ground. Fewer than half the dry campsites in the park were occupied. A tow-behind RV was parked across the road from my site. The occupants were not at home.

While I busied myself at my table, a young man on a bike pedaled in and parked at the site opposite mine. Shortly after that, a man and his wife in a pick-up truck parked in front of the camper at the other site.

I walked across the road to say hello to my bike-riding neighbor. He was sitting at his picnic table, boiling water on a one-burner butane stove. He invited me to sit down. I took the bench on the other side of the table. He broke up some spaghetti and dropped it into the pan, cut up a tomato and added it to the boiling water. His one-man tube tent pointed into the wind and his bike leaned against the picnic table.

As his meal simmered, James stirred the pot and told his story.

"I'm from South Bend, Indiana. I finished my PhD in Physics in May. I've always wanted to take a long bike trip. This seemed like a good time to do it."

"It's hard to get time off for a long trip. What's your job?" I asked.

"That's why I can go now. I don't have a job. After I graduated, I submitted a bunch of applications. I'm waiting to hear."

"How far are you riding?"

"As far as five thousand dollars will take me. I'm headed to San Francisco. Then I'll loop north to Oregon and Washington. If I get a good job offer while I'm on the road, I'll go back. Otherwise, I'll just keep going. I've got no return ticket and I don't mind biking west, then all the way back home."

"What will you do when you get back?"

"Look for work if it doesn't find me on the road. My girlfriend is a single mom. She wants to get her degree too. We'll figure out how to make that work."

James' bike and gear were a study in efficiency with side saddlebags, front-frame-mounted waterproof containers and a handlebar pack with a waterproof, see-through map holder. He told me the bike and gear weighed about a hundred pounds.

"It's not an RV but it takes a lot of pasta to push," James said.

"If no job offers materialize, what will you do when you get back to South Bend?"

"I plan to volunteer to support Pete Buttigieg. Do you know who he is?"

I shook my head, no.

"Buttigieg resigned as mayor to campaign in the Democratic Primary for President. I believe in his platform and – who knows, maybe something (like a job) will come of it."

"Sorry, I have to admit, I don't know Buttigieg."

"He's the first openly gay candidate for President."

James paused as if waiting for an argument. I waited for him to continue. He seemed relieved when he did.

"He's in favor of national healthcare and financing for university students. He supports the Paris Climate Agreement and campaign finance reform limiting lobby and political action committee money. He's also opposed to separating immigrant parents from their children and of course the wall."

"You know, I've always wondered why health care is such a volatile issue in the U.S. I live in The Netherlands. We have a national healthcare system. It's affordable and it seems to work pretty well," I said.

"People say that system won't work in America. They say Americans have a unique culture that functions best with a private, for-profit medical system. That's bullshit."

James was stirring his pasta faster as he grew enthusiastic.

"Did you know that America has one of the least effective and most expensive healthcare systems in the world?

"No."

He continued: "It's true. And Americans believe it's the best. It isn't. It's set up for profit. And it hurts everyone so a few can make big money. It's about greed, not health care or civil rights, or free choice or any of that crap. It is a chaotic financing system that's profitable, but not efficient or effective. The chaos is by design. There is no oversight of medical costs, no one responsible for keeping prices down. So they keep going up."

"Well, I know people here pay a lot more than I do for health insurance," I said.

"You better not get me going about it. It's a real sore point for me. And I hope Buttigeig can do something about it. And I'll help if I can."

"I'll look up Pete Buttigieg when I get back."

"He's a good guy, very popular in South Bend."

I left James to his meal and walked to my campsite. A little later, I visited the neighbor occupying the campsite next door, where I heard an entirely different story. He attracted my attention with the two big flags flying from the back of his all-terrain-wheeled pick-up truck. A red, white and blue American flag was fixed to one side of his truck bed. I didn't recognize the other flag.

I walked over to say hello and introduce myself. We shook hands. Bart and his wife spend every Fourth of July holiday at the park to celebrate Turner Days. He competes in the annual fishing tournament, and they watch the fireworks display over the reservoir. Their home town is forty miles away. They were high school sweethearts who grew up together, married and lived in the same town all their lives. Bart is a truck driver. He thinks James is crazy and a road hazard. He's shorter than James, stocky with dark hair and a beard. James is thin, with short, thinning hair. Both men are in their early thirties.

I briefly explained that I lived out of the country and did not know the meaning of the blue and white "MAGA" flag.

Bart: "Not everyone likes it. But I'm proud to be a Trump supporter. It stands for: "Make America Great Again". A lot of people support Trump but are afraid of criticism. I'm not. I think he's doing the right thing. I'm all for the wall. We can't afford to support all those immigrants. I know he's not popular. A lot of people don't like him, but he's turning this country around. We need somebody to stand up for American ideals."

His wife did not get up to meet me or say hello. She hardly turned her head while I spoke with her husband. I didn't get a good look at her. She sat by their campfire in a plastic lawn chair, holding what I assume was a baby wrapped in a blanket. Two mongrel dogs sniffed at my feet as we talked, beside Bart's new, eight-cylinder Dodge Ram.

He continued: "I know he does things people don't like, but even the people who say they don't like him know he's right. He's putting Americans back to work. He's protecting our borders and he's stopping the Democrat tax give-aways, like Obama Care and environmental regulations that are bankrupting our country."

"Is there a big illegal immigrant problem in Kansas?" I asked.

"Not yet, but there will be if it's not stopped. There are ten million illegal immigrants living in America now and more than a thousand new ones sneak across the border every day. A hundred thousand came in last month. They come here with nothing and expect us to support them. Half of them are criminals, illiterate, poor with no skills. They claim to be refugees."

"I spoke with someone who said immigrants have to pay someone to get across the border. It takes them years to save enough. Seems like they are pretty motivated," I said.

"They just want to live for free. If they were skilled, or educated, they could make it in their own country. Well, I'm not going to pay for it. Free medical, free schools, free housing. The Democrats want to give away this country. Trump wants to save it for Americans." Bart answered.

"Didn't we take it from the first Americans? I mean, aren't we all immigrants?"

"That was hundreds of years ago when this country was practically empty. There's a big difference."

"You mentioned Obama Care. Isn't that national medical coverage for everyone? What's wrong with that?"

"It's socialized medicine. It's another Democratic give-away. Trump is going to stop it."

"But what about people who can't afford insurance? What can they do?"

"They can do what they do now. They go to the emergency ward in the hospital and get free treatment."

"Free?"

Bart continued: "You get a bill, but you don't have to pay it. And they can't do anything about it. It's the law. If I don't pay, my insurance gets canceled, or they sue me. But if you don't have any money, like you're an illegal immigrant, then you're golden. Your kid is a U.S. citizen because he's born here, and you get to stay free and don't have to pay the hospital bill. Trump is going to stop that.

"Because, who's paying for it? The working man, that's who. Me. And there are fewer of us now than ever. Fewer people to pay for more people getting free rides. Figure it out. It doesn't add up."

"If somebody goes to the emergency room, then doesn't pay the bill, how do the doctors get paid? The nurses? Hospitals have expenses. How are they covered?" I asked.

"I guess the federal or state government pays the bill."

"So taxpayers pay for it."

"See what I mean. We pay for everything." Suddenly he switched topics:

"Global warming, that's a lot of bullshit. Nobody proved that's real. There's no real proof that it's happening. And even if it is, that doesn't prove man's causing it – or can fix it. A famous scientist, I forget his name, said an alignment of the planets is causing it. It happens every five or ten thousand years. It causes changes in weather. It's temporary. It's happened before.

"There's nothing we can do about it. These international environmental agreements are just an excuse, a communist plot to strangle the American economy."

"Are you saying global warming is caused by an alignment of the planets? Mars is causing climate change?" This was not the first time I'd heard this about climate change.

"I know it's not a popular opinion. But I'm not afraid to have an unpopular opinion. Galileo said the world was round. That was unpopular. He was criticized for it, but he was right. Someday people will know I'm right."

"Galileo didn't . . ." I started, then stopped.

"What?"

"So are you saying that climate change isn't happening? Or it is but man is not causing it?" I asked.

"Both, I haven't seen warmer winters in the last five years or less snow. Even if it is getting warmer, isn't warmer better? So what does a couple of degrees matter? If you ask me, if global warming is happening, and I'm not saying it is, it would make things better."

He walked over to the back of his truck and spread out the blue-and-white MAGA flag.

"Nobody's going to take it from us. Not the Russians, not the tree huggers, the immigrants and not the goddam Democrats."

I looked over at his wife, just a few feet away, staring silently into the fire holding the baby. I wondered if she shared her husband's opinions. I hadn't been introduced and she did not move or say anything. Dusk was settling in. The air was getting moist. The mosquitos were waking up and my gear was still spread out on the grass around my campsite.

"Well, I have to get back, get organized and get some food. You certainly gave me something to think about. It was nice to meet you. Enjoy your long weekend."

He wished me a good trip and walked back to stand beside his wife and baby. They watched me walk across the road to my campsite.

I pushed my sleeping bag and pad into the tent to protect them from the damp evening air, then sat on the bench at my table to write in my journal. The darkness and mosquitos coerced me into seeking shelter. I crawled into the tent and continued my notes from the day's conversations. The dramatic difference between my two neighbors was striking. The two men were about the same age, yet worlds apart. If I had met only one of them, my conclusions would have been simpler. Having met both, how could I reconcile their views and describe a "typical American" to my Dutch friends? Which one represents America? Of course, they both do. No country is homogenized and no one person can serve as the representative for a society. But these guys seemed totally different.

James was a Democrat, Bart a Republican. James pedaled a bike; Bart drove big rigs. They didn't share a view of what America should be, how America should be governed or who should govern it. They didn't agree on who should live there nor how they should live. They didn't agree on the wall, guns, religion or climate change. They didn't agree on gay marriage, the death penalty or abortion. They didn't even agree on who should use the public roads. Bart considered James on his bike, a road hazard. While I was there, they didn't share a conversation. James stayed on his site and Bart kept to his.

I yawned, put away my notebook, turned off the flashlight hanging over my head and settled in for the night. It was a hot night, so I stretched out on top of my sleeping bag. Just as I was dropping off to sleep, I felt the uncomfortable, familiar tickle of an insect crawling on my stomach. I slapped it. It didn't move. In the dark, I used my fingers to find it and pick it off my skin. It still would not move. I had left my sleeping bag and pad on the grass during the day.

Warm wet weather is ideal for insects, and ticks love the tall, damp grass. A tick must have hitched a ride on my bag when I dragged it into the tent. Its heat-seeking radar had found me.

I sat up on top of my bag, groped for the flashlight hanging over my head and turned it on. In the wavering shadows cast by the slowly spinning light, I found the tick. It had not yet settled in for its meal. I picked it off with my thumb and forefinger. I pinched it and held it in place with my right hand. If you know about ticks, you know they are almost impossible to crush by hand. I didn't waste my time trying to pinch it to heaven. Instead, I unzipped the screen door of my tent. I pushed my hand outside the tent and flicked the tick out into the darkness then quickly zipped the tent closed.

I settled down to cool off and get back to sleep. I took a drink of water from my bottle. I lay on my back, congratulating myself on finding the tick before it sank its blood-sucking fangs into me. Then a disturbing thought occurred to me.

"What are the chances only one tick got in?"

I imagined a herd of silent, prowling arachnids, searching blindly inside my tent, seeking my flesh. I untied the flashlight, held it in my mouth and began my hunt. It is a small tent, but the search took most of an hour. I turned my bag inside out, examined every inch. I pulled open my sleep sack. It is dark brown, a good background if you're searching for butterflies, not so good when you're hunting for ticks. I squinted at it in the shadows and passed my hand over its silky surface. I peered at and carefully felt every square inch of the tent floor, under my sleeping pad and all my gear bags and clothes.

"No ticks."

"OK, maybe there was only one."

"Do you really believe that?"

"What else can I do?"

"Lyme disease is curable if it's diagnosed early."

After a fruitless search and with nothing else to do, I gave up, turned off the flashlight and laid down on top of my bag. In the dark, I listened for the sound of tick hoofbeats. I heard none and again, started to drop off. Then I felt the familiar tickle again, this time on my neck.

"Shit."

"Told you."

"Shut up. We have to do it all over again."

It was a repeat of the prior hour, pinch the tick, flick it out the door, then mount a search and again, find nothing. I have no idea what time it was when I finally gave up. I don't think I slept more than an hour or two and was happy to see the tent brighten with the rising sun after the night of the ticks.

In the morning light, I inspected my body for uninvited guests and found none. I hoped I had found the only two who sneaked into the tent, or only two had found me. Neither enjoyed a meal. Lyme disease takes a few weeks to present symptoms. By then, I would be back in Holland. I resigned myself to a Dutch national healthcare system-sponsored Lyme disease treatment sometime in the near future.

CHAPTER 26: STORM

*Put on your big boy pants and
get your ass back on the road.*

Friday, July 5

At seven-fifteen when I rode away from Cross Timbers State Park, the weather was overcast and steamy. I chose a route that would take me south of Kansas City. I wandered onto the southern truck route across Kansas. I traveled through treeless farmland that stretched to the horizon, buffeted by walls of wind from the passing trucks delivering produce that fed a country.

I rode through the heart of America's Bread Basket. I rode across the southern expanse of Kansas from west to east, through vast fields of crops swaying in the ceaseless wind. I passed tractor dealerships, feed stores, truck and tractor repair shops and miles of irrigation equipment. The whole region was dedicated to agriculture. In his dystopian classic, Aldous Huxley described a future in which the middle of the country was a huge farm preserve, fenced and guarded by the military to secure the country's food supply. This Brave New World of industrial agriculture was overwhelming.

I felt very much an outsider, an interloper in this working community, a tourist and an intruder. I rode a toy on a highway built for powerful commercial vehicles driven by hard-working people. Dusty, dented pick-up trucks, tractors, backhoes, bulldozers on trailers and dumps, horse trailers, pig, cattle and corn haulers, coal, oil and propane tankers, lumber, feed and construction trucks, big-box eighteen wheelers blew by me on their way to America's meat-packing plants, grain-processing factories, supermarkets and grocery stores. A billboard beside the road advised: "Choose life, your mother did."

The road surface bounced and jarred my spine with its patches and bumps. The pavement was scarred, grooved and slick with oil. The concrete and asphalt patches were poorly mated. My tires squirmed and twisted on long, thin, black snakes of tar. Ahead, the sky was darkening. In addition to the almost constant buffeting from the passing big rigs, a wet wind smeared my face shield. Low, purple clouds raced to intercept me.

My destination, Mark Twain National Forest, was a hundred miles away. Rain was threatening and getting closer with every mile. I deceived myself with optimism, hoping it would hold off till I reached my destination and was safely inside my tent. Reality told me otherwise. The storm was closing in fast.

The familiar damp, sweet, earthy scent of an approaching storm grew by the second. Sometimes rain starts slowly and spits little drops, it's a mist, maybe a drizzle. Sometimes the drizzle fizzles and fades to humidity. Sometimes the mist builds strength, gets heavier, turns to rain. Sometimes a motorcycle rider has time to consider options; keep going or look for a place to pull over and wait out the storm. This rain didn't start with a mist or a drizzle, it started with an angry downpour. The clouds opened and dumped an ocean of water on the road. Ever the optimist, I thought, "Maybe it'll pass by quickly."

Wrong, the downpour increased. The sky darkened. Water poured down my helmet, obscured my vision, dripped inside my face shield and streaked across my windshield. Water sprayed off my tires, up onto my legs and soaked my pants. The other vehicles on the road, shrouded in the downpour like ghosts, sprayed water that flooded over me.

The road was a blur. I swung my face shield up, out of the way, squinted to see. I leaned forward and low behind the windshield to protect my eyes from the fat, heavy, sixty-mile-an-hour bullet rain drops. I slowed. The angry storm turned noon into midnight. Water flowed down my rearview mirrors. Fuzzy headlights approached from behind. I was a rolling roadblock. I prayed the drivers behind could see me through the rain. I feared a collision, skidding crash or a hydroplane slide into a ditch.

A car passed. It might have been red. The taillights shimmered and glowed. Then it immediately cut in front of me, throwing a waterfall of tire spray into my face. For a few seconds I was blind. I slowed, then slowed more. It was too dark to see the speedometer. I didn't need it to know that I was traveling too slowly. Sightless in the deluge and tire wash, I was down to road survival basics. I followed tail lights. The lane markers were obscured. Directional signs were invisible. Lightning cracked jagged arrows through walls of water. Thunder boomed and the world trembled.

I had to get off the road. I was an accident waiting to happen. But there was no haven in sight, no sheltering overpass, no escape exit and the berm beside the pavement was a rushing river of muddy water. I was about seventy-five miles from my goal, but I couldn't go on like this. I was soaked to the skin. Staying alive became my single priority. The torrential rain, heavy traffic, submerged road surface and almost total lack of visibility were a deadly combination. I began to write my obituary in my mind. It opened with a headline,

"Too stupid to stop"

Finally, I spotted an exit sign through the sheeting rain. I almost passed it in the darkness. The words were obscured. Maybe it offered some relief, possibly shelter until the rain stopped. I scooted right onto the exit ramp, too late to use my turn signals. I banked right, surprised my tires held the road. I slowed and cruised up the ramp.

It did not lead to a town. It was a side road that ended in an industrial park and a professional building parking lot. I pulled into the parking lot; thankful it was paved. A river of water ran across the asphalt into a drainage culvert. Below, a swelling retention pond foamed with white water rushing in from four sides. There was no shelter in the parking lot. I sat on my bike in the rain and took stock.

On the plus side, I was still alive. I was no longer risking my life on the highway. From my perch above, the traffic didn't look as busy as I thought. Maybe because I was not blocking it anymore or maybe because I was safely parked out of danger. It also didn't seem to be raining so hard. Again, maybe it just felt that way because I was no longer riding straight into the storm. Rain always seems heavier when you are riding. A road sign ahead offered hope: "Lebanon, MO 10 miles". If I could make it that far, I could stop and rent a motel room. I decided to try ten more miles.

"This is going to be tough."

"Wah, Wah! Put on your big boy pants and get your ass back on the road."

Still I was reluctant. It was safer to talk to myself than to get back onto the highway. Low, misty clouds obscured the horizon. A new wave of lightning cracked the sky and rolling thunder echoed through the valley. I looked up, into the falling rain. There was no place in the sky to imagine the sun breaking through. The rain wasn't going to stop.

"You can't sit here forever."

"I know I have to move forward."

"It is dangerous."

"I'll be careful."

"What's your plan?"

"Don't get killed."

"Good plan."

I pushed the starter. For the first time the engine hesitated. It seemed Harley didn't want to do this either. Then it coughed and finally caught. We rolled down the ramp through the downpour to merge into the twin rivers of water and traffic. It was a ten-mile battle of endurance and patience. It seemed to take forever, but the Lebanon exit sign finally came into view. I circled off the highway, up the ramp and turned into the service complex. It included a fuel station, general store and a McDonald's restaurant. I stopped beside the pumps. When the tank was filled, I sloshed into the restaurant for shelter and food. While waiting for my burger and fries, I asked Google to help me find a motel.

I was dripping from head to foot. Water pooled under my

stool and onto the table where I searched for a motel on my foggy phone. I made squishing sounds when I walked. Water squirted out of the grommet holes in the sides of my boots. My jeans were pasted to my legs and black with water. Three layers of weather-proof motorcycle rain gear had failed to keep my shirt dry. I was soaked to the skin. My hair dripped water onto my phone screen. I used my sodden handkerchief and paper napkins to wipe my wet face. The skin on my fingers was pale white, wet and wrinkled. Little rain rivers flowed down the restaurant windows. Gusting wind blew the rain sideways. The window rivers shifted like tides. My stoic Harley waited bravely outside under inadequate cover.

While I dripped onto my fries, I found a Holiday Inn Express nearby offering a room for fifty dollars. I called to make a reservation and got through to the front desk.

"Yes, we have a room available. The price is $129."

"What about the $50 price offered on the internet?"

"That must be an old offer."

"Why is it still on the internet?"

"Well, if you can find a room for that, good luck. Do you want the room?"

"No thanks."

Even soaked, cold and tired I could not surrender to this blatant bait-and-switch extortion. I continued my search and munched cold fries, while the pool of rainwater beneath me got larger. I gazed out the window at my gear, bungeed to the bike and absorbing water like a sponge.

Another motel nearby offered a $59 smoking room for $65 plus tax for a total of $71.44.

"I'll take it."

"OK, What's your name and address?"

"My name is Robert Barra. Can I just fill out the rest of the form when I get there?"

"OK, but I can't reserve the room without a credit card."

"Do you have rooms available?"

"Some."

"OK, I'll be there in five minutes."

I finished the last of my cold fries with trembling fingers and shivered as I climbed back into my rain-soaked jacket. I zipped it up and squished back outside to my dripping bike. I recalled the longing look from the RV driver in Vail, Colorado as I rode off into the sunshine. Nobody gave me longing looks as I rode out of the McDonalds parking lot in Lebanon, Missouri.

The motel was five minutes across the highway and down the ramp. I parked under the shelter of the reception area to check in. It was one-thirty in the afternoon. The clerk allowed me to park the bike under the overhead shelter near the office. We had a brief conversation.

"This isn't supposed to be happening today," said the desk clerk. "The weather report said scattered showers."

"Yeah, it made my life more interesting," I admitted.

"There is a laundry room down the corridor. You can dry out your stuff if you want. It takes quarters."

"Does it have a coin machine?"

"Yes."

"Great. I guess I have a new plan for the day."

"Have a good one."

I spent the afternoon inspecting, washing, drying and then repacking my clothes and gear. Hot air discharged from a ventilator high on the right side of the ice machine in the laundry room. I removed the laces and used them to hang my dripping boots from the air vent. All afternoon, I shuttled back and forth from my room and fed quarters to the hungry machines. By evening, the rain had stopped, and my gear and clothes were clean and dry. Any concerns I had about tick hitchhikers were washed and air-dried away.

During a break in the rain, I walked to Dowd's Catfish House and treated myself to a rare steak and a beer. In the evening, I repacked my clothes and gear while warm, dry air from the ice machine flowed over my boots. I was feeling down. Maybe the bad weather had gotten inside me too. I felt chilled and damp from the day's ride. I was tired from a month on the road. I felt very far from Han in the Netherlands, Mike, in California and Matt in Massachusetts.

CHAPTER 27: HYPOCRITE

*The crazies and fringe groups
have taken over the country.*

Saturday, July 6

By morning the rain had stopped. I collected my warm, dry boots from the laundry and began a ride that took me on a meandering path over quiet county roads through towns with names like Sleeper, Gascozark, Buckhorn, Devils Elbow and Doolittle. I had no idea where I was or where I was headed but the day was gorgeous, and the road was paved.

I weaved along routes marked TT, 645, M, 709, Z, AA, V, 713 and Y that offered no destination, compass direction or hint where the next town might be. Cell towers had not been introduced to the neighborhood, so my phone and navigation were useless and I didn't care. I zigzagged through the rolling wilderness maze, up, down, through and around. The forest views, river crossings and quiet, remote lakes were peaceful and serene. The weather was mild. I enjoyed the aimless motion and hum of the powerful motor with no concern for a goal or destination.

I was riding through hilly country, winding roads threaded through the forest. I followed the contour of the earth all morning, down, up and around long sweeping curves, enveloped by and emerging from the soft morning fog. Caution signs warned of sharp left and right switchback turns.

Posted speed limits were too conservative for my mood. I pushed faster, accelerating, leaning into the curves, drifting to the center to glimpse the way ahead. I was alone on ribbon roads, the only traveler through the forest faeryland. The morning evaporated in the joy of the ride.

"Have you thought about fuel? We've gone about 150 miles."

"I just wish I had a clue where I was or what direction I was headed."

"I'm pretty sure we're still in Missouri."

"It feels like we're riding west."

The sun hid behind an overcast sky, on State Highway Y, I could only guess my direction.

"There's a sign."

"Y goes left, V heads straight. Maybe there'll be fuel when we get to A."

I picked at random. Six miles further on, I found the Cherryville General Store and Post Office. I rolled the bike into the gravel parking lot, tossed my plastic kickstand plate on the ground, set it in place with my boot then climbed off and stretched.

A rough-planked farmer's porch with a wide railing spanned the front of the old building. Weathered steps led to a screen door that squealed on rusty hinges. My boots echoed on the wide pine floorboards. The shop was roughly divided; to the left, the general store, straight ahead a three-table restaurant and to the right, a post office. The postman lurked in the shadows behind a caged window.

I walked directly forward to an unoccupied table, took off my jacket and hung it over the back of a chair. The air smelled subtly of cinnamon, coffee and bacon. A boy of about ten years old played a hand-held video game while his father looked on. At the other table a thin man sipped coffee, reading a newspaper. All three were wearing clean, worn, work clothes and baseball caps.

A woman wearing an apron invited me to help myself to coffee. I nodded a greeting as I passed the boy and his father and to the other man who looked up from his paper. A full coffee pot simmered on a hot plate in front of the counter. I selected one from a mismatched collection of chipped, porcelain mugs and poured. The lady at the grill offered to cook me breakfast. That was how she asked, "Can I cook you some breakfast?" More than an invitation, it felt like a generous offer and a welcome at the same time. I gratefully accepted.

I sipped my coffee as I strolled through the general store. It was an eclectic collection, no doubt the result of long years of serving local needs. I browsed the shelves of canned and packaged foods, functional clothes and bins of bulk goods, onions, potatoes and flour. A brass cash register with ivory keys perched on a rough wooden service counter waiting patiently as it had for the last hundred years.

The cook scooped butter from a tub and dropped it onto the griddle. Steam sizzled off the hot surface and disappeared inside the stainless-steel hood. I sipped my coffee till she delivered my eggs, home fries, homemade sausages and biscuits with a friendly smile. I spent the next few minutes savoring the best breakfast I'd had since, Hell, I don't remember when.

I eavesdropped while the men and the cook, who I suspect was also the owner, discussed local events. From what I gathered; the town had closed the elementary school. Starting in September, all the Cherryville school children would be bussed to a nearby town. The older children were already bussed to high school.

The screen door screeched on rusty hinges. A general store customer wandered in, the door banging closed behind her. The discussion ended when the waitress/owner/cook glided across the room to greet the shopper. I helped myself to a second cup of coffee and introduced myself to the man with the newspaper. I asked if I could join him, and he invited me to sit down.

Henry was a truck driver, local not long distance. He wore a blue, denim uniform with his name sewn in yellow on the shirt pocket. He was tall and thin with quiet, strong, thick hands and forearms. He spoke slowly, if a little sadly but clear enough so I could hear every word.

"It's bad news about cuts in school services all over the county. They're shutting down art and music but keeping basketball and volleyball. Class sizes are goin' up because they're laying off teachers. They're gonna close the local elementary school and bus the kids twelve miles to Steelville."

The cook stopped on her way to the kitchen and added, "Next year'll be the first in living memory we have no school in town."

I asked why.

Henry explained: "It's about the mines. There's lead in this part of Missouri. In the seventies the mines put a lot of money into the local towns. People moved here for the work. Towns grew, schools too. There was plenty of money. Now the mines are fighting taxes. While it is going on, years in court, the towns don't have money to pay for services. So they fire teachers and close schools.

"Half the people around here don't have anything, no money, no house, no jobs so they don't pay taxes. The kids got free lunch at school, breakfast too. For some, if it wasn't for the schools, they wouldn't get any. Now, the mine owners don't want to pay. So half the town is paying for the other half.

"What are you going to do? Nobody wants to pay more taxes. So there's thirty-five kids in a class. Teachers don't have time. So they pass kids, just to move them on. What kind of education is that?

"And all these people voted for Trump. Why? Because they thought he was going to turn the economy around and get them jobs. What are they going to have when it's done? They'll have no jobs, no schools, no roads. I don't know what's going to come of it."

Henry gave me directions to a nearby campground and a fuel station in Steelville. I thanked him for his time, bid him goodbye and rode away with the feeling I was deserting them.

I found the campground halfway up a mountain in a southern Missouri pine forest at about three o'clock in the afternoon. The sun had burned away the cloud cover and the day had turned sticky hot. I rode a slow circle around the eight-site campground. I settled on a site that overlooked Red Bluff Hollow and the Root River. A tow-behind RV occupied the adjacent site.

I changed to shorts and sandals, then set up my tent. I strung a line between the trees to hang my sleeping bag in the sunshine. I explored the campsite on foot. It offered a pit toilet, no shower and no drinking water. Mountains to the west shadowed the valley. Far below, a river wound through the lowland and disappeared behind the hills. I walked a wide circle around the campground to search for a path to the river.

A river swim would be perfect on this hot day. However it was not meant to be. All the routes toward the river led to one great, steep cliff. No doubt, spring runoff formed an impressive waterfall. Hot and sweaty after several unsuccessful attempts to discover a route to the river valley, I accepted defeat and returned to my campsite. I settled down to enjoy the sunny day, warm weather, write in my journal and read. I peeled off my damp t-shirt, hung it in the sun and unpacked my pipe, pen and notebook.

My neighbors arrived about an hour later. They drove a brightly polished, white four-wheel-drive SUV. Bermuda shorts, white sox, sneakers and a pastel polo shirt exited the driver's side. A middle-aged woman similarly dressed climbed out of the passenger seat. I observed them from my accustomed reading position on the picnic table bench. My cold pipe rested on the table beside me. I turned ready to wave and say hello. They glanced in my direction once as they unloaded several plastic grocery bags and four one-gallon water bottles. They locked the car, unlocked the door of their RV and disappeared inside without acknowledging my presence.

The camper bounced on its springs while they busied themselves. The window curtain moved aside once, then snapped back into place. After about fifteen minutes, they exited the RV and strolled around the campsite. I got the impression they were performing a security check. I reclined on my bench watching, waiting to greet them. They each carried a stainless-steel drinking cup.

I closed my e-reader and focused on my neighbors. This was getting interesting. I watched them openly while they, just as openly, ignored me. I was the only other human in the campsite and just fifteen yards away. Yet they behaved as though I didn't exist. Their clean, expensive clothes, the new SUV, and late-model RV spoke of affluence. The man was tall, soft, overweight, but not yet fat. She was softer, with coiffed, blond hair, matching red nail and toe polish, and wearing leather sandals.

A white nylon awning stretched atop five aluminum tent poles shaded the picnic table. A floral plastic sheet, secured with aluminum clips, protected the table top. Two glass vases rested on the table top, each containing one red and one yellow plastic flower. Plastic and aluminum chairs with drink holders in the arm rests sat in the shade under the trees. The couple disappeared behind the camper. When they returned, he poked a stick into the cold fire pit. They continued to ignore me. I continued to watch them.

My meager campsite must have told them something about me, just as theirs gave me hints about them. Maybe my motorcycle, shirtless, lethargic pose, or bare feet put them off. I watched as the man walked to his car and rattled the door handle to verify it was locked. He returned to the RV. My eyes connected with his wife when she peeked over her shoulder at me then quickly looked away. He exited the RV, ignoring me and spoke quietly to his wife. I wondered why they didn't sit in those comfortable chairs in the shade. Then I realized, the chairs were turned toward their fire pit, away from me. They probably didn't want their backs to me. I chuckled. Finally, my bad boy Harley persona had impressed someone.

I began to consider where they lived, what they did and speculated on their politics. It was fun, but I was not on this trip to speculate. As amusing as this dance was, I decided it was time to shake something loose. I made a small production of my movements. I wanted them to be prepared when I walked over there. I set my e-reader on the picnic table, sat up and slowly strapped on my sandals. I climbed off my bench, unhooked my sun-dried t-shirt and pulled it over my head.

I stretched, picked up my half-liter water bottle and walked five steps across the campsite to say hello. They affected surprise, like they just noticed me. Each took a step back as I approached.

"Hi, nice rig you have," I said. "It looks comfortable."

"Hi, yes, it is. We like it. We just got it this year."

"Looks great. Is it heavy to tow?" I asked. "This is hilly country."

"Not with that."

He pointed proudly to the SUV parked nose in. "I can pull two of these if I had to."

"Is that a solar panel?"

"Yes."

"What do you use it for?"

"It recharges the battery when we are camped."

"Plenty of sun for that today."

"It's already recharged to full. It powers the lights, TV, computer, phone chargers, even the microwave."

"You have a microwave in that thing?"

Asking about their equipment was usually a good way to break RV ice. He seemed to be thawing.

They stood side by side and had not moved closer, so I kept my distance. They had not invited me into their campsite, and I did not want to impose. But carrying on a conversation from ten feet seemed silly.

I stepped toward them and held out my hand.

"I'm Bob Barra."

He paused, then stepped forward. He transferred his drink to his left hand and took mine, she followed.

"I'm Matthew, this is my wife, Dorothy."

"Hi," I greeted them.

I paused, not speaking or moving forward or back. I just stood looking at them. Sometimes silence encourages the other person to fill the empty space. This time it seemed like a long wait, but it was probably my imagination. He looked from me to his wife and seemed to make a decision.

Have you ever talked with someone who seemed to be sizing you up, deciding about your opinions and framing their conversation to fit his guess of your opinion? That's how it felt talking to Matthew and Dorothy. They seemed guarded, reluctant to tip their hand before they knew where I stood. Like they were putting out feelers to test me, accumulating hints to guide them.

It was easy for them to form an opinion about me. My dirty, old motorcycle, small tent and general scruffy appearance gave them some hints to my social status. I made no attempt to dissuade them. I mostly listened to the story Matthew delivered.

After a pause Matthew started.

"I used to work in this area when I was in college, clearing land for the county, cutting trees, and cleaning up trash in the state parks. It was hard work, but fun. We were all college kids working to make extra money between semesters. There's great hunting and fishing around here. I hunted here for years. Now we just camp. I come here every year with my wife and daughter. What about you?"

His eyes shifted, appraising my campsite.

"Looks like you're on a trip. Where are you headed?"

"I'm on my way to the East Coast to visit my son," I explained. "It's been a while since I got out and traveled the country. Now seemed like a good time. You hear a lot on the news. I wanted to go out and see it for myself."

Matthew and Dorothy sipped from their silver cups. I sipped from my plastic bottle till it was empty. We stood in the dust, outside their campsite under the intermittent shade of the scattered pine trees. They took turns refilling their drinks in the RV. During the two hours we spoke, they never invited me to sit down and never offered me a drink.

Matthew worked for a St. Louis reinsurance company.

"Insurance companies contract with reinsurers to minimize losses. Hurricanes, floods, tornados, forest fires, any kind of natural disaster can mean retail insurance companies lose money. So they hedge their bets by subcontracting some of their risk with reinsurers."

"So, reinsurance companies are the insurance companies for insurance companies?" I asked.

"I guess that's one way to put it. Even though most people have never heard of us, we control the insurance industry. We dictate auto, real estate, health, business, liability, virtually all insurance standards. What kind of garage door to buy, when to put on a new roof or have termite inspection, floodplain boundaries, smoking, weight, prescription coverage, if you don't meet the standards, you don't get insurance."

"I got a letter last year about my house. The insurance company sent an inspector. The roof was twenty years old. It had to be repaired or replaced or they wouldn't insure me."

"We work with industry and trade organizations to set standards."

"So I had to put on a new roof even though I had no leaks, and my roof was fine."

"We set standards to protect investments."

"Whose investments?"

Matthew smiled, "Ours."

Matthew and Dorothy lived in a part of St. Louis where houses start at a million dollars. He complained that even though it's a gated community, they are often annoyed by people who target affluent neighborhoods.

"We choose to live in a gated community to insulate ourselves from undocumented workers and salespeople."

"Undocumented?"

"There are lots of people who try to sell us everything from magazines to lawn and roofing services, who have no documents. No business credentials, no licenses, no insurance, many aren't even citizens. I don't want them knocking on my door. I know these people have to make a living, but you can't trust them. And, I don't want to worry about them breaking into my house when I'm not around. Safety is the main issue. I protect my family. When I need something done, I hire someone who I can trust. An American with a license to do the job. Then I can depend on getting the job done right."

"You have your own wall."

He paused from sipping his drink. "What do you mean?"

"I mean, isn't the wall like making a big, gated community out of America?"

"That wall won't work any better than our gate," Matthew answered. "It won't be able to keep everyone out. Some will still find a way in."

He walked back into the RV. I stood with his wife in the sun, holding my empty water bottle. She was silent up until now. I asked about their daughter.

"Lisa's a teacher. She is studying for her Master's Degree in Special Ed."

"I was a teacher," I said.

"Oh really." I could tell Dorothy wasn't impressed.

"Lisa teaches third grade. This is her second year. She wants to get into Special Ed because there are better chances for a job. She plans to move to California."

"I just came from California."

"Oh."

When Matthew rejoined us with a frosty, cool drink, Dorothy turned without a word and walked to the RV. She returned a few minutes later with her drink refilled.

We continued to talk in the hot sun, standing between the two campsites. Shade under their nylon awning was a few feet away. There were plenty of seats at the picnic table where a gallon bottle of water called to me. I was reminded of a legend that said a vampire can't enter your home and suck your blood if you don't invite him in. Maybe they thought I was a vampire.

"You were saying that the wall won't work," I prompted.

"There will always be people desperate enough and clever enough to get by the wall. As you said, just like the gate around our place. People still find a way in."

"Are there a lot of immigrants in Saint Louis?" I asked.

"Not as many as in the south. But they are increasing."

"Isn't that why we are here? I mean, aren't we all immigrants?"

"Yes, but this is different. This isn't a wave, it's a flood from the south that just keeps coming. We can't afford to support all the illegal immigrants coming in." Dorothy was nodding, while Matthew spoke.

"But isn't the history of our country a series of waves, or floods? Waves of immigrants came here from other parts of the world: The Spanish, French, British, Irish, Italians, Polish, and we brought the Africans here. In the eighties, people were worried about the Cuban wave. Even native Americans migrated from someplace else. We're a country of immigrants. When you think of it, isn't that how the globe was populated?" I asked. "Tribes migrated to where the game or food was plentiful or the weather was better."

Matthew sipped, then continued.

"The country is paralyzed. The government can't get anything done. The Democrats and the Republican won't work together so Trump writes executive orders. Instead of dealing with our problems, the Democrats are trying to kick Trump out. It's a waste of time. They can't win. The Senate will never vote him out of office."

He sipped from his frosty silver cup. I was starting to fantasize about a cool, frosty drink.

"There used to be moderates. Now, there is just one side or the other. You have to find out how people feel about the issue before you can talk to them. Every side has its facts, sound bites and lies. They don't listen to your facts. You don't believe their facts. The facts are different. Whose facts are right? Where do all these facts come from?"

I said, "False news is not new. It's just that the internet spreads information faster and wider."

At this point, Matthew and Dorothy's daughter arrived driving a red, compact convertible. She was a tall, thin young woman with brown hair, wearing sandals, jean shorts and a red top.

Dorothy greeted her with a smile and tried to introduce us but forgot my name.

"I'm Bob." We shook hands.

"Hi, I'm Lisa."

"Your mom tells me you're a teacher. What do you teach?"

"Third grade."

"How long have you been teaching?"

"I just finished student teaching. I'm going to get my Master's in Special Ed. But there are no jobs around, so I plan to move to California."

We stood in a circle at the border between our campsites with their RV behind them till evening approached. They left our discussion in turns for brief visits to their camper. My empty water bottle remained in my hand. They returned to the discussion with fresh, frosty drinks. They sipped from stainless steel camp cups, drops of condensation flowed down the sides. I ran my tongue over my dry lips.

After Lisa joined us, Matthew changed direction.

"This is Trump country – why? He's taking away all the social programs that keep people alive. He's cut budgets on education, environment, health care. He's abolishing Obama Care. He's opening the national parks to mining and forestry."

Beside me, Lisa was nodding.

"Teachers have to teach creationism in public schools. It's the law. They say it's an alternative theory to evolution, supported by the Bible. So people keep their guns, teach creationism and outlaw abortion. But they don't have a job or health care.

"Have you heard about 'bug out' bags?"

"No. What are they?"

"Backpacks, they sell on the internet with everything you need to survive; food rations, knife, compass, who knows what else. What are they thinking? Do they think the government can't find them? Or that they can fight the army? But idiots buy them."

Matthew sipped his drink, warming to his topic.

"Internet and phone calls are tracked by advertisers so they can sell stuff. They can track where you are. If you go into the mall, you receive an SMS advertisement for the store. But the police can't get your location without a search warrant. The crazies and fringe groups have taken over the country."

He sipped from his dewy thermos cup. Hypnotized, I watched a drip land on the front of his polo shirt. I rolled my tongue over my parched lips.

Sip, drip. The hot sun beat down on my head. My empty water bottle made my hand sweat.

Lisa walked back to the camper, opened the door and disappeared inside. Her drink must have been empty. Matthew continued.

"And how are the police supposed to do their jobs? They have video cameras on their cars, in the cars, even pinned to their shirts. Every criminal has a cell phone. When they arrest someone there are people all around with cameras recording everything. So what happens? The police go on trial, not the criminals. How can they work like that?"

"And who do the police have to deal with? Homeless people, drug addicts and illegal immigrants who don't even speak English. They arrest them and we have to support them. We pay for the jails, their food and medical care, get them a lawyer and even pay for a translator."

Lisa returned and Dorothy left. My hand sweated. I was sure my lips were cracking. Maybe they'd offer me water if they saw blood.

"We had to add private security for our company and our neighborhood. The city has extra police patrols because of break-ins. It's drug addicts. No jobs means more drug addicts. It's simple. Everybody knows that. More drugs, more crime. So Trump promises jobs. Everyone wants more jobs. But there are thousands of immigrants coming into the country illegally and they don't pay taxes. There are fewer workers paying taxes for more and more people who don't."

Dorothy returned with a dewy silver cup. The sun burned

through the thin pine branches above my head. My tongue felt like sandpaper. My feet were tired from two hours of standing in the dirt. My head needed a hat.

"That's why everyone is afraid of the wave of illegal immigrants. We're already paying high taxes. Nobody wants to pay more for illegal immigrants that come to this country and want everything free."

All three sipped from their cups as if on cue. I fantasized about cool lakes and waterfalls. As dusk fell, mosquitoes joined our group. Matthew called an end to our social circle. "Well, it's time to cook the steaks."

He walked back into the RV. His wife looked at me but said nothing.

It was a clear message for me to leave. No steak for me. But I was stubbornly determined to elicit one small bit of hospitality, or failing that, force them to refuse. Matthew opened the door of the camper carrying a plate, its bulky contents covered with aluminum foil. He seemed surprised I still existed.

I smiled and held up my empty bottle. "Could I trouble you to refill my water bottle?"

He pointed to a gallon water jug on the picnic table and turned toward the fire pit.

I filled my bottle, bid them good night and walked five steps back to my site. A little later the aroma of sizzling steak drifted on the breeze. I sat at my picnic table without a plastic cover, spooning a can of Chef Boyardee ravioli, considering life in the high rent district of St. Louis.

CHAPTER 28: GARDEN OF THE GODS

They were quick, little bastards and shrewd.

Sunday, July 7

At five-thirty it was already a warm Sunday morning. I woke atop my sleeping bag. My neighbors' RV was silent. I had been breaking camp each morning for more than a month and by now, it had become a comfortable routine. I dressed in the tent, then packed and closed my bags. I maneuvered my equipment into position by the door. I unzipped the tent door slowly and as quietly as possible. Then I tossed my gear onto the ground outside. I carried the two gear bags and set them on the ground beside the bike. Like setting up camp in the evening, breaking down and packing in the morning was a no-mind activity. My body performed the motions. It was so practiced it no longer involved the front part of my brain.

However, this morning my body played a trick on me. It unexpectedly demanded attention. Dressed, still inside the tent, I reached over to drag my packed duffel to the tent door. I had moved and carried this bag every day since leaving Delft with no ill effects. This time, when I leaned over to drag the heavy bag across the tent, I twisted something in my back. I must have over-extended my reach.

"Oh shit!"

I had been lucky so far. I had suffered only minor discomforts during this trip. Even my crash landing in Pennsylvania left me relatively healthy. When I felt my back spasm, I was afraid my luck had changed. I let go of the bag and carefully stretched out on the floor of the tent to assess the damage. I slowly turned my shoulders from left to right then from right to left. I felt the familiar burn at the base of my spine. It was a fresh injury, warm, new and just getting started. It had not yet declared its intention. With early back pain, I can't tell if it will sort itself out with a little rest, or if it will blossom and grow like a mushroom cloud. I've experienced both. This might be just a warning.

I couldn't stay where I was. I carried no food and not enough water for more than a day. My Tylenol was long lost in New York or on the road with my bag's new owner. If the pain became more intense, I'd need to find a place to rest and heal. I needed to buy some food, water and pain medication. But first, I had to break down camp, carry the gear and load the bike before the pain blossomed.

I continued the decamping process, slowly and carefully. I felt no guilt at six-thirty when I fired up the Harley and roared out of Matthew, Dorothy and Lisa's life. For in reality, I know I never entered it, except maybe as an anecdote over cocktails behind their gate.

I rode out of the campground, waved a farewell to the insurance guy and his family, undoubtedly watching me from inside their air-conditioned tin can. trying to ignore the hot coal burning into the muscles of my lower back and the image of the fragile twig that was my spine. I didn't know if my journey would allow me to continue my journey or force me to stop, rest and heal.

It was a smooth ride and hot. I followed alphabet roads all day; V to C to Y, and then Z. I had no idea where I was, but it was pretty country. The roads were smooth and well paved. They wound through green, forested countryside and wide fields of crops. Missouri farmland is not like Kansas. Families lived here. Cows grazed near green tractors parked in front of red barns. Freshly painted white picket fences with rainbow flowers embraced houses with clothes hanging from lines in the sun. Rail fences sectioned fields. I imagined scenes of children collecting eggs with dogs trailing, wagging their tails, cats sleeping on porches, pies cooling on windowsills. It was a pleasure to ride through this slice of America.

I stopped for fuel and drugs. I swallowed a few Tylenol with some water in the gas station parking lot, then climbed back onto the bike, hoping for the best. I headed east, back across the Mississippi River and into Illinois. I was sorry to say goodbye to Missouri. I had loved riding through the picturesque, Rockwellian landscape.

Back roads take longer, but it's a peaceful ride. The four-lane gets you there quicker but it's intense. It's a quality-of-life choice. Do you want to save time with four hours of fast, straight, highway riding and arrive earlier but exhausted? Or do you want to ride five or six hours peacefully through beautiful scenery and reach the campsite relaxed, wanting to ride more? I chose the latter and was always satisfied with the result. At noon I bought a cold-cuts sandwich and ate half for lunch.

I rumbled into the Garden of the Gods campground at two o'clock in the afternoon. It was 90 degrees with 99 percent humidity. The campground was quiet and almost empty. Of the twenty or so campsites, only one other was occupied.

I selected a campsite in the shade, backed the bike into the parking area, shut off the engine and set the kickstand plate. I peeled off my riding gear and spread it out on the picnic table to air out. I slowly set up my camp, listening for messages from my back. It felt weak, like my upper torso was supported by a brittle twig. But it was not more painful than in the morning. I took that for a good sign.

There was no shower or sink in the campground, only a single stroke well pump that gushed fresh, cold, chlorinated water. A sign beside the pump prohibited water use for bathing and dish washing. I was hot and sticky in the extreme. I thought, "There was no shower or water at Mark Twain yesterday. There's no shower here. Maybe the Gods don't need showers, but I do."

I opened my saddlebags and collected anything that would hold water and carried it all to the pump. I pumped clear, cold water into all my water bottles, pans, even the red plastic ice cream container that held my coffee maker. When everything was filled, I shuttled them all to my campsite and set them on top of the picnic table to warm in the sun.

While the water warmed, I pulled out a change of clothes, my soap and towel. I bathed at the picnic table and washed my hair in the sunshine, cooling and cleaning in one satisfying operation. I donned clean underwear, shorts, sandals, a clean t-shirt and felt like a new man.

I never met my neighbors. They must have been off hiking, fishing or shopping. I reclined at the picnic table with my e-reader and pipe. I ate the other half of my sandwich with a bottle of water for dinner and gobbled Tylenol for dessert.

The biting flies arrived soon after I finished my sandwich. Every campsite hosted its designated predators. Some emerged on the scene at dusk, others preferred the light of day. I suspect they've negotiated insect treaties that permit them to hunt in species-specific shifts. At more than one camp it was mosquitos. At others, it was midges or no-see-ums. At another campsite I was plagued by big green head flies, still another by fleas. Ticks at one campsite kept me awake most of the night. The Garden of the Gods campground was haunted by small, black, biting flies.

They circled like sharks, occasionally landing on bare skin, wiggling their wings, ready to spring away if threatened. The pipe smoke kept them at bay for a while. But I'm only good for one bowl at a time. More than that, especially in the hot weather and my tummy protests. When the pipe went out, the flies returned. It was too hot for a campfire, so I tried vigilance, speed and stealth. I learned to respect my enemy. They were quick little bastards and shrewd.

Instead of relaxing in my comfortable reading position on the bench, I sat up and placed my reader on the table in front of me. This left my hands free and gave me more room to move quickly. Biting insects are annoying, mobile predators and territorial. When a predator zeros in on a victim, he (or is it a she?) establishes a primitive exclusivity. The other predators mostly stay away. So the prey (that's you and me) must deal with only one hunter at a time. This is of course not true with mosquitos and other lower forms of life. But the big ones, the green heads and the black biting flies that plagued me at Garden of the Gods, were certainly in the union.

From one perspective, this makes it easier. I only had to deal with one predator at a time. On the other hand, we're talking about extremely motivated and skilled hunters who are in a fight for survival and think three-dimensionally. I just didn't want to get bit. The fly wanted to eat, live and continue the species. Theirs was the higher evolutionary goal. It was a struggle for survival.

The sad truth is, there was no way for me to win. If by some accident of mistiming or quirk of fate, I got lucky enough to slap one of these vicious animals to bug heaven, there was another waiting nearby to immediately step in and take his (or her) place. Then the hunt started again. And there were millions of them and only one of me. The struggle would only end when I admitted defeat, collected my gear and retreated into the tent for the night. Which is what I finally did after suffering several nasty blood lettings. I'm sure that I nourished the continued survival of whatever species I fed that night. I itched in my sleep till sunrise.

CHAPTER 29:
MAMMOTH CAVE

*I've got whiskey. If you
want to stop by later.*

Monday, July 8

Kentucky is a thousand miles from Massachusetts. I'd traveled
seven thousand miles since the start of my trip. But far from
being tired, I felt energized. The motorcycle and I would roll to
a stop in my home state too soon. I wasn't ready. There was so
much more to see, to experience and to learn.

I rode across the Ohio River then 175 miles through forested hills dotted with graceful country houses in southern Illinois and Kentucky. This stretch of road more than any other, affirmed that I had settled into my comfort zone. I glided through the scented breeze beneath a cloudless sky swaying with the music of the road. The motorcycle rumbled and purred smoothly. We turned and banked as one through the mottled forest shade. We glided on silk ribbons past fields of rich, black soil blanketed in yellow wheat and green corn. The elegant homes and verdant pastures whispered an invitation to a quiet life of peace and contentment. This little piece of Kentucky touched my heart. It must be a wonderful gift to live there.

In a week I'd emerge from the wilderness and rejoin civilization. It was not an appealing thought. I'd grown accustomed to my clock- and calendar-free life. I was bound by no schedules, no obligations, and only myself to consider. When I rejoined the world, I'd co-ordinate plans to reconnect with friends and family. We'd check agendas, synchronize appointments, and organize plans hours and days in advance. I'd sleep under roofs in guest rooms, or on sofas, and eat regularly. The weight of responsibility felt overwhelming.

A burden returned to my thoughts and my heart. I had tucked it away in a storage box in the back of my mind for most of the trip. But it would not remain buried. I had to pull it out into the sunlight and face it. I was racing toward an onerous decision. I faced a painful separation from my trusted friend, the Harley. I had become attached to the roaring metal beast. I wanted to keep it: I wanted to keep it in America; I wanted to take it back to Holland.

Where could I store the Harley in the U.S.? Matt, Jim, Dan, Paul all owned homes with a garage, but I wasn't comfortable imposing upon them to store my motorcycle indefinitely. And I could not rely on Paul's registration and insurance forever. I'd need my own paperwork to ride it legally. And of course, when would I return to the U.S. to ride it? I thought of shipping it back to The Netherlands. I already owned a cruiser. I certainly didn't need a second one. One would have to go. Which one? The Harley was ideal for an American cross-country road trip but ill-suited to the narrow, winding cobblestone roads in Holland. If I didn't store it in America or ship it to The Netherlands, I'd have to dispose of it. How would I sell it? I'd avoided these questions for six weeks.

A subtle, sweet fragrance drew me from my melancholy reverie. I didn't recognize the ripe, sweet, heady smell. As I rode on that warm day past sleepy farms, I tried to identify the crop that filled the air with perfume. I came upon a stretch of road beside a field of leafy plants with purple flowers. They grew about knee heigh. Their sweet fragrance filled the air. I added agriculture to geology on my "wish I knew more list".

I stopped at the next gas station/general store, bought a bottle of water and asked the clerk about the plant with the perfume. She knew right away.

"Soybeans."

"Soybeans, I never would have guessed."

"Kentucky grows about as much soybeans as corn. It's a big cash crop," she added.

I thanked her, walked to my bike and continued to enjoy the sensory pleasures of the Kentucky back roads all the way to Mammoth Cave National Park.

I arrived at about noon and weaved through the Visitors' Center lot looking for a parking place. After two days of riding on almost deserted country roads, I was stunned by the swarms of people and fleets of cars, trucks and buses. The parking lot was full. The only open spaces seemed miles from the building.

In Europe, motorcycle riders park their vehicles pretty much any place they can fit; sidewalks, beside buildings, in public squares, under trees. The authorities allow this because it leaves more spaces for cars. Similarly, in traffic, motorcycles can travel between lanes when the commute slows to a crawl. Usually, car and truck drivers move to the side to let them pass.

In the U.S., motorcycles must observe the same rules of the road as cars. They must park in legal spaces and ride in designated travel lanes. Cars and trucks do not part in traffic to allow motorcycles to pass. I made a second circuit through the packed lot. Though there were plenty of "European" spaces, near the building entrance and around the perimeter, they were not "U.S." legal. I longed for the flexible European attitude toward motorcycles.

Mammoth Cave offers dozens of tours into sections of the vast underground vault. I booked the late afternoon tour into the main cavern. The departure meeting point for the tour was an open-sided, post and beam building. A park ranger greeted our group and delivered a brief introduction. We boarded three yellow school buses for the ten-minute ride to the cave entrance.

Spelunking speaks to the adventurous side of my nature. Exploring dark caverns, seeking passageways, mapping routes and finding connections sparks my imagination. My back injury reminded me I'm no longer fit for heavy lifting. But I'm excited by the history, adventure and remarkable discoveries of cave exploration. I was thrilled to visit Mammoth Cave, the largest and most dramatic example of underground exploration in the U.S.

I jockeyed for a position close to the ranger to better hear the stories. For two hours we walked through the cavern while the ranger/guide described the discovery and history of exploration of the network of caverns. Our tour began with a descent of about two hundred steps to the cavern floor. We wound our way around, over and through rock formations, boulders and ancient passageways. We followed a narrow, irregular, winding and sometimes wet man-made path. We ducked under low cliffs, twisted and turned around massive rock formations illuminated by the dim light of weak bulbs at irregular intervals. The air was cool and damp, the floor and walls sometimes slippery and the cave was always spectacular. My stiff back muscles protested but did not mount an embarrassing revolt or diminish my enjoyment.

For the most part, visitors near the ranger/guide followed in silent awe, to absorb the history of discovery that became Mammoth Cave National Park. Not all of us enjoyed the walk in quiet contemplation.

A squat, dark-haired woman wearing jeans and a brown sweater followed close behind me supervising her ten-year old son.

"David, hold on to the handrail or you'll slip." "David, watch your head."

"David, don't go over there." "David, stay close."

"David, put your sweater back on." "David, be careful, it's slippery." "David, keep up."

"David, be careful of the steps."

Only my stubborn determination to listen to the ranger's ongoing description of the cave kept me close. Otherwise, I would have dropped back to avoid the annoying woman.

Ten-year-old David was either a mute, or patient as a saint. He never protested, argued or commented on his mother's suffocating attention. Three-quarters of the way through the tour, I discovered David had a father.

Mother: "David, stand over here by me."

Mother: "Take a picture of us in front of this rock."

Mother: "We're not supposed to use a flash in the cave. Make sure the flash is turned off."

Mother: "Never mind. Here, give it to me."

David's father said two words. "Yes, dear."

In spite of the irritating shrew haunting David, I enjoyed Mammoth Cave. I envisioned explorers climbing, sometimes swimming, through narrow passageways, to emerge into underground caverns so vast that even their powerful headlamps could not measure them. The exploration of Mammoth Cave continues today. New passageways, caverns and the connections between them are still being discovered.

The temperature in the cave was a constant fifty-four degrees. We toured an area about 250 feet below the forest, slowly working our way up to the surface. The ranger explained that the lowest-known section of the cave was about 150 feet below where we walked. Flowing water was still creating new caverns and tunnels, though very slowly. The process of carving a cave takes centuries.

We returned to daylight where the outside temperature was thirty-five degrees warmer than below ground. We boarded the buses that delivered us to the Visitors' Center. I walked to the camp services building and invested a dollar fifty for a four-minute warm shower. I shampooed my hair and soaped my body, then rinsed. There was still time to press my hands against my spine under the warm water after the wash-up. My sore muscles were stiff but not screaming. After the shower, I stopped at the camp store to buy calories for two nights and a day. The grocery bag was large enough to stuff in my wet towel and underwear for the walk to my camp.

My legs carried me toward my campsite while I struggled to make sense of what I'd learned so far on my journey. My mind drifted across topics; the slow process of geological events that create caves and deserts, climate change, migration, cultural traditions, wealth, security and fear. My feet followed a path across a wooden foot bridge and through a stand of pine trees. I stepped on a branch and a back spasm reminded me of the fragility of the human body, age and small luxuries like a warm shower. The walkway emptied onto a paved camp road that turned uphill. I was lost in thought, wandering to my campsite. The sound of a voice interrupted my reverie. I turned and saw a dark-haired woman with smiling eyes. She was seated beside a tent, holding a paperback. I stopped.

"Hello. Did I wake you?"

"Hi. No, well maybe. I guess I was daydreaming," I admitted.

"Sorry to interrupt."

I pointed to her book. "What are you reading?"

"Ken Wilber, do you know him?"

"No, what does he write?"

"Philosophy."

I crossed the road and stood in front of her campsite. She smiled, her tanned face innocent of makeup. She braided her hair in a ponytail. It hung over her left shoulder below her breast. She wore a light blue, cotton sundress snug against her figure. Her bare arms and legs were sun browned. Open leather sandals exposed red toenails.

She smiled. "I didn't mean to interrupt you."

"I guess I was woolgathering."

"About the cave tour?"

I hesitated.

"I was on the same tour. Didn't you notice me?" She asked. "I saw you."

"Well, there were a lot of people," I said, "and it was dark."

She smiled at my discomfort.

"Did you like it? Or were you woolgathering then too?"

"Yes, I loved it. I'm a fan. I mean I like caves."

She pointed at the bag hanging from my hand. "Been shopping?"

"Oh, yeah. Got some supplies at the camp store."

"Looks like you bought plenty. You plan on staying the whole summer?"

"My towel's in there too."

"And your underwear too, it looks like," she said.

"You're very observant."

"Where are you camped?"

"Up the hill." I pointed.

"There's a path through the woods. Follow the stream. It'll save you some steps." She pointed behind her tent.

"Thanks."

"What are you doing, traveling, camping?"

"It's a bit of a story."

"I've got time, why don't you sit down?"

"Well, I was going to heat up some food. And maybe, put on some underwear."

She flashed a smile. Her eyes sparkled.

"Too bad. I've got whiskey. If you want to stop by later."

"OK, but I have one condition."

She looked at me with open curiosity.

"I want to hear your story."

"What do you mean?"

"Well, a pretty woman, camping alone, reading philosophy in

the woods; there's got to be a story in there."

She laughed; it was a mellow chuckle. "My name is Ruth."

"Hi Ruth, I'm Bob."

"Hi Bob."

Her hand was warm and firm.

"OK, Ruth. Let me warm up my dinner and I'll be back a little later."

As I was preparing my dinner, a man approached my campsite, carrying a section of watermelon. He was about sixty-five years old, gray haired and stocky. Two dogs the size of hamsters hopped at his feet on leashes he held in the not-watermelon hand.

Walter was returning to Indianapolis from his annual road trip. He towed a camper behind his red mini-SUV. His wife passed away two years ago.

"Now it's just me and the girls." He glanced affectionately at the dogs weaving between his feet. As if just remembering, he held out the watermelon.

"I bought more than I can eat and wondered if you want any."

"I'd love some, thanks very much."

Walter looked at the water boiling on my one-burner, said he didn't want to intrude and walked back to his campsite. While my pasta cooked, I cut the melon into bite-sized pieces and filled a stainless-steel cook pan.

A little later I carried the watermelon to visit my new friend. Ruth saw my approach and ducked into her tent and came out with a bottle and two camp cups. We met at her picnic table.

"I hope you like watermelon. It's a gift from my neighbor."

I set the pan on the table and opened the top.

The setting sun silhouetted the soft curves beneath a thin

sundress, her only garment. She poured generously into both cups, sat on the bench opposite me, lifted her cup and smiled.

"Here's to new friends."

We touched cups and sipped Tennessee bourbon. It was the golden hour, quiet and warm, with the sun low to the horizon. Our only neighbors were yellow-topped pine trees and the bubbling creek.

"It is beautiful here, so peaceful," I said.

Ruth followed my gaze. "It is."

"So, what are you doing here all by yourself, reading philosophy?"

"Right, this is story night."

She smiled and raised her cup. I raised mine, we sipped and sat for a moment.

"Why don't you start? What are you doing here so far from New Hampshire?"

I told her of my cross-country trip, reconnecting with my sons and my country.

"That's a cool thing to do. Have you learned anything, Dorothy?"

"I'm struggling. I've talked to people everywhere and still have a hard time getting a grip on what's going on. I don't know if I'll ever get it."

"What do you mean?"

"OK, let me give you an example. I met a couple of young men at a campground in Kansas. They were about the same age and basically from the same part of the country, but they viewed America from completely opposite sides. One was an ultra-conservative, Republican Trump supporter. The other was a progressive Democrat. Both held strong, opposing opinions and supported them with their own 'facts'. Both strongly believe that the other side is completely wrong and will destroy the country if it gets its way. I met a guy from Reno who said nothing has changed and nothing will, until he doesn't get his TV and beer."

We sipped our drinks.

"When my Dutch friends ask me what is going on in America, what can I tell them? How do you reconcile those two, actually three, opinions?"

"What makes you think I can make sense out of it?"

Her smile started in her eyes.

"I hoped a philosopher would be able to help me."

She leaned back and took a breath that stretched the thin cotton tight against her breasts. She followed my eyes, smiled and picked a piece of watermelon from the pan.

"I'm not a philosopher, I'm a cougar."

"Thanks for the warning. But I'm older than you. I think I'm safe."

Her eyes sparkled. "A cougar doesn't do safe."

Her eyes held mine, I sipped my drink.

"I'm from Michigan. I'm fifty-one. I thought I'd get that right out front."

"Fifty-one's a perfect age."

"My soon-to-be ex-husband came home one day while I was cooking, took a beer from the fridge and said he wanted a divorce. The love was gone."

"I'm sorry."

"I was shocked, never saw it coming. I cried, promised I'd change. We talked all night. I said I'd be whatever he wanted. He agreed to give it another try. He even told me what to do. You know, like those women on the television shows from the fifties, cooking, vacuuming in sexy clothes, fixing drinks. He drank beer so that was easy. Have you ever handcuffed a woman to the bed?"

I took a slug of Jack.

"I'm a nurse at a big hospital, a shift supervisor. I'm good at what I do. When I got home, I became his toy. His puppy. His maid. Call it whatever you want. I felt stupid. Trying so hard to be someone's slave. After a month of trying, failing and feeling stupid, I decided to split. That was a year ago." She paused.

"I moved into an apartment with two friends. He doesn't like them. They're gay partners. They cleared out a spare bedroom and told me I could stay as long as I wanted. I felt relief right away. I still feel good. I can be myself. Do what I want with no apologies. I forgot what it was like to be happy. I've been happy since I left. I feel like I rejoined the world. We were married twenty-four years. I asked my therapist why I'm not sad. She told me I've been grieving my marriage for two years."

She paused and sipped from her cup, looked at me.

"You're not drinking nearly enough for this conversation, and I can't do it all myself." The bourbon was silky smooth. She smiled.

"Now, I'm doing fine, but things didn't turn out as well as he hoped."

"What do you mean?"

"He thought that by divorcing me he'd find a perfect wife, be happy. He has these ideas of a perfect, simple life. He wants the world to fit his fantasy. Like he saw his parents. Except his fantasy is fifty years old. It doesn't work that way anymore. It probably never did. But he hasn't caught on. The world moved on and left him behind."

Dusk was falling. The dim streetlights cast little spotlight circles along the edge of the road. I waved absently at a few mosquitos and twisted on the wooden bench to relieve the stiffness. I thought about a time when American women wore long dresses and high heels to do the housework. Had they ever really done that or was that somebody's myth? Ruth walked to the tent and returned with a citronella candle. She lit it and set it on the table. The image of Ruth handcuffed to a bed sprung into my head. I hastily sipped my drink, relieved she couldn't read my mind.

"Are you OK?" Maybe she could.

"Just thinking about your story. We haven't got to the philosophy part yet."

"He started by isolating me from my friends. He doesn't like gay people or blacks, immigrants, Arabs, the list kept getting longer. I don't care what they are if they're nice people. He told me the world was a dangerous place and he could protect me from it. He built a wall around us. He said it was to keep me safe. It was really a prison."

"When we broke up, I lost everything. But in another way, I gained everything. I lost my husband, my house, even my dog. Did I tell you I loved that dog?" She smiled.

"I had no money, no place to live and nowhere to go. I should have been terrified, but I wasn't. I was free."

We sipped bourbon. She continued.

"See, my ex wanted the world to stop, stay simple, even get simpler. But that's not the way things work. Everything changes, nothing gets simpler. That's the philosophy part. When I got married, I was young, just out of nursing school. He became my world. I thought that was the way marriage worked. But I guess I changed. I wanted more. My ex got angry when I talked about it. The angrier someone gets when they argue, the weaker their argument.

"I don't blame him. He liked his life the way it was. He wanted what his parents had. His mother never worked outside the home. His father was king of the house. He wanted the same thing.

"We argued over politics. He's a Trump guy all the way in case you didn't guess. He doesn't believe government should interfere in people's lives. I look at things differently. Every day, I see sick and injured people, kids and babies that need help. I think we should help them. He doesn't.

"He wanted our marriage to fit his image of it. He didn't consider my image of it. We're only two people. It took twenty-five years of him trying to change me and me trying to change him.

"Imagine how long it takes a country with 360 million people to change. Half the country wants one thing. The other half wants something else. No party or partner can have its way all the time. Neither party will ruin the country because the other half of the country won't let them. That's why change is glacial."

"Wow. I'll have to think that over."

I sipped my Jack. Ruth sipped hers. The level in the bottle had dropped with the sun. We were quiet for a minute.

"What's the matter with your back?"

"What?"

"I'm a nurse. I notice things."

"I twisted it this morning. It's a little stiff."

She smiled again, her bright eyes reflecting the candlelight.

"I told you I'm a cougar. I didn't tell you it was accidental."

"What do you mean?"

"I have a boyfriend who is twenty years younger than me."

"Congratulations." I held up my cup.

"He pursued me. That's the accidental part."

"He's a lucky guy."

She flashed a bright smile.

It was full dark. She leaned over and sloshed liquid into my cup. I leaned forward and looked in her eyes. We clicked rims and sipped. The street lamp highlighted the outline of her figure beneath the flimsy fabric. I tried not to stare.

"One last thing about my ex, then I'm done. There was a neighborhood barbeque. My ex showed up with a thirty-something Barbie on his arm, shocked when he saw me with John.

"One of my friends walked up to John, right in front of everybody and said, 'So, have you got an Oedipal complex, or what?'"

"John smiled and said, 'No, I'm just into exceptional women.' My friend slapped him on the back and handed him a beer. It was great!"

She paused and smiled.

"I'm doing something now that I never had the courage to do when I was married."

"What's that?"

She spread her arms wide and looked from left to right.

"This, traveling on my own. I just packed the car and took off. John wanted to come with me, but I wanted to do it on my own. He worries about me."

"That's kind of our job. Must be in the genes."

"I thought my ex was trying to protect me. He was just keeping me under control. I don't want anyone to protect me. Nice as John is, and I know he's worried, I'm sick of that. I'm a big girl. I can take care of myself."

She leaned close to me and poured into my cup. I admired the view. "So you didn't notice me on the cave tour. I'm hurt."

"You were really there?"

"Don't you remember? I saw you before we got on the bus."

"Sorry. Did you enjoy the tour?"

"I was worried it would be too hard, you know, climbing all those stairs and hiking through the cave. They warn that if you're not in good shape, it could be dangerous. But the new me said, 'Go for it'."

"It would be hard to carry someone out of there if they had a heart attack."

"Especially with your back."

"Sad, but true."

"Maybe you need a massage. Have a drink. Think about it."

CHAPTER 30: AMERICA IS BROKEN

The first sign of eco-failure is migration.

Tuesday, July 9

The next morning, I lingered over breakfast of oatmeal, raisins, honey and two cups of coffee, then set out to explore the campground by foot. Ruth's camp was deserted, except for the empty bottle of Jack Daniels on her picnic table. She was an exceptional woman. I never saw her again.

In grad school I studied a course called Introduction to Occupational Health and Safety. I expected a summary of government regulations. It turned out to be a fascinating study of the health factors connected to job-related stress. Most of us recognize and accept the psychological impacts of stress. This course focused on the physical aspects of stress, the way the body responds. Heart disease and high blood pressure can be directly related to job stress. Heart attacks, strokes, alcoholism, drug abuse, anxiety, asthma, cancer from smoking have all been linked to job stress.

The readings, lectures and discussions identified job conditions that create and reduce stress. Stress is not related to how complex, difficult or important our job is, or how simple. It's also not connected to how much money we make. The biggest factor in job stress is workers' freedom to make decisions about how they do their jobs. If someone tells you what to do, how to do it, how fast to do it and when it has to be done, what is there left for you to decide? You are responsible but someone else makes all the decisions. This is what causes stress; responsibility but no control. However if you have freedom to make decisions and choices, you will experience less stress. It is no surprise therefore that one of the most stressful jobs is machine-paced assembly line work. One of the least stressful jobs is to be a handyman.

My watermelon neighbor was sitting at his table with his two gerbils scampering in the leaves under the picnic table. I walked over to say hello and thank him for the treat. Walter was seventy-three, eight years older than I had guessed. He was writing in a little notebook.

"I'm a handyman outside of Indianapolis. I've been away for almost a month. I have jobs waiting when I get back. I'm trying to set up appointments so I can get right to work."

"Are you retired and do this part-time?" I asked.

"Hell no. I work for four real estate management companies

and also have my own clients."

"So there's enough to keep you busy?"

"I've got more work than I can handle. I don't advertise, it's all from referrals."

"If you don't mind telling me, how did you get into it? I mean it's not a conventional job, like with a salary and benefits, insurance and a pension. Is it?"

"You're right, it's not for everybody. I got into it by accident. I retired from the Navy, with no job and no prospects. Someone asked me to help them fix up their apartment. I had the time, so I helped. I ended up taking over the job. Someone in another apartment saw me working and asked me to look at their dishwasher. I fixed it. Suddenly I was in business. That was thirty years ago and I've been doing it ever since."

"So you must like it."

"I wouldn't think of doing anything else."

"I have a son who I think would be perfect for this kind of a job. What would you tell him?"

"This generation doesn't want to get their hands dirty. They buy small condos and townhouses in the city. They like to live near bars, stores and restaurants. They spend their time going out. If something breaks, they don't know anything. They just want it fixed so they call me. There is always a need for someone who can fix things."

I thought of Mike in Lake Tahoe. It seemed to me that this job was a great fit. Who lives in Lake Tahoe? Rich people who are there to play. They don't want to fix things. Mike's a natural handyman. He can fix anything. And he's smart. What he doesn't know he can figure out. I made a mental note to call him with the idea.

Walter invited me to share lunch with him: hot dogs on sticks over the campfire. I had two with mustard on bread – delicious.

According to Walter, the economy is fine. He's got no financial worries and no plans to retire.

After talking with Walter I walked back to my campsite. I checked my phone and was surprised to see I had cell service. So I emailed Mike with the handyman idea. I think he'd be perfect for it. He likes figuring things out, he's good with his hands and not afraid to get them dirty. He likes being his own boss and he's personable. If I were younger . . .

I thought, "In my next life."

Wednesday, July 10

Most of the campers at Mammoth Cave were families and couples. But there were four singles, Ruth, Walter, me, and I met the fourth Wednesday morning, David. I saw him drive in a couple of days before but hadn't seen him around much since. At seven o'clock I was preparing to fire up the Harley when I saw him crawl backwards out of his tent. I walked across the road to say hello.

David was long and loose from his gray hair and his untucked Hawaiian shirt to his baggy madras shorts above leather sandals. He was leaning into the hatchback of his light blue Prius when I approached from behind. I said hello to warn him I was nearby. He turned with a laptop computer in one hand.

We shook hands. "David."

"Nice to meet you. I'm Bob. I'm camped just over there." I pointed.

He looked behind me up to my motorcycle, packed and ready to go. "Nice bike."

"Thanks, nice Prius."

"It is actually. I like it."

"Where are you from?"

"Oregon."

I looked into the packed car.

"It looks like you've been on the road for a while."

"About a month. I'm headed to Chicago. I just retired. I'm tracing my family's genealogy, and sightseeing along the way."

"Nice. So, you like the Prius?"

"It's a good car, comfortable and I'm getting fifty miles a gallon, all the way from Oregon."

"Fifty miles! I'm only getting forty on the Harley. And it doesn't have a trunk."

"The car's running fine, but I got delayed here. I was on a tour of Mammoth Cave and Ieft my laptop in the car. It got fried. I guess, like dogs and kids, you can't leave them in the car in the hot sun. I spent yesterday in a computer shop in Glasgow trying to recover my data. I didn't succeed. My computer is gone. So I bought a new e-computer. But this morning when I booted it up, the screen went black, blank screen, nothing. It's brand new."

"Is the battery charged?"

"I think so, it was last night. I've got no computer experience. I lived the last twenty years in a log cabin without electricity, phone or the internet."

"You've got to tell me about that."

David explained that he lived in a worker-owned co-operative colony in the Cascades. It was very successful and had grown to more than one hundred people. He boiled his political interests down to one point: climate change.

"I've got children and I'm worried about the world they will inherit. I can't believe more people aren't concerned and doing something about it."

"Lots of people don't think climate change is real," I said.

"It's a real problem, bigger than just the temperature."

"What do you mean?"

David explained. "The first sign of eco-failure is migration. Animals – and that includes people – migrate from unsustainable ecosystems to better environments. A lot of the world is on the move now. People are starving so they move to where they can find food. Countries with food want to protect it for themselves. That's why there are border patrols and walls."

David described his ride from Oregon to Kentucky. He took a northern route, drove back roads and stopped to visit his son in Montana.

"Every fifty miles or so I came to a picturesque little town with pretty architecture, pedestrian walkways, lots of space and parks. But half the store fronts were boarded up, closed, empty, for sale. Nobody needs a local shoe store. They buy online. The children are moving away. People are frightened. They want this to change. Hillary offered more of the same. Trump offered change."

David told me he attended one of the ranger's talks about Mammoth Cave National Park last night.

"The ranger described the history of how the park was formed. She said they took the private land by eminent domain. The owners relocated. So what was private property with restricted access became a national park for everyone to enjoy."

David paused and asked me, "Isn't that socialism? I didn't ask the ranger. But what else can you call it? And the ranger was proud of it. But don't call it socialism."

We talked about climate change and unsustainable lifestyles. David said a lot of West Coast retired people fly to Mexico for the weekend. That generates huge CO_2 emissions.

"Sustainability is not just about the environment. It's not just about clean air and water. Of course, that's part of it. But a sustainable society also has an economy that works and that means social programs. Like better city planning to include cluster housing and more open spaces. Like corporate responsibility so companies don't just suck resources then leave the region barren and move on. They should be building something for the community, not just taking."

I mentioned the lead mines in Missouri, the schools closing, and the strip coal mines I saw in Pennsylvania.

"Yes, but we're talking on a global level. Like what corporations are doing to the forests in South America and fishing out the oceans. Here in America, the President is talking about opening the National Parks and Forests to cut the trees, mine the minerals and drill for oil. Eighty percent of the world's resources are being exhausted to support 20 percent of the world's people. This can't continue."

"You are right. It's complicated," I agreed.

"Maybe capitalism is not the answer. The practices that make capitalism work create the tragedy of the commons. The world's resources go to fewer and fewer wealthy people."

David continued, "America has become more of a business than a society. Society and socialism are bad words. We've taken rugged independence and created a culture of selfishness. Taking care of the sick, old and poor has become anti-American. They call it socialism, and that's one short step away from communism. America is the only modern nation that doesn't support universal healthcare. Why should only rich people be healthy?"

"I live in Europe. We have a national healthcare system. It works pretty well. People I've talked to say it won't work here. But they don't say why."

"Because the pharmaceutical companies, HMO's, doctors, insurance companies and the politicians they own won't let it work. They are making trillions on private healthcare. They tell people it won't work because it's their cash cow."

David paused, took a breath, then went on.

"That's why I stick with climate change. I think America's broken. There's just too much that needs fixing. I can't deal with all of it. I'd get crazy. So I try to stay with climate change for my children."

David was anxious to return to the computer store. And I was ready to ride to Daniel Boone National Forest. We said our farewells and went our separate ways, him at fifty miles per gallon with a roof and me at forty miles per gallon without one.

My destination was 175 miles east. I stopped at Betty's Country Cooking in Columbia for eggs, over easy, bacon, home fries, toast and coffee. My meals for the last couple of days had been adequate to keep the lights on, but Betty's breakfast was a welcome feast. I arrived at Laurel River Lake at two o'clock in the afternoon.

The unusually wet spring that flooded the Mississippi River in Missouri and drowned campsites in Kansas, also cultivated the insect-rich habitat of the Daniel Boone National Forest. Noisy crickets chirped till long after dark. No-see ums, mosquitos and flies swarmed and bit. Butterflies fluttered in the woods and festooned the undergrowth. Fireflies sparkled and blinked in the darkness. Spiders cast gossamer webs that tangled in my hair, legs and arms. Fat, slow black ants and tiny, quick red ones scampered over the ground and up the sides of my tent. My little patch of gravel was a chaos of crawling, swooping, fluttering, blinking, buzzing and chirping. The insects were ubiquitous, hungry and horny.

My skin was itchy, hot and blotchy with insect bites.

Something nasty and hungry had crawled into my sleeping bag and spent the night chewing on me. My left arm, both legs, back and left buttock were dimpled with swollen, burning, itching boils that leaked clear fluid when I scratched. It was a sneaky bastard. I hadn't felt the bites. I slept like a rock but suffered the poisonous aftermath in the morning.

The campground management provided each campsite with a bear box bolted to a concrete footing. I set up my camp and secured my food in the steel container. I did not encounter any bears during my stay. I assumed they were deep in caves, hiding from the voracious insects that infested the forest.

In the afternoon, I ambled down the road to the lake wearing sandals and a bathing suit. A grassy clearing sloped down to meet the water. I laid my towel and shirt over a rock and waded in. After the heat and humidity of the campsite jungle, the lake water was a welcome relief. I spent an hour alone, floating contentedly in the cool lake, relaxed.

Thursday morning found me drinking coffee at the picnic table in front of my tent. Instead of getting lighter as the day awakened, the sky darkened, and the wind was rising. The morning was warm and heavy with moisture in the air so thick, my skin felt sticky and damp. Rain was approaching. It is one thing to be caught in an unexpected thunderstorm while riding a motorcycle. That may be unavoidable. But it is quite another thing to set out riding when you know there is a thunderstorm on the way. That is foolish. I was under no deadline to be someplace in a hurry. The approaching storm convinced me that Daniel Boone National Forest was a good place to sit out the storm and give the motorcycle a rest.

The campground offered all the amenities I'd need for an extended stay; a drinking water pump nearby, a shower down the road and a lake to relieve the heat. I decided to delay my departure and wait for the storm to pass.

Thunder from the north confirmed my decision. I checked that the tent stakes were secure and my gear was buttoned down and zipped for heavy weather. The wind continued to rise in advance of the approaching storm. I sat at the picnic table with my coffee, expecting to finish it in the tent.

My tent rested on a raised, graveled rectangle about 10 feet by 20 feet, bordered by railroad ties. The space was large enough to include a picnic table and a fire pit. The wind battered leaves from the trees. Absently, I watched a long-tailed wasp drag a green leaf as big as my hand along the railroad tie. The wasp trudged backward, pulling the leaf, struggling to hold it against the rising wind. I sipped my coffee, watched the wasp and waited for the storm to descend.

A few minutes later, I left the wasp to his business and retreated into the tent. I sat cross-legged under the dark sky. The rain poured and pounded against the thin nylon fly and washed down the sides. I wondered if the wasp had abandoned his leaf or had sailed away to Oz. Lightning flashed, followed instantly by booming thunder. The explosive flashes brightened the twilight sky. Rain hammered the tent, the trees and the ground. Lightning cracked so close I could smell the ozone and thunder crashed almost simultaneously. Pools of water formed on the gravel island outside my fragile shelter. Inside, I crouched, surrounded by my bags and gear. The willowy tent swayed in the gale. Only a fragile nylon sheet stood between me and the storm, but it was enough.

The sky darkened. After thirty minutes, my knees and back cried for relief. I spread out on the tent floor to ease my aching muscles. I rested my head on a duffle bag. I dug out my flashlight and e-reader but found the weather more entertaining than a novel. The storm passed over my position from northwest to southeast. Lightning, thunder and rain surrounded me for a half an hour. After thirty minutes the rain tapered off. The thunder faded, the lightning retreated beyond sight and the wind quieted.

Peace returned to my world and the sky brightened to overcast gray. I climbed out of my refuge to assess the damage and stretch my cramped muscles. The thunder was a memory, and the air was still. Shallow pools of water surrounded my tent. Leaves, beaten from trees, some still attached to broken branches, littered my gravel island and the surrounding ocean of forest. I walked around to explore, avoiding the puddles that had formed in every depression. I followed the path to the parking lot to check my motorcycle. My loyal friend was dripping wet in the dismal weather leaning on its kickstand, patiently waiting.

From the northwest distant thunder rumbled. The wind rattled the trees and scattered leaves like confetti. The sky faded to charcoal as the next wave of thunder clouds advanced. In a half-hour, fireworks would light up the sky and the deluge would drown the forest. If it followed the pattern of the last burst, another half-hour would see it pass. It seemed the wisest course of action was to wait out this storm system. During a pause in the rain, I walked to the main entrance to reserve a second night's stay.

I met the campground caretakers. Dave and his wife, Mary, were retired. They worked in the National Forest six months each year, cleaning campsites, registering campers, "Whatever it takes." They were on their way to the shower/toilet building with a golf cart packed with cleaning equipment and supplies. Dave told me he had wrecked his BMW motorcycle and bought a Harley Softail Custom, "modified to look like a Road King." They volunteer with an NGO aid program to work in disaster relief. Mary explained, they want to give something back, make a contribution. Another wave of clouds was fast approaching. We scrambled for cover.

When the rain stopped, the wind died down and the insects returned to my campsite. I waved ineffectively at mosquitoes and searched for my DEET. I applied the oily liquid to my exposed skin and watched a National Geographic documentary play out at my feet. A biting fly was attacking a bright green grasshopper. The grasshopper was trying to hop away, but the fly landed on its back and nipped at its body. The grasshopper tried to scratch it off with its leg, but the fly positioned itself out of reach. The grasshopper made a hop. The fly jumped off, then immediately landed back on the grasshopper for another bite. The grasshopper walked, jumped, rolled over and crawled to no effect. Every time the grasshopper moved, the fly stayed with it, either flying low and landing on its back or hanging on while it moved, then biting again. I was mesmerized by the duel. The grasshopper rolled in the sand, but the fly hung on. The grasshopper was struggling for its life against a tiny fly and the fly was winning. The grasshopper was tiring. Its jumps became shorter, hops slower and it was rolling on the ground more than jumping.

The combatants were unaware of my presence. My sympathies were with the underdog. My body was a constellation of insect bites, old and new. I had been swatting and scratching for weeks, never free from the damn blood suckers. Without reservation, I was rooting for the grasshopper, who in spite of its greater size was clearly losing this battle.

I watched the duel and began to form a plan. I timed the intervals of the attack-defend sequence. Jump, fly, land, bite. Roll, fly, land, bite. Scratch, hang on, bite. I planned my intervention to intercept the fly during a grasshopper jump. It seemed the best chance to swat the fly and let the grasshopper escape. I watched and waited for the right opportunity. The grasshopper was slowing. The fly was becoming bolder, hanging on longer, even during jumps. Then I saw an opening. The grasshopper jumped; the fly hopped off its back. I stamped down with my sandled left foot to kill the fly and save the grasshopper.

I missed. I was shocked how quickly that fly reacted. I've

missed swatting lots of bugs, many of them on this trip. But this wasn't OK. The fly, apparently incensed by my interference, turned its wrath from the grasshopper to me. It attacked my ankle. I swatted at it with my hand. It jumped off and landed on the back of my knee. I slapped and missed again. I turned around and around, searching for the little bastard. He kept coming after me. I did what the grasshopper did, I hopped and ran away. The fly came at me from everywhere, buzzing, landing, I slapped at it. It jumped off and landed again. I looked for the grasshopper, maybe for help. The fly intensified its attack. I turned, slapped and ran from the campsite along the path into the woods waving frantically at the air and swatting blindly at my body. I continued to run and slap fifty yards along the path through the woods to my motorcycle in the parking lot.

Somewhere along the way, I lost the demon bug. I didn't kill it and it didn't kill me. But given time, I'm sure it would have. I walked a circle around the perimeter of the parking lot, to be sure it wasn't hiding and to quiet my hammering heart. When I thought it was safe, I cautiously walked back to my campsite, terrified the evil beast was lurking in ambush. I approached the campsite slowly and carefully, peering through the trees ahead for any sign of attack. I didn't see it. I walked toward my tent, still cautious. I kept a wary eye open for Beelzebug for the rest of the day. Thankfully, I never saw that homicidal maniac or the cowardly grasshopper who deserted me. I feel no shame at my undignified retreat. It was him or me. And I'm just happy to be here to tell the story.

I have fond memories of Daniel Boone National Forest. Camped in windy, overcast and thunderstorm weather doesn't sound much like a pleasant way to spend a couple of days. But the campground offered handy drinking water, showers, toilets, a cool lake and quiet forests. I liked it there. It was a beautiful woodland and a relaxing respite during a long trip. Though I enjoyed the area, the scenery and the campsite, I was anxious to move on.

CHAPTER 31: FRACKING

America is Tahoe writ big.

Friday, July 12

By morning, Daniel Boone National Forest was enveloped in a gray fog. The shadowy forests beyond the road were obscured in a murky cloud. The heavy veil muted sound and absorbed light. Its weight muffled the rumble of the powerful Harley engine. The morning ride was like a dream. Nothing was tangible, only hints of reality surfaced briefly, then melted away. Other vehicles materialized like ghosts then disappeared into the swirling mists. The world was gloomy, mute and dim. Time stood still while the earth hid in the haze. The vibration of the engine communicated my only sensory input.

Suddenly the curtain parted, the mist thinned, and then was gone. The sun shone and color returned to the universe. The earth woke. Birds soared in a blue sky. Wind rustled green leaves on saplings. The engine roared. My spirits rose, time restarted.

Hunger crept in and stabbed my stomach. My belly clock never quite synchronized with a likely diner. I encountered a multitude of fast-food factories along the main road, but few independent diners or restaurants. I suppose the franchises could afford the expensive main street real estate. The "mom and pop" shops moved to the side roads when the rents went up. The locals know where they are, but they aren't easy for a visitor to find. Too often, I settled for something semi-edible from a gas station snack bar, or a fried food franchise.

I discovered a solution in the second week of my trip. It happened on an impulse almost by accident. I had been riding since seven-thirty in the morning. My belly alarm was sounding loud and clear. I passed several fast-food restaurants but no place with a welcoming personality. At about noon, I stopped for fuel. Flush with my success navigating the gas pump credit card identification process, I left my bike at the pump and walked into the building. I picked up a bottle of water and posed my question to the friendly, middle-aged woman behind the counter.

"Can you tell me where I can find a diner or restaurant for breakfast? – Not fast food, I want a sit-down meal."

"Hmmm." She thought about my question. "Which way are you headed?"

"I'm headed to the diner."

She smiled.

"OK, well, I know a good one that's a couple of miles from here."

"Sounds perfect. Where is it?"

I found the restaurant two miles from the main road and realized I'd hit on the perfect solution. It turned out that most of the good, local diners were not far out of my way. And a couple of miles was always worth it. I enjoyed talking with the local customers, the friendly service, good food and reasonable prices for breakfast, lunch and (once or twice) dinner.

Wayne National Forest is in southeastern Ohio, not far from Kentucky and West Virginia. I arrived at the Lake Vesuvius Recreation Area at about two thirty. I unloaded the bike and unpacked. My sleeping bag was damp from two days and nights of thunderstorms in Kentucky. The tent was a soaked sponge when I packed it in the morning. It didn't get any drier on the ride. I strung a nylon line between two trees. The warm sunshine made a quick job of drying my wet gear. I set up my tent and threw in my duffel bag, motorcycle jacket, gloves and helmet. I settled down on the picnic table to read an Elmore Leonard novel in the shade.

I was about eight hundred miles from Massachusetts. The end of my trip was in sight. Though I looked forward to seeing my family and friends in New England, I didn't feel ready to end my trip. It felt like I was just getting started instead of coming to the end. I didn't feel like I had done all that I set out to do. I was hungry for more road.

Saturday, 13 July

Leith Run Camp is situated on the western bank of the Ohio River. The river was high, fast flowing and muddy from the recent rains. A half mile of water separated my campsite from the West Virginia shore. Barges pushed heaping loads of coal in three, four and five boat trains. Campers fished from the grassy shore all day and with lanterns after dark. The campsites were booked six months in advance. I was lucky to find one vacant. I was accidentally in the right place at the right time. Someone didn't show up and I got their site.

Once again, my motorcycle and tent were matchbox toys surrounded by mammoth SUVs and RVs, homes away from home. Terry and Sheri occupied an RV in the campsite beside mine. They invited me for dinner. She was a radiologist and he was a physician's assistant. They were happy with the economic direction the country is going. They talked about their work. They described how uninsured patients used the emergency room instead of a doctor they couldn't afford, even for pregnancy tests.

Sheri's insurance requires a $250 co-pay for emergency room use. They asked about the Dutch medical insurance system. I told them we have a national healthcare system. Everyone pays and everyone is covered.

Terry: "That wouldn't work here. There are more people in America."

They conceded that Trump shouldn't use Twitter for foreign policy statements. But were satisfied by his hard line with China. "Now they are ready to make a deal."

Terry said the area economy needs a boost. He was looking forward to the coal mining operation Trump promised for West Virginia and,

"Fracking will be great for the economy."

"Fracking is pretty hard on the environment," I suggested.

"People around here are more concerned with putting food on the table than saving a spotted owl."

They planned to retire in a year and travel around the U.S.in their RV.

At this campsite, there were swarms of flies in the air. They looked like biting wasps with wide, translucent wings, but they were harmless. They flew, hovered and landed in pairs. Their only function seemed to be mating.

Then they died, blanketing the exterior of my tent. In the morning, I brushed off the bodies of hundreds of spent lovers.

Sunday, July 14

From Leith Run campground early Sunday morning I rode northeast for fifty miles. My route paralleled the Ohio River with Ohio on my left and West Virginia on my right. I turned east at Glen Dale. I followed secondary roads through forested hills and small towns whose names I didn't know. I wound my way north and east through West Virginia to the Pennsylvania border south of Pittsburgh.

By nine o'clock, I had traveled a hundred miles and found myself seated in a red imitation-leather booth in a franchise restaurant and wondering why. What makes a franchise successful? It isn't quality. Maybe it's name recognition; people know what to expect. The food may not be dynamic or innovative, guests may not even like it much, but it's dependable. The family-operated, no-name diners were risky. Their menus were not standardized. There were no regional managers to maintain service and quality levels. They took a little more effort to find. But they were far superior in ambience and flavor, and the prices were competitive. Unlike franchise restaurants, the 'mom and pop' diners even felt more real.

The restaurant was a stand-alone building in front of a shopping mall. I did not see a name and thought it was an independent. There were a dozen cars parked in front, usually a promising indicator. I negotiated a U-turn into the parking lot. At first glance, it appeared to be a family restaurant. I discovered it was a franchise with a farm theme. I was hungry so I decided to give it a try.

The food was uninspiring and tasteless. Their name was proudly displayed on every surface inside the building, on the menu and the posters. They offered souvenir mugs, key rings and stuffed toys, all proudly trademarked. But there was nothing special about the restaurant, no ambience or character. It was efficiently laid out, air-conditioned, clean, but a bit worn. The interior was decorated with professionally printed marketing graphics displaying images of food that looked better than it tasted. The waitress was apathetic, the coffee weak and the prices high.

Is dependable mediocrity better than a risk? My Styrofoam breakfast and watery coffee dropped me into melancholy thoughts. Neither the servers nor the customers seemed enthusiastic. All appeared to be fulfilling a role assigned to them. The customers ate listlessly in silence. The servers moved slowly, unsmiling, with lifeless eyes. I ate only as much of my meal as I needed, paid the unsmiling hostess and was on my way.

My thoughts turned to seniors stalling change. Baby boomers, and I'm one of them, have accumulated houses, cars, boats, RVs, lawn mowers, pensions and investments. We've got our TV and beer. We worked hard for all these things but they're a trap. We embrace them, nurture them and protect them. We fight to keep them safe. We dig in our heels and hold on tight. We fear and fight any change that threatens to take anything away. I began to consider the possibility that we are holding back progress.

My meal and fuel stops brought me in contact with young service people. What chances did they have? Their options became more limited each year they worked at dead-end jobs. The patrons they served in the restaurants, fast and slow food, breakfast, lunch and dinner, were baby boomers with money. I felt a pang of guilt, supporting a system that subjugated a generation. I thought of Mike and his girlfriend. I wondered if they found a place to live by their July 15 eviction. A feeling of concern grew with a worrying thought. America is Tahoe writ big.

I was riding through the forests, rivers, lakes and mountains of Appalachia. It's a land of environmental wonder, also a region notorious for moonshine, clan feuds, ignorance and widespread poverty. The ride through Kentucky, West Virginia and Pennsylvania was breathtaking, but somber. In spite of its many resources, this part of the country is in a historic struggle with poverty. A brief economic recovery introduced logging, mining and the steel industry to the area in the mid-twentieth century. It was a short-lived boom. Industry withdrew, mechanization dried up jobs and conservationists established national parks and forests that sent the lumber industry into suspended animation. The prosperity that blessed most of the United States over the last fifty years passed by Appalachia.

The buildings and roads were decaying. Closed and abandoned shops lined the main streets in town centers. Roadblocks restricted travel across acres of unrepaired, crumbling potholes and washouts. Even the Jersey barriers were worn, cracked, eroded and discolored with age.

Countless families lived in unfinished foundations, capped and roofed with tar paper and black rubber when the building money ran out. Others called aluminum boxes mounted on cinder blocks home.

In West Virginia I rode by a two-mile industrial complex beside the Ohio River. Cooling towers belched clouds of steam that drifted for miles. A coal-coke debris pile, three stories high and a mile long bordered the river awaiting transport. Sooty buildings served as office spaces.

Filth-streaked trucks rumbled over oil-stained bumpy streets. Smokestacks spewed gasses high into the clouds and methane flames flared out of exhaust pipes like candles on a sooty cake. The dust and coal/oil stench coated my clothes and skin. My lungs burned and eyes teared from the foul air.

I thought of Terry and Sherry's enthusiasm over the West Virginia and Ohio shale oil reserves. They were excited about a plan to develop the world's largest fracking operation.

"Fracking will really boost the economy. We will replace coal mines and steel mills with fracking plants. It will provide a whole generation of young people with employment."

The ailing economy in the tri-state area was desperate for a shot in the arm. The deplorable condition of the infrastructure attested to half a century of subsistence living. Riding through this part of the country, it was easy to understand why injecting chemicals, sand and water into subterranean rock formations to extract gas and oil seems like a good idea. The choice between economic prosperity and environmental protection was a simple one for the people who struggled to survive here.

I arrived at Trough Creek Campground in Pennsylvania Sunday afternoon. The weekend campers were on their way home. Only five of the twenty-nine campsites were occupied. I chose a remote site within walking distance of the pit toilet and adjacent water pump.

This section of the campground was deserted. It was a warm and sunny afternoon. I set up my tent in the shade of an old oak tree and went about organizing my camp. I collected some sticks for a campfire. The ranger stopped by at about five o'clock on his way out for the day. He told me there were only five parties in the whole campground and none near me.

Soon after the ranger drove away, a double-axle pick-up truck with Pennsylvania license plates arrived. It rumbled and bumped down the dirt road and stopped beside the water pump. A middle-aged man and woman and two dogs climbed out. I watched from my seat at the picnic table. They parked their camper, dumped their water and spent forty-five minutes refilling their tanks. I walked over to say hello. I asked why they were dumping water and refilling. They explained that they filled up at another site, but the water was brown. This water was clean.

I learned to recognize the signals of people who wanted to talk. These two sent the other signals. When my attempts to draw them into a conversation failed, I gave up and walked back to my campsite and reclined on my bench with a Lee Child novel.

The couple finished filling their tanks and backed their RV into the site diagonally across from mine. They set up their camp, tended to their two dogs and ignored me. They fired up a gasoline generator; which chugged all night, presumably to power the roof-mounted air conditioner and the TV I glimpsed flickering through their window blinds.

An hour after the first couple settled in, two more SUVs arrived, towing similar RVs. My secluded site had grown into quite a little community. Once again, I was surrounded by the giants of modern comfort camping. The new group entertained me for a half-hour while they struggled to wedge their oversized campers into undersized parking places, backwards. One man accomplished his task quickly, but the second driver struggled. Two women and the other man surrounded the vehicle. They pointed, waved and offered high volume, helpful, sometimes conflicting and increasingly animated directions.

I observed from my seat in the shade while the driver attempted to back his camper into the narrow parking space. I could empathize with his dilemma. I'm no good at steering a trailer. I used to own a garden tractor with a tow-behind trailer for hauling leaves and brush. The trailer was a handy tool, very useful for big yard jobs and small ones. Any garden work is more fun when you use a tractor. But I never got the hang of backing up that trailer.

My brother has no trouble with trailers. He owned a similar tractor and trailer. He also owned a boat. He made it look easy when he backed his boat down the ramp to launch it. But I'm hopeless. No matter how slowly I drive, how careful I am, every time I try to back a trailer into a spot, I make a mess of it. Back, forward, turn the wheel the other way, try again, forward, back. The trailer always ends up sideways.

My camping neighbor reminded me of my little tractor and its handy trailer. For twenty minutes, he tried to negotiate his RV into the parking space without success. Back, forward, try again, then again.

The RV clamped to the back of the SUV, rolled forward and back, turned from side to side, stopped diagonally, then rolled back out again. I watched the driver make several attempts, peering in the side mirrors to guide the big metal box. He was aiming for the narrow, level space with trees on one side and the fire pit and picnic table on the other. After several attempts and retries the driver stopped, climbed out and turned the job over to his friend. The second man was more experienced. To my disappointment, for I was enjoying the show, the second driver was successful on his first attempt.

The sun had set by the time both RVs were parked. The couples busied themselves with the conventional RV camping activities. They plugged into power, turned on their flood lights and stereo. They set up a folding table and lawn chairs. They set out food and drinks. Then they sat outside, talking till long after dark. Once again, mine was the only tent in sight. While they talked, I sat by my campfire, smoking my pipe trying to tune out the noise and lights next door. I thought of walking over to say hello, but it seemed to me they were old friends, enjoying a sociable night. I didn't want to intrude.

An hour later, a car drove around the bend and stopped beside their campsite. The lights from the new arrival shone directly on me and my campsite. I could see the driver in silhouette when he climbed out of the vehicle. He left the lights and engine running and walked over to talk to the people sitting in the lawn chairs.

Instead of a quick visit, he lingered, socializing with the group. I sat on the bench at my picnic table, spotlighted by the car's headlights, while the newcomer talked with my neighbors. The laser beams were an annoying distraction from my contemplative campfire.

Finally, I walked over to his car. He walked away from their RV to intercept me. I was surprised to see it was a tall, thin, freckle-faced park ranger, complete with uniform, badge, Sam Browne belt and wiry, red hair sticking out from under the edges of his campaign hat, with a brim that barely extended beyond his sun-blistered nose. We met beside his car. He was about thirty years old.

"Hi," I said.

"Is there something I can do for you?"

"I'm just surprised. The other ranger had told me he was leaving at five o'clock. He implied I'd be alone all night."

He stood by his car and made no response.

"I didn't expect another ranger to be around. Will you be here all night?"

He became evasive. "We do different things."

"Oh, so you are here all night."

"We're around all the time."

I thought but didn't say, 'Who does this guy think he is, the Secret Service?'

He tugged the belt of his brown uniform pants and brushed some imaginary lint off the green shoulder patch.

"Can I see your camp receipt and identification?"

"The receipt is mounted in the post at the front of the campsite. That's what they told me to do when I registered."

"Will you go get it and show it to me, and your identification." This was not framed as a question.

I walked back to the front of my campsite and pulled the folded paper from the plastic holder on the post. From my pack on the picnic table, I retrieved my passport. Then I walked to the car where he was waiting.

I handed him both documents. He glanced at them and handed them back to me. "Is there something you wanted?"

"Yes, I wonder if you could turn off your lights. They're shining right on my camp."

He looked over at my little tent, as though it was the first time he noticed it. Then back at me. "Is there anything else?"

"Nope, that'll do it." I waited.

He stood looking at me. I stood looking at him.

He reached into the cab and turned off his headlights, not the engine.

"Thanks."

He walked back to the group at the RV without a word. He left the engine running for forty-five more minutes while he talked with my neighbors.

I smoked my pipe and considered my plans. I had plenty of time before I was supposed to meet my cousin. I thought about staying at this campsite for another day, but the place didn't give me good vibes. I decided to leave in the morning, find someplace that felt better.

The interior of my tent was bright from the glow of my neighbors' roof spotlights. I laid on my sleeping bag, closed my eyes and tried to ignore the music, the generator and the barking dogs. With the lights from my three neighbors flickering, I lamented the invention of the RV, electricity, gasoline, dogs and officious park rangers till sleep carried me away.

CHAPTER 32: IT'S THE JOURNEY

If the Democrats win, maybe
we can stop the bleeding.

Monday, July 15

When I selected Trough Creek for my camp stop, I thought it might be a hospitable place to relax for an extra day, explore the area, maybe find the creek and go for a swim. I was 450 miles from the end of my trip. I had a few extra travel days before I was expected in western Massachusetts. But I developed the feeling that this was not the campsite for me, so I decided to get back on the road and put Trough Creek in the rear-view mirror.

My gear was packed and my bike loaded, ready to ride, but I was not yet sure where I was headed. I sat at my picnic table to look at my road atlas. My glasses, pen, notebook, bottle of water and e-reader were spread out on the table in front of me. All my neighbors were awake and busy around their camps. A clear-faced, tanned middle-aged man wearing hiking boots, khaki shorts and an untucked flannel shirt, walked in my direction. He approached and stood on the grass between our two sites.

"Good morning. I'm Joe. I see you're all packed and ready to go. Do you have time to come over for a cup of coffee?"

"Hi, I'm Bob. Sure, that sounds good. Let me get this stuff organized and I'll be over in a minute."

I gathered all the things on the table and packed them into my gas tank pack and zipped it shut. I picked up the atlas and walked over to greet my four neighbors. They were sitting at a picnic table, beside one of the RVs.

I met Joe, Marci, Meredith and Tim.

Marci had curly, sandy hair. She was wearing cargo shorts, sneakers and a black, sleeveless t-shirt. "Would you like a cup of coffee?"

"Yes, thanks."

They were friends and work colleagues.

Joe explained, "Pennsylvania has over a hundred state parks and twenty forests. That doesn't count the national stuff; parks, memorials, wildlife refuges and recreation areas. There is a lot of recreation land in Pennsylvania. We all work for the Pennsylvania Department of Conservation and Natural Resources."

"Must be a cool job. Is this a business trip?"

Joe laughed. "No, well kind of. I have to visit a lot of state campgrounds. We thought we'd make a long weekend of it."

"So you all work together?"

Marci: "All but Tim, he's in IT. He's not really an outdoors guy.

Did you see him park the RV?"

"I didn't notice."

"Right. Well it's a rental. First time he's driven it."

"You look like you're on a trip," Joe observed. "Where are you going?"

"I live in The Netherlands. I'm taking a cross-country trip, from NH to California. I'm on my way back now."

"I knew you had a story! So you've already been to California and now you're riding back?" she said.

"Yup, I have a son who lives near Lake Tahoe. I rode out to visit him."

We covered the basics about what I was doing on the trip and the conversation came back to Pennsylvania.

Marci: "We're worried about the open spaces. The federal government is defunding the national forest system and selling leases to private developers to cut the lumber. The state is laying off staff and closing parks. A lot of parks have reduced access. Some are closed two days a week because there aren't enough rangers to keep them open."

Joe: "Pennsylvania has a long commitment to public forests, parks and recreation areas. But the federal government is strangling the budget, so it impacts state services too. We're worried. Once you lose a state forest or park to development, it's gone and never comes back."

Me: "What do you think is going to happen?"

Joe: "It all depends on the next election. If the Republicans win, we'll lose a lot of wilderness land, maybe our jobs too. If the Democrats win, maybe we can stop the bleeding."

We sat in silence for a minute, sipped our coffee, each with our own thoughts. Then Joe asked, "Where are you going today?"

I looked down at the Rand McNally atlas spread out on the table between us. It was opened to the Pennsylvania pages.

"Northeast."

"That's it, northeast?"

"Yah, I'm not sure where I'll end the day but I'm on my way to New England. So northeast." They looked back and forth at each other. All of them smiled.

"Did I miss something? What's funny?"

"It's just that most people have a destination. You don't. You're just headed in a direction. It's all about the journey, that's pretty cool."

"I hadn't thought about it."

"That's what's cool."

"So, you don't know where you're going today, or where you'll be staying tonight?"

"I figure I'll ride till I'm tired, then find a place."

"That's great."

"Riding a motorcycle, you never really know how far you'll get. You start with a direction in mind and deal with whatever happens. Maybe it'll rain and you have to pull over. Or you see someplace nice and decide to stop for a while. I don't lock in on a destination."

Marci: "You traveled across the country and didn't make any plans?"

"That's not entirely true. I started with an itinerary. But it didn't work. After the first week I put it away."

"What about reservations for motels or campsites?"

"I made one reservation for a night in New York City. That was at the end of the first week." "So you just showed up and asked for a campsite and got one, all across the country?"

"Arches National Park was full when I got there late in the afternoon. But I found a place close by."

Joe: "So, this morning, when you leave the park, which way will you turn?"

"Whichever way takes me northeast."

Joe: "If you want a very nice state park, you should try World's End. It's northeast of here."

Marci stepped into the RV and returned unfolding a map of Pennsylvania. She spread it out on the table and pointed to World's End State Park.

"It's up here in the northeast corner, near New York. It's only about a hundred and fifty miles but there's no direct route. It's all back roads and farm roads."

"It sounds like just the ride I'm looking for."

"I think it's one of the nicest state parks we have. If you're going in that direction, I think it will be worth the trip."

We said our farewells. Marci wrote her email address on a sheet of paper. I promised to write when I got home.

The route to World's End took me through Amish country, an example of how resisting change can be beautiful. Wandering the hills of central Pennsylvania was a voyage to an earlier time. It was a peaceful ride through winding, rolling, sometimes mountainous roads. There were few other vehicles, some were horse-drawn carriages. The drivers waved as I cruised by, idling the Harley engine in deference to the horses. The sun was warm and the air smelled rich and clean. I passed freshly painted, two-hundred-year-old homes and farms where horses pulled plows through thick, black earth in straight rows.

I arrived at the campground early Monday afternoon. The

variation between state and national parks and forests, even within the same region is striking. They all provide picnic tables, fire pits and tent sites, the level of maintenance and service varies greatly. For example, Trough Creek offered drinking water and stinky pit toilets, no showers. World's End, a few hours away in the same state, offered clean drinking water, restrooms with sinks, showers and flush toilets. Maybe there was a creek at Trough Creek, but I never saw it. World's End provides a grassy slope so campers can walk into the clear, flowing river to swim, raft or canoe. The camping fees don't seem to relate to services. And all the state parks I've stayed in cost more than the national parks and forests.

World's End was my first experience with an untidy campsite. I guess that speaks to the efficiency of the park caretakers across the country. They spend a lot of time and effort cleaning up after people who don't. All of my previous campsites in state and national facilities were neat and well maintained.

That is why the World's End campsite took me by surprise. It was a mess. The previous campers had used the firepit for a trash barrel. It was piled with unburned trash and garbage; Styrofoam coffee cups, a half-full box of pancake mix, a plastic coffee creamer bottle also half full, wipe rags and charred, wet newspapers; thankfully, no dirty diapers.

The clutter was not confined to the firepit. The whole campsite and the surrounding area were littered with candy wrappers, empty plastic water bottles, an empty Red Bull can and wet tissue paper. I considered returning to the registration office to complain and request a new site. But something piqued my curiosity. So, before I unpacked my gear, I began to put the site in order. The previous campers had abandoned a half-full trash bag behind a nearby tree. I used it to collect their debris.

I wondered who stayed there and for how long. What kind of people were they and where were they from? I donned my camp gloves and collected the forensic evidence.

I discovered an arrow in the woods behind the picnic table. It was short, with bright plastic, orange and white flights, a toy for a child's bow. It was new. The metal point was slightly dented from hitting rocks. Beside the arrow, lay a limp pizza box. Someone had drawn three rings on the inside for a target. The open box was slumped on the ground, against the base of a tree, not nailed or hung with string. The box was punctured only once, outside the rings. In the underbrush rested a brown, plastic toy sword sheath without the sword.

Red, green, pink, yellow and blue plastic beads with little holes were scattered on the table and the ground; the kind of trinkets children use to make toy bracelets and necklaces. A box for plastic swim floats was abandoned in the woods.

I found a box with a price tag for a one-person hammock, four-hundred-pound capacity. They must have taken the hammock with them. They abandoned or forgot a package of All Natural Kiln Dried Firewood in the woods behind the tent site.

I paced around the campsite, no longer collecting trash, but clues. I found two small, steel tent stakes, the ends curved like question marks. They were bent by someone who used their foot to push them into the hard-packed ground. I kept returning to the fire pit. It was a treasure trove of evidence. I excavated two large Styrofoam coffee cups, coffee stirrers and a half-melted coffee creamer bottle, a half-full box of pancake mix and a few filter cigarette butts, two different brands, no lipstick.

It took me an hour to clean up the campsite, but I continued to discover new clues during my two-day stay. I pieced together my theory about the family that used the site.

The two, large coffee cups and two different brands of cigarettes told me it was a couple, probably a man and a woman. They had two children, a boy who played with the bow and arrows and sword and a little girl who crafted plastic jewelry and was not a strong swimmer. The swim floats were pink.

The new bow-and-arrow set, hammock and swim floats boxes told me they went shopping before they arrived. So my guess is they lived nearby. Dad made a target with the empty pizza box. But he didn't help his son shoot. Or he was a bad shot too because there was only one hole in the box. Mom made jewelry with the little girl. Mom was neater than dad because there were only a handful of plastic pieces littering the table and the ground beneath it.

The pancake mix box was half full. That means only one breakfast. They didn't cook dinner because they left the pizza box but no food cans in the fire pit. So they stayed only one night.

There were several signs this family probably didn't camp often. The tent stakes were new and of poor quality – and they forgot two. Experienced campers buy good ones and don't lose tent stakes. It's lucky it didn't rain while they were here. It was probably a low-quality tent. They bought firewood even though there is plenty of deadfall scattered everywhere around. They abandoned or forgot a package of expensive firewood, so they didn't stay long enough to use it, or bought more than they needed.

Their fire pit was long cold when I arrived early Monday afternoon. They probably arrived Saturday and left Sunday afternoon. This is a non-electric site, so they came in a car, or a van, not an RV.

Here's my profile and reconstruction of events from the evidence at the campsite:

- A local, thirty-something couple with a boy, eight years old and a five-year-old girl arrived Saturday about midday in their van after shopping for food, toys, a hammock and swim floats.

- They probably didn't get an early start, so they live

within fifty miles of this site.

- They stayed one afternoon and night.

- They set up the tent, probably for the first time and the hammock. The tent wasn't new because I didn't find a tent package.

- After that, they went down to the river for a swim by the campground general store. They bought pizza for dinner.

- While the boy played with the bow and arrow, the mother and daughter made jewelry at the picnic table.

- At night they lit a campfire and burned one package of wood. They didn't cook marshmallows or hotdogs on sticks over the fire. I didn't find any burned marshmallows, hotdogs or sticks.

- Sunday morning, they cooked breakfast of pancakes on a gas stove on the picnic table. They threw their garbage and trash in the smoldering fire pit. They collected their children and as much of their gear as they could find and drove away just after noon on Sunday.

Even after I cleaned up the campsite and set up my tent, I continued to turn up new clues about the people who stayed there. I spread some of their debris on the picnic table and looked it over to absorb their aura. I wonder if they'll ever go camping again. I don't think they did much before this. The biggest clue of their inexperience was the chaos they left behind. Experienced campers leave little or no trace of their passing. I hoped these parents wouldn't teach their kids to leave campsites the way they left theirs.

I carried the bulging trash bag to the campground toilet building and deposited the trash in a common receptacle. Then I changed into my swimsuit. I hiked through the woods to the shallow river nearby. The afternoon found me reclining in the cool, bubbling water, watching the sun shimmer on the rippling surface and wet rocks.

In the morning I rode twenty miles to Dushore for breakfast. I was sitting in the booth in a local diner enjoying eggs over easy, hashbrowns and bacon when an unfamiliar noise reached my awareness. It took me a few seconds to realize it was my phone. Its primary function on my journey was for navigation. I had almost forgotten it had a communication mode. By the time I recognized the annoying beep and reached into my bag for the device, it had stopped. The pop-up screen informed me that my cousin Jim had tried to contact me. I called him back.

He'd been following me on Google Maps and saw that I was three hundred miles from his house. He warned me of an approaching rainstorm headed my way and suggested that I leave tomorrow. He assured me I could make it to his house in one day. It would get me there a day earlier than we planned. I told him if he was ready for a visitor, I'd leave tomorrow. After breakfast I found a local supplier and bought a bottle of single malt whisky as a house gift.

Suddenly it was the last day of my road trip. I couldn't really believe it. Civilization, clocks, calendars, appointments and responsibilities thrust themselves upon me. As painful as it was, I was forced to consider selling the motorcycle I had come to love. That responsibility could no longer remain tucked away in a back corner in my mind.

Thunderstorms drove me into the tent early. At seven o'clock I was lying on my sleeping bag, reading by flashlight. It rained most of the night.

Wednesday, July 17

The last day of the trip, I woke early to a cool, gray day with the trees dripping in the light breeze. I'd have to start early to get to Jim's before the storm. I bundled into my rain gear hoping I wouldn't need it. I promised myself if the rain hit hard, I'd stop. With thunderstorms on the way, it was safer not to move. I didn't know if it was the dismal weather or the end of the trip that darkened my mood. Regardless, it was time to go.

At six o'clock in the morning my neighbors were sleeping peacefully. So I muscled, wrestled and rolled the bike out of the campground without using the engine. The Softail was a comfortable, tireless cruiser, but it was an uncooperative beast to push on gravel and damn heavy. The first part of the campground road was mercifully flat. There was a slight uphill grade where I dug my boots into the surface and leaned over the handlebars to push. The rest of the winding exit was downhill. Once on the main road, I fired it up and cruised away in low gear. I followed U.S. Routes 17 east and 88 east in New York.

These were terrible motorcycle roads, all scratched and patched. Bone-jarring bumps at irregular intervals pounded my spine and sent electric shocks from butt to brain. This part of the ride was painful and dangerous for motorcycles. The irregularities in the road pounded the bike with sharp and sudden shocks that struck, too often without warning. I hung on and kept a vigilant eye on the tarmac and concrete. But it did no good. I was continuously shocked and jarred. My teeth rattled, my neck ached, and I gripped the handlebar with cramped hands and numbed fingers. Mercifully, the traffic was light and the rain held off.

I turned onto Jim's driveway in the afternoon, thoroughly beaten and tenderized. Jim greeted me from his seat on the front steps. He had been following my progress on his mobile phone. We hugged, smiled and had just enough time to roll the motorcycle into the garage before the rain started.

CHAPTER 33: FAMILY AND FRIENDS

Your credit card was used in Dallas.

Jim and Cindy had remodeled the basement of their three-bedroom ranch into a two-room guest studio. It was complete with a private bathroom and laundry. I unpacked and spread my gear all over the studio to sort and clean. My dirty clothes turned and thumped in the washer and dryer. I even washed and dried my sleeping bag and tent.

Thursday, Jim and I cleaned the bike and topped off the oil. We drove into town. It was my first ride in a car since California. Jim bought sandals and some garden mulch; I sat for a haircut. We played nine holes at the local golf course. In the evening, Jim barbecued steaks and we watched the Red Sox on the tube.

The trip had come to an end.

I phoned Mike. They had not found an apartment. They had moved into a single room in a condominium with two roommates. They were cramped, uncomfortable and stressed. It broke my heart. I offered moral support and encouragement. It felt weak.

For two weeks I reconnected with friends and family in New England, visiting for an hour, a day or two. I rode from western Massachusetts to Cape Cod; after that to Marshfield, Hull and Abington. I visited Matt and Jessica at their new house in Bolton. We toured their house and backyard forest. He described twenty-five years of ambitious plans to clear, clean, build, plant, and renovate. I was struck by the similarity between his new home and the one where he grew up. We parted unconnected.

My friend in Marshfield put me in contact with a man who was interested in buying the motorcycle. I rode to southern New Hampshire to show it to him. He told me motorcycle riding in America is a dying hobby. It's only old guys like us who still buy motorcycles. That's why the market is shrinking. The kids all want new cars with air conditioning. It broke my heart to part with my trusted friend.

* * *

I will not recount conversations with my friends and family during my last two weeks, not because they were private or irrelevant, but because there were no new revelations. Friends and family expressed the same polarized political views as the strangers I'd met on the road. Democrats in New England believed the liberal news, Republicans subscribed to the conservative spectrum. The gulf between their views was wide and deep, with strong emotional currents.

However, I would feel remiss if I did not briefly summarize three conversations that occurred during my final week. They fit with a characteristic of U.S. life that I had come to recognize. From an elderly shut-in and her caregiver, I learned about fear of widespread telephone scams that prey on the vulnerable. The perpetrators of these frauds use a database of the names of senior citizens.

They open the conversation with a threat:

"Your credit card was used in Dallas."

"Your social security number was used to authorize…"

"Your computer has a virus."

"This is the IRS; your taxes are overdue."

"Your mortgage is overdue."

"Your electric bill is unpaid and we will shut it off."

I assembled a list of fifteen different phone scams that threaten to halt service, foreclose or initiate legal action. The purpose of the phone call is to elicit as much personal information as they can trick the victim into divulging; credit card numbers, social security number, date of birth, age, middle name, anything that will help them access financial resources, empty bank accounts, pensions and savings. The eighty-seven-year-old lady I spoke with was afraid to answer the phone for fear she would be tricked into poverty. Her caregiver told me they received several of these calls per day.

Two other conversations focused on the U.S. healthcare system. Two emergency room nurses explained how the U.S. healthcare system is manipulated to access free medical care.

Uninsured patients drive directly to a hospital emergency room with ambiguous complaints like chest or abdominal pain. The subsequent diagnosis and treatments are ultimately subsidized by taxpayer dollars, not insurance companies. And a hospital administrator described the complex and chaotic hospital financing that supports an expensive, disjointed, yet profitable healthcare system with no responsible oversight to keep costs under control.

He said, "Americans live and die with the most expensive, least efficient and most profitable medical healthcare system among all developed countries. And surprisingly they don't know it."

I spent my last evening with my niece and her family. In the morning they drove me to the shuttle that would take me to the airport for my flight back to Amsterdam.

CHAPTER 34: CLOSING THOUGHTS

*My feelings are just as
valid as your facts.*

In the summer of 2019, I rode a Harley Davidson motorcycle from New Hampshire to California and back. I set out to reconnect with my country and my sons. I immersed myself in the American way of life. I refreshed my view of America. I developed a bond and affection for the motorcycle by learning to adapt to its qualities. And, I visited both of my sons.

I experienced America as a citizen and as a visitor from another land. I rode through the forests of New England, the farmland of middle America, over the Rocky Mountains and across the western deserts. I felt the texture of the land under my wheels; every bump and crack and downhill thrill. I sweated in the heat, shivered in the cold and soaked in the rain surrounded by the fragrance of rich, wet earth, desert sage and Ponderosa pine. Along the way I listened to the stories, hopes and fears of the Americans I met. I gained a new perspective on my country and its people.

I grew to love my ride. It was powerful, heavy and loud, a wild beast but not my enemy. It was mighty but not angry. It leaped to life with a throaty roar each morning. It was strong, healthy and hungry for the road. It leaned eagerly into turns and cruised the open road tirelessly. It was a powerful lion, not an agile antelope. Gravel, sand and loose earth were not our friends. I wish we had met when we were both younger.

My other goal was to reconnect with my sons. Matt is a homeowner starting a family, an engineer with a Master's degree married to an engineer with a PhD. By all standards he is well on his way to a rewarding life. He was polite and respectful but distant and detached. We did not discuss the issues that divide us. I can only guess that his memories of the life we shared are very different from mine. Matt responds to my emails occasionally and sends links to family photos. I'm sorry we can't have more. We did not reconnect.

Mike is another story. He and I have a complex relationship. He's sometimes close, sometimes distant. When he's out of touch, I know he's in trouble. I think our relationship was strengthened by my visit. He welcomed me into his home and shared his life. He's chosen a challenging path. I wish I could help but I respect his decisions. I provide what support I can and hope it's enough. I didn't so much reconnect with Mike as reinforce our bond.

ROBERT JOHN BARRA

I listened to Americans from east to west and back. Some were retired, some working, young, old, men and women; a pattern emerged. Common themes threaded through every conversation: fear and insecurity. People expressed fear for themselves, their families, for their safety and for America. Financial security was foremost. Some feared for their safety, some feared for the environment, others feared for their health.

Almost everyone I spoke with expressed fear in one way or another. My new perspective is that America is a place where people live in a continued state of insecurity. Even product price tags and restaurant menus can't be trusted.

The political climate was polarized. Republicans expressed fear of losing what they had and concern over being prevented from getting what they wanted. Most people owned lots of personal possessions, toys, stuff, and continued to collect into their senior years. But no matter how much, it wasn't enough, and they didn't want to give up any of it. Democrats feared America was losing its soul to greed and selfishness. The two opposing sides didn't speak with each other, they argued, accused and threatened.

The Republican message was simple. They blame America's woes on four main villains: immigrants, criminals, welfare recipients and Democrats. According to Republicans, immigrants represent a tidal wave of poor, unskilled, beggars, thieves and rapists invading from the south that will bankrupt and ruin the country. Criminals are Oxycontin and methamphetamine addicts who attack and rob innocent victims without conscience or remorse. Most immigrants are also criminals. Welfare recipients are the generations of lazy, non-working poor. Immigrants are future welfare recipients. The Democrats are socialists who support the give-away programs that will steal the country from working people and surrender it to immigrants, criminals and welfare recipients.

It's a simple message with an easy-to-understand solution.

The Democrats message is more complex. They say that the country is decaying because of Republican selfishness, greed and corruption. They want a sustainable society with more schools than prisons. They endorse affordable health care, equal justice, environmental protection, transparent financial systems and an end to special interest lobbying. They want to improve the quality of life for the whole country, not just the rich. It's complicated, with no simple solution.

Both sides demonize their opponents and subscribe only to "facts" that support their opinions. A question, often repeated in varying forms by both sides, highlights the proliferation of false facts, gossip, rumors and the need for reliable information.

"Why are their facts correct and my facts are not?"

Another statement was more troubling because it implies a moral justification for every form of bigotry: "My feelings are just as valid as your facts."

I viewed almost no commercial television during my stay in the U.S. The TV "news" I heard in restaurants, motels and travel stops seemed different from what I remember. I grew up watching Walter Cronkite, Dan Rather, Tom Brokaw, Chet Huntley and David Brinkley. I thought of them as people who cared about what was happening in the world who shared information I could trust. But maybe I see things differently after so many years.

The news readers I heard during this visit to America made no pretense of impartiality. The main function of popular news media is not to inform, but to fan the flames of fear and incite discord. Americans subscribe to information sources based on the message; conservative or liberal. American "news" has become a collection of opinionated editorials, crafted to appeal to a biased audience. Carefully selected sound bites are woven together to create emotional messages. There is no clear distinction between fact and opinion. Objectivity is not part of the "news" presentation.

The political dialogue in the U.S. reminded me of a line from the Rudyard Kipling poem, "If":.

If you can bear to hear the truth you've spoken twisted by knaves to make a trap for fools . . .

I met with and spoke with many seniors across the country, the baby boomers, former hippies. They've aged, matured, become settled, comfortable, and too many are frightened. These aren't the dynamic social changers who marched on Kent State. I can't blame them. They have too much to risk. They want to live out their final years in comfort. They aren't speaking out for social justice, equality and opportunity. They support the status quo. They don't want anything to change.

They worked for a lifetime to build a comfortable retirement. They fear a change will threaten their social security. They resist any risk to their investment funds, retirement pensions, IRAs and Roth accounts. They are jealous of their expensive homes, recreational vehicles, ski vacations, motorboats, SUVs, guns and summer cottages. The retired Reno fireman summarized it best when he said:

"As long as I have my TV and beer at the end of the day, I don't care what the politicians do."

I came to the conclusion that seniors are holding back progress. Deeply invested in the accumulation and maintenance of wealth, the older generation is afraid change will cost them their stuff. Seniors control America's wealth and power and they vote. Some grudgingly admit change is needed, but they resist it out of fear. They are content to leave the changes for their children and grandchildren.

The young people I met don't watch commercial news, they don't read newspapers. They receive their information online.

They subscribe to podcasts, tweets and blogs. They instant message (IM), post on Instagram and rely on social media for current events. They express their opinions with less energy and anger and more fatalism than the seniors. And they listen more readily to the opinions of others. These young people weren't non-political, they were apolitical, less interested in political parties than the results. They want reform, but know they are not the ones in charge. They recognize that social and economic disparity in America is growing. Young, old, black, white, immigrants, Christian, non-Christian, rich, poor; the polarities are powerful. They know change is needed. They are waiting for their turn.

I set out to get to know America again. This visit exposed me to a new view of my country. I saw it as an outsider. I grew up using the American standard measuring system with inches, quarts and miles. It worked fine. In Europe I learned the metric system with centimeters, liters and kilometers, that works fine too. It's only when I try to merge the systems that I run into trouble. What's an inch in metric? How many liters in a gallon? Why isn't there a metric healthcare system in America?

Maybe I've grown used to living in Europe, so the American standard feels strange. I've heard that when you move to a new culture, you never go all the way back. You always have one foot in each country.

When I grew up in the U.S., I did not recognize the pervasive insecurity I observed on this trip. I don't know if it has always been there, or if it's new. I don't know if I felt it but didn't realize it.

The recognition of this fear was the biggest take-away from my trip. Americans live a fragile, insecure life. The insecurity takes many shapes and expresses itself in many forms. Insecurity subtly dominates the thoughts and actions of many people and diminishes the quality of life in America. There are many American institutions that profit from, even provoke a pervasive climate of fear; first among them is the insurance industry, in its many forms. It is a wealthy, powerful force for inertia.

I spoke with David at the Mammoth Cave campground. He said America is broken. There is a lot that needs to be fixed, too much for him to troubleshoot all at once. So he focuses his energies on one issue, climate change.

I agree with David, there is a lot to do in America to make it better. But the one issue that I feel would make the biggest difference is a national healthcare system. It seems like a hundred years ago, when I was in college, I was introduced to Maslow's theory of human development. He outlines five categories of needs humans must satisfy to reach their full potential. According to his theory, human needs are universal and must be fulfilled in a logical sequence. That is how a healthy person develops. The second stage of Maslow's hierarchy is safety. Bodily safety is a human need that must be fulfilled before a person can evolve to fulfill more conceptual needs like love. Only when a person feels safe can they evolve and develop to their full potential.

Health, like education, is a universal need. Universal education is a fact of life in America. Universal or national healthcare is not. Inequalities in health services diminish the value of life, establish a hierarchical social culture and cultivate insecurity. The uninsured, under-insured, including those with astronomically high deductibles, avoid, postpone, and fear doctors' visits because they are not affordable. These people are essentially making a food or heat choice during a blizzard. Why is the health of a wealthy person more valuable than that of a poor person? Affordable healthcare for everyone is a great equalizer.

I think a national system of affordable healthcare is the single most important change needed to diminish the pervasive insecurity that many Americans express.

Now that the trip is finished, I miss the road, the Harley and my sons. I was often alone but never lonely. I miss the freedom, the day-to-day simplicity of the journey. I miss the smell of the forests, the mountains, the deserts, even the cities. I miss sleeping in the tent, surrounded by my gear with my ride framed in the tent window. I miss the deep, rumbling roar of the motorcycle that I came to love. I even miss the artillery shell explosion when it started in the morning. I miss the afternoons in the sun with my pipe and journal. I miss evenings, staring at the flames of the campfire and the quiet mornings with a cup of coffee and a map.

I thought when I started the trip that I had fallen out of touch with America. I wanted to understand the volatile political climate that divides it. Both sides fear the other will destroy America. This is the truth I learned: it is the conflict that creates a balance that keeps America stable. Neither side is strong enough to do much damage. The other side won't let it. If one side goes too far, the majority opinion shifts. That's why social change is glacial; like the process of carving a cave, it takes centuries.

EPILOGUE

Most of the writing for this book took place in a small apartment in St. Francois, Guadeloupe during two holidays. The tropical island was a welcome relief from the windy, wet, gray Dutch winter. The lapsed time gave me perspective, first to draft, then to edit the story down to something I hope is readable.

Much has happened since the events described in this book. This is not a historical record, so I will not detail every event. I will only touch on some of the U.S. and world events that relate to this chronicle. I'll also follow up on some personal information in case the reader wants some closure.

Joe Biden beat Donald Trump in a Presidential election that left

America with even more wounds, controversy, violence and criminal prosecutions. There was no reconciliation between Democrats and Republicans and no compromise. Trump held a rally in Washington DC to protest the election results on January 6, 2020. He delivered a fiery speech claiming to have been the victim of a Democratic plot and election fraud. He said that, in times of national crisis, force is needed, a show of strength. Thousands of right-wing radicals marched from the rally to storm the Capitol building. Congress was in session, certifying the election results. The protesters attempted to stop the certification process. The National Guard was called in to restore order. This is the first time in American history that the peaceful transfer of power was challenged by a losing candidate and his followers.

Donald Trump left the White House never conceding defeat or congratulating the new President. Instead of attending Biden's inauguration, he returned to his resort in the Florida Keys. After two years and 61 failed lawsuits, he continues to claim to be the victim of a stolen election. Trump's followers staunchly continue to support his claims of election fraud. The country remains as divided as it was when I rode across it in 2019, maybe even more so.

The right-left controversy is not uniquely American. In the U.K., a popular referendum forced the government to withdraw from the European Union. Boris Johnson led the 'Brexit' campaign and stepped in as Prime Minister. The Brexit movement in Britain was a reactionary movement, like the Trump presidency. A dissatisfied and protectionist voter base demanded change. Similar candidates ran for public office in several European countries including, France, Germany, The Netherlands and Hungary. The re-election of protectionist Viktor Orbán as Hungary's Prime Minister points to a global, populist, right-wing shift. People everywhere are afraid.

A few months after I returned from America, an outbreak of

an unusually deadly flu occurred in China. In the three years since my ride across America, the COVID-19 pandemic spread around the world. It was a lucky happenstance that I chose 2019 to make my trip. It would not have been possible one year later. Since the outbreak of the virus, over six million people have died worldwide. The United States accounts for over one million deaths – a disproportionately high number. This is due in part to a plethora of false information, popular disbelief of scientific evidence and a healthcare system poorly suited to meet the needs of its population.

Health organizations, governments and citizens of the world are still struggling to deal with the global impact of the virus. Global travel restrictions grounded planes around the world. Each country and each U.S. state established health and safety protocols that were a compromise between economic and safety priorities. Personal protection measures varied widely from country to country and state to state. For example, China established a zero-tolerance policy for the virus. In Shanghai and other cities, total lockdowns have isolated people in their homes for months at a time. Their front doors were padlocked. The cities were closed down. Even the supermarkets were closed.

In Florida, college Spring Break festivities and motorcycle Bike Week were celebrated as usual, ignoring all medical advice. The Republican governor challenged a federal law that required people to wear masks to prevent the spread of infection. He won and the masks came off in Florida. In Michigan, three men were arrested and convicted for plotting to kidnap the governor over her support for COVID-19 restrictions. In the Netherlands, right-wing activists claimed there was no pandemic. The government was using the health scare to gain more control over the citizens. The belief, "My opinion is just as valid as your facts." helped spread the COVID-19 pandemic in the U.S. and around the world.

Russia, under the leadership of Vladimir Putin, invaded Ukraine. He claimed it was a "special military action" to deNazify Ukraine. To the people in Ukraine, it was a declaration of war. The government-controlled Russian media claims it is a freedom initiative. Millions of war refugees have fled Ukraine to seek safety in neighboring Poland, Slovakia, Hungary and Romania while Russian troops bomb Ukrainian cities to rubble, rape the women and shoot civilians in the back and bury them in mass graves. The Western world supports Ukraine and has established economic sanctions against Russia, Putin and his inner circle of super-rich supporters. China and India have until now remained on the sidelines.

Putin has shattered the 75-year-old world order and balance of power agreement established after World War II. No western country wants to risk World War III. They support Ukraine with money, humanitarian aid and weapons, but not troops. Russian media is strictly censored, as is the country's internet. Meanwhile, a vast amount of false information is spread through Russian-based internet hackers. The internet, social media and public news sources are so compromised that it is almost impossible to separate fact from fiction. A world economic crisis is looming. World trade agreements, petroleum products, natural resources, agriculture and manufactured products that were only recovering from the pandemic shockwave have tumbled from the earthquake that is the war in Ukraine. Economists are predicting a period of increasing prices with decreasing production. They call it stagflation. A lot of people's TV and beer is threatened.

During the last three years, while the United States and the rest of the world seems to be in a race to chaos, my son Matt and Jessica became the proud parents of two daughters. They live in a beautiful home set in a rural suburb of Boston. Theirs is an oasis of serenity in a desert of conflict. The COVID-19 travel restrictions have been lifted and I met my granddaughters for the first time in July 2022. It was my first visit to the U.S. since the outbreak of the pandemic. The one year old was curious and observant from her seat at the kitchen table. The two year old is a bright, precocious little girl. She was excited, busy and talkative. She eagerly posed for photos and took me by the hand to show me her toys and drawings. My daughter in-law explained that she always acts that way with strangers. I am a stranger in my son's home.

Mike and Leah seem to have found an economic foothold in the Lake Tahoe culture. They rent a one-bedroom cottage with a long-term lease, which they can afford as long as they both have jobs. Their financial foothold remains fragile, strained and insecure. I hope the recent improvements are enough.

The three years that have passed since my cross-country revisit to America will offer scholars a century of research in a multitude of disciplines. From technology, science, education, medicine, finance, economics and epidemiology to psychology, communication, politics, history, culture and religion, every tree in the forest that makes up our world has been singed by the fires of the last three years.

Some social scientists claim our political and cultural institutions are inadequate to deal with the complexity of the evolving world. I can only wonder if the glacier of change is melting. Or will it continue to be true to say that nothing has changed?

Now that I can close the book on my U.S. trip, I have started to consider a back-roads journey through Europe to better understand the cultures of the people with whom I now live.

15 March 2023

APPENDIX

Appendix

Clothes
2 pairs long pants
1 pair shorts
2 long-sleeved shirts
3 t-shirts
4 pairs of boxer shorts
5 pairs of socks
1 river shirt
1 sweatpants
1 bathing suit
towel
Tilley hat
Gloves
flashlight
e-reader

Toiletries
toothbrush
toothpaste
floss
toothpicks
soap
shaver
brush
Q-tips
toilet paper
paracetamol (Tylenol)
allergy medicine
moisturizer
nail file
nail clipper
Chapstick
bug dope (DEET)

First Aid kit
ankle wrap
athletic tape
Band-Aids
gauze
antibiotics
Vaseline

Camping toolkit
Knife
lighter
matches
candles
rope and string
clothes pins
sew kit
stove repair kit
nails
compass
shoelaces
padlock

Bike toolkit
metric wrench set 8–17mm,
U.S. wrench set hex keys, ⅛"- ⅝" screwdrivers, pliers,
long nose pliers, channel lock pliers, wire cutters,
spark plug wrench, 5/8" spark plug gap tool
electrical wire
alligator clips
cable ties, assorted sizes, bailing wire
funnel for stove fuel
fuses
black electrical tape
small box of assorted hardware: screws, nuts, wash-
ers, electrical connectors, mounting hardware and
cables to recharge phone, Bluetooth and e-reader

Kitchen kit
cook kit (pans)
stove kit
fuel tank
coffee pot
cooking utensils
3 plates
2 cups
scrub pad
steel wool
soap
tea towel
ziplock bags

coffee and tea
rice
bouillon
salt and pepper
oatmeal
raisins
honey
olive oil
garlic salt

On the road

4. Large nylon duffel bag strapped to the back: Tent, sleeping bag w/ liner, sleep pad, bungee cords, sneakers and sandals.

5. Gas tank pack: maps, camera w/ tripod, notebook, pencil/pen, legal papers, wallet, water bottle.

3. Harley tour box behind me on the seat: Clothes and e-reader.

2. Saddle bag 2: Tools kits, pipe kit, rain gear, stove fuel, motor oil and water bottles.

1. Saddle bag 1: Kitchen kit and food.

ABOUT THE AUTHOR

Robert J Barra

Robert Barra is an educator and an environmental scientist. He taught public and private schools in the U.S. and The Netherlands. In 2001, he was working as an environmental scientist when terrorists attacked the World Trade Center in New Your City. He led a disaster recovery team at Ground Zero for six months.

In 2003, he moved to The Netherlands where he worked in competence development for the IKEA organization. He traveled in Europe, Asia, Africa, Australia and North American for business and pleasure. He retired in 2018.

He is an avid motorcyclist, and wilderness canoe and camping enthusiast, who paddled the Allagash Wilderness Waterway in the North Maine Woods more times that he can count and the Yukon River once.

In the summer of 2019, he spent two months riding a motorcycle from Massachusetts to California and back to relearn what it was like to be an American.